MAKING THE GRADE

MAKING THE GRADE

CANADIAN EDITION

A GUIDE TO STUDY AND SUCCESS

Iain Hay
Dianne Bochner
Carol Dungey
Nellie Perret

OXFORD
UNIVERSITY PRESS

OXFORD
UNIVERSITY PRESS

Oxford University Press is a department of the University of Oxford.
It furthers the University's objective of excellence in research, scholarship,
and education by publishing worldwide. Oxford is a registered trade mark of
Oxford University Press in the UK and in certain other countries.

Published in Canada by
Oxford University Press
8 Sampson Mews, Suite 204,
Don Mills, Ontario M3C 0H5 Canada

www.oupcanada.com

Original edition published by Oxford University Press
253 Normanby Road, South Melbourne, Victoria 3205, Australia
Copyright © Iain Hay, Dianne Bochner and Carol Dungey 1997, 2002, 2006

Library and Archives Canada Cataloguing in Publication

Making the grade : a guide to study and success / Iain Hay . . . [et al.]. — Canadian ed.

Includes bibliographical references and index.
ISBN 978-0-19-544350-9

1. Study skills.   2. Academic writing.   3. Academic achievement.
4. College students—Canada—Life skills guides.   I. Hay, Iain

LB2395.M35 2011   378.1'70281   C2011-906545-2

Cover image: Ocean Photography/Veer

Oxford University Press is committed to our environment. This book is printed on
Forest Stewardship Council® certified paper and comes from responsible sources.

Printed and bound in Canada.

1 2 3 4 — 15 14 13 12

MIX
Paper from
responsible sources
FSC
www.fsc.org   FSC® C011825

Contents

Figures and Tables

TABLES

Acknowledgements

I would like to acknowledge the guidance and support of numerous friends and colleagues: Patrizia Albanese, Leslie Barker, Teresa Biderman, Scott Browning, Kathy Chung, Michelle Fost, Chris Garbutt, Corey Goldman, Susan Hopkirk, Tamar Kagan, Victoria Littman, Christiane Martin, Sam Minsky, Paul Moore, Gail Noble, Roz Spafford, Lorne Tepperman, and Jamie Thompson. The wisdom, kindness, and collegiality of Margaret Procter and her colleagues at the University of Toronto's writing and academic skills centres have been invaluable. The intelligent and carefully conceived contributions of Stephen Kotowych, Mary Wat, and Maria Jelinek at Oxford University Press have been considerable and are greatly appreciated. The authors of the Australian edition of this book—Iain Hay, Dianne Bochner, and Carol Dungey—have produced a wise, well-informed, and informative guide. Chapter 7 has greatly benefited from the updates and revisions contributed by Gillian Eldridge, liaison librarian for science and engineering at Flinders University Library, Adelaide, Australia. I also appreciate the feedback from the following reviewers, along with those who chose to remain anonymous, whose thoughtful comments helped to shape this book:

Reuben L. Gabriel, University of Northern British Columbia
Nancy Marenick, St. Francis Xavier University
Robert L. Nelson, University of Windsor
Mark Barrett, University of Prince Edward Island

I am grateful to the many students I have taught and counselled at the University of Toronto for their unstinting candour, good humour, and grace. Mostly, though, I am well aware that my own contribution to this book would not have been possible without Murray and Ariel Pomerance, whose patience, generosity, and wisdom have been in this, as in all things, my mainstay.

From the Publisher

In preparing this edition of *Making the Grade*, we have kept one important goal in mind: to produce the most complete yet accessible study and communication guide possible, specifically for Canadian students. The tips and strategies offered in this text can make a world of difference to students encountering a university course for the first time. As you browse through these pages, we hope that you will see why we believe *Making the Grade* is the most exciting and innovative guide to study and communication skills available to Canadian students.

SIX THINGS THAT MAKE THIS A ONE-OF-A-KIND TEXTBOOK

1. A CANADIAN TEXTBOOK FOR CANADIAN STUDENTS

References to Canadian examples and research reflect the kind of information Canadian students will encounter during their studies. This text also provides a window into life at Canadian universities, the expectations Canadian professors have of their students, and the facilities and resources available on the average campus.

2. CLEAR AND USER-FRIENDLY

Sample student notes, carefully chosen figures, and examples from real textbooks are just some of the elements that invite students to apply the techniques described in the text to their everyday studies. A tear-out weekly scheduling grid and templates for reading logs, flashcards, and checklists provide the tools students need to get started.

3. AN INCLUSIVE APPROACH

Students starting university face a variety of personal and academic challenges. These two themed boxes appear throughout the text to offer concrete advice and insights to students of English as an Additional Language (EAL) and to students with learning challenges

4. AN AUTHOR WHO UNDERSTANDS THE CHALLENGES FACING STUDENTS TODAY

Dr. Nellie Perret has crafted exercises and written expert advice for this text based on her 20 years of teaching and coaching experience in the area of student success. At the University of Toronto's Academic Success Centre she continues to work with professors to assess the needs of their classes, providing practical, hands-on advice. In addition, she works with students on a one-on-one basis and lectures to over 2,500 students every year on the importance of study skills and time management to student success.

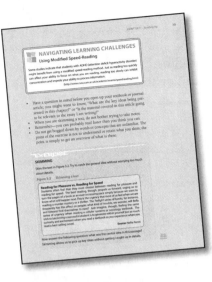

5. A WEALTH OF EXERCISES

Exercises throughout the text illustrate and reinforce important concepts, while icons direct students to an online database containing self-grading quizzes and exercises for additional study and review.

6. ONLINE RESOURCES

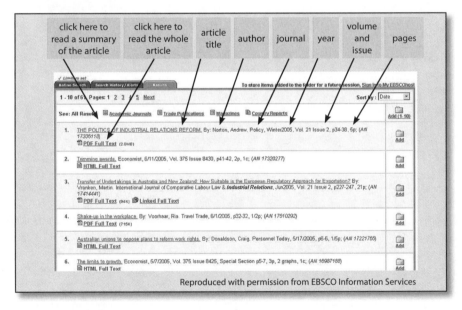

Reproduced with permission from EBSCO Information Services

FOR INSTRUCTORS

- A detailed **instructor's manual** provides an extensive set of pedagogical tools and suggestions for every chapter, including chapter overviews, key concepts, teaching notes, homework assignments, and additional print and online resources.
- Classroom-ready **PowerPoint slides** incorporate graphics and tables from the text, and may be edited to suit each instructor's individual needs.

- **Podcasts** featuring short talks from Nellie Perret are carefully matched to each chapter. Topics include "Making the most of your lectures," "Tracking your time," and "Strategic reading."
- A comprehensive **test generator** enables instructors to sort, edit, import, and distribute hundreds of questions in multiple choice, short answer, and true/false formats.

FOR STUDENTS

The **student study guide** includes:

- **Chapter summaries**
- **Key terms**
- **Printable activities**, including templates for note-taking and samples of effective notes
- **Self-grading quizzes** featuring true/false and multiple choice questions, with a complete answer key.

Successful Study

Starting Out:
University Study and You

They know enough who know how to learn.

Henry Brooks Adams, 1907

Deciding to begin on a course of university study is a big step. Like most people, you have probably found the process of enrolling and working out what is required of you more complicated than you expected. You might be wondering what other surprises are in store for you in your new enterprise. This book is designed to help you with communication and study skills that might be new to you and that will be important for all the subjects you are studying at university. You can read the book from front to back, look up particular topics as you need to, or use just one section that you find useful. Each section is self-contained and deals with a different aspect of the skills necessary for successful university learning.

This first chapter offers advice on how to approach some of the new teaching and learning experiences you will encounter at university. It also deals with some of the skills you will need to get the most out of lectures, **seminars, tutorials**, and workshops. An important part of achieving academic success is learning to make the most of the communications you *receive*. Much of the teaching we get at university concentrates on how we should send messages and takes our ability to receive them for granted. For successful study and work, however, we spend most of our time listening to, or reading messages from, other people, and our ability to learn depends to a great extent on our ability to understand and respond to the messages we receive.

WHAT IS UNIVERSITY LEARNING ALL ABOUT?

This might seem a silly question. Most of you have enrolled in university to learn about history, psychology, geology, engineering, drama, and other subjects you are interested in or that you hope will help you find an engaging job. But as well as learning about the body of knowledge that makes up the core of these **disciplines**, what else do you need to know? What else are your professors trying to teach you by setting certain kinds of assignments and structuring your courses in particular ways?

Of course, the specific answers to these questions will vary from person to person and course to course, but there are some general aspects of learning that government, academics, and employers agree are vital for all university students. It is not enough to know about the specific content of mathematics, English, or biology. You must know how the disciplines you study are connected and be able to do something interesting with the information you have learned.

Surveys of academics have shown that the most common objectives for university faculty and academic support staff are teaching students how to analyze ideas or issues critically; developing students' intellectual/thinking skills; and helping students comprehend principles or generalizations.

Different subject areas have their own specific objectives, as well, but these general principles underlie all university learning. This kind of learning, and the skills it develops, never become outdated and can be applied to other aspects of your life outside university study. This kind of learning (often called **transferable learning**) will help to develop your imagination, judgment, and problem-solving skills.

Academics also value communication skills very highly as an essential part of a university education, as do employers of university graduates. Surveys in Canada, Britain, and the United States show that employers of university graduates look for thinking and problem-solving skills in their employees and value good communication skills highly. They expect students at university to learn how to speak and write well in their chosen profession (Conference Board of Canada).

So, teaching at university aims to

- provide you with a body of knowledge in your chosen field;
- stimulate you to enquire, analyze, and make decisions;
- encourage you to be flexible and creative; and
- develop your communication skills.

It is important to remember these aims when you are studying and completing the tasks set for your course. If a professor sets an essay topic, for example, he or she will want more than a regurgitation of information. In your essay, you should be trying to show not only that you have done careful research and understand the most important and relevant facts but also that you can use them to develop a new idea or to see unexpected connections between different ideas; that you can explain your ideas in a clear and interesting way; and that you can make some decisions about them on the basis of what you have learned.

LEARNING: HOW DO YOU GO ABOUT IT?

You cannot have learning administered to you like a dose of medicine or a massage. *Learning is something you do.* You must be active in your learning tasks to get the most out of them and to enjoy them. It helps if you are interested, not only in what you are studying but also in the process of study itself. Think about the way you study and give yourself feedback on it. This will help to make you a more effective learner. In the same way that golfers work on their swings, hockey players work on their stick handling, and tennis players work on their serves, students should work on their technique for studying in order to improve it. Your study skills will not improve just by themselves.

Researchers have established a number of factors that improve the quality of student learning and a number of factors that reduce it. Some of the factors that improve learning are listed in the statements below. You will find learning more effective if the following statements apply to you:

- You process information rather than store it; that is, you think about what information means and how you can apply it.
- You have a personal interest in the topic you are studying; it is much easier to remember something you are interested in.
- You have some personal goals in mind; you will work harder if you can see how your learning will help you to achieve some personal ambition.
- You can develop some of your own ideas; people don't work well if they are just following orders.
- You can put something into practice; you need to see how it works.
- You use social processes; you discuss your work with others, either formally or informally.
- You can establish a positive relationship with one or more professors or teaching assistants; getting to know some of your teachers will help to give the subject you are studying a human face.
- You share in the responsibility for learning; you do not wait for that magic knowledge pill.

> **TIP**
>
> Successful learning is *active* learning: process information; discuss ideas with others; set goals; experiment; reflect.

> **TIP**
>
> Online discussion groups can be a great way to interact with other students if you simply cannot find the time to get together any other way.

- You can work independently; you do not need someone to tell you what to do.
- You feel free to take reasonable risks; if you do not, your learning will be limited.
- You see learning as a process of change rather than an end product; you will never learn everything.
- You reflect on the way you are learning; you are aware of your own learning characteristics.

LEARNING IN LECTURES

Lectures, live or online, still provide the basis of university teaching, and you will find them very different from the kind of teaching you have been accustomed to in high school or in the workplace. They are, in many cases, the most efficient and cost-effective way to expose a large number of students to world-class scholars talking about significant ideas and research in their subject areas.

For students learning online, lectures are often provided as written text. Information about learning by reading is contained in chapter 3. For students on campus, or learning from podcasts or webinars, learning in lectures means learning to listen, sometimes in difficult conditions.

The forms of lectures vary and some professors are more interesting than others, but, in general, live lectures will involve minimal interaction between professor and students. For some students, and particularly for those sitting in large and noisy lecture halls, it can be hard to concentrate. This is true for professors as well as students. The larger the audience and the more crowded the classroom, the harder it is for the professor to maintain contact with individual members of the audience. This means that *you* have to work at getting the most out of lectures.

The following sections of this chapter look specifically at listening and note taking in lectures and small groups, but below are a few practical introductory tips to help you get the most out of lectures.

The main purposes of lectures are

- to provide a framework for your course by indicating the areas you should cover and the order in which you should study them;
- to supply, in summary, the essential knowledge in those areas and to indicate where you can find further information;
- to present a particular point of view, or a number of different points of view, on the major areas of concern to the course;
- to explain areas of difficulty or controversy;
- to allow an expert in your field to outline original ideas or research; and
- to give a practical guide to how to carry out a task or procedure.

KEY CONCEPTS

Getting the most out of lectures

- Arrive early so you can get a good seat where you can see the professor, the PowerPoint slides, and the black/whiteboard. Some classrooms are very crowded at the beginning of the semester, so if you are late you might end up not getting a seat at all.
- Sit near the front of the classroom. This will help you feel more involved in what is going on as well as making sure you can hear, see, and avoid distractions from people arriving late, leaving early, and so on.
- Make sure you know what the lecture is about before you go so that you do not spend the first ten minutes wondering what is going on.
- If slides or lecture notes are posted online, look them over before class or print them out and take them with you to class so that you do not waste time writing down the information that they contain.
- If your professor posts lecture notes or PowerPoint slides, don't just "fill in the blanks" if you bring them with you to lectures: listen for ideas that are outside the scope of the posted notes as well as for material that develops what has already been sketched out for you.

It is important that you recognize the purposes of different lectures so that you can respond to them appropriately. In some, you might want to take detailed notes of what the professor is saying. In others, you might want to concentrate on listening or noting comments to consider later. The titles of the lectures should give you some clues to their purpose. If they do not, try to work out the purpose from the professor's introductory remarks and plan your noting strategy accordingly. Lectures are an important fact of university life. Do not expect them to be stand-up comedy acts. Think about the purpose of each one and be active in getting the most out of them.

LEARNING TO LISTEN

Reading and listening are the two language channels through which we receive information. Studies have shown that the average adult does about three times as much listening as reading and that we spend more than half our working day listening (Wolvin & Coakley, 1996). In spite of this, we get very little instruction in listening. Perhaps this is because we tend to equate listening with hearing, and we assume that listening is an inherent ability rather than a skill that needs to be learned. Effective listening, however, requires concentrated effort. Many people are poor listeners, and for them the whole process of communication becomes very difficult.

One of the main difficulties with listening is that many people regard it as a passive process, whereas listening must be active if the listener is to get the most out of any oral communication. You need to be aware of possible problems in listening effectively, as well as your own listening habits and how you can improve them.

Barriers to effective listening

Many people have difficulty with listening, especially over an extended period of time, for example, in a lecture. If you are aware of the major barriers listed below, you might be able to try some deliberate strategies to overcome them.

- *Thought speed*: This is a problem because the average talking speed is about 125 words a minute, and intellectually you can process about 400 words a minute. This means that your thoughts can be very far ahead and far away from the speaker's words.
- *Failing to see listening as work*: Listeners who do not understand that listening is an active process see any failure in their understanding as the fault of the speaker. Unless your purpose for listening is relaxation or entertainment, you must be active in assimilating the message the speaker is giving you.
- *Prejudice of various kinds*: Your attitude to the speaker might colour your understanding of what is being said. If you like the person who is talking, for example, you might be prepared to accept whatever he or she says uncritically or to interpret it in a favourable light. If, on the other hand, you dislike something about the speaker, you might switch off completely or interpret the speaker's words in a negative way. This can have unfortunate effects on any learning situation.
- *Lack of interest*: It is easy to let your thoughts drift if you do not care about the speaker or what he or she is saying.
- *Distractions*: Anything, from more important thoughts to noise outside the room, can be a problem if you let it.
- *Difficulty understanding*: If English is not your first language, you might find that the speaker lectures too quickly for you to follow the argument; once this happens, it's very easy to get lost and to just stop trying to understand what is being said.
- *Physical discomfort*: Heat, cold, crowding, noise, light, and uncomfortable furniture can all cause difficulties in any listening situation.
- *Physical comfort*: Sometimes a classroom can be *too* comfortable. Finding adequate and appropriate space, particularly for large first-year classes, has become a challenge for many Canadian universities;

> **TIP**
>
> Effective listening requires effort and practice.

sometimes lectures are held in theatre auditoriums where dim lights and soft chairs make it difficult to stay awake, let alone to pay attention to what the professor is saying!

Techniques for effective listening

Try using some of the techniques listed below to improve your listening skills.

- *Concentrate.* Use the time lapse between your thinking and the speaker's words to anticipate what the speaker will say next. Even if you are wrong, it will focus your attention on what is being said.
- *Analyze the message.* Look for deeper meanings, think about evidence for or against what is being said, try to think of additional points or contrary ones.
- *Review.* Go over the main points the speaker has already covered, and summarize the information or argument so far.
- *Ask questions.* This is one of the most helpful ways of keeping your concentration, and it encourages the speaker. In a large lecture where you feel you cannot question the speaker, write down your questions to refer to later. Most large lectures have tutorials where you can bring up any questions that you might have had.
- *Be objective.* Do not make hasty judgments. Listen to what is being said before making decisions about it.
- *Find a motivation.* If you do not find a speaker intrinsically interesting, look for something you can use as a reason for concentrating. Ask, "What is this person saying that can be useful to me?" The answer might be in terms of short- or long-term goals or economic or emotional satisfaction. It does not matter what your **motivation** is, just as long as you are listening.
- *Stay physically alert.* If you are too relaxed physically, you will not be mentally active (and will in any case give a bad impression to the person speaking). You should be physically comfortable but not ready to doze. Sit upright, lean forward, and make an effort to respond to the speaker in an appropriate way, not as a favour to the speaker (although it is likely to produce a more interesting talk) but as a way of helping yourself.

Effective listening in lectures

Lectures present a particularly difficult listening situation: there is no personal contact between you and the professor; fifty minutes (or sometimes ever longer!) is a long time to maintain silent concentration; classrooms are often stuffy, noisy, and uncomfortable; and some lectures are not inherently entertaining (particularly if you come to class unprepared!). This means that you have to work at getting the most out of the lectures you attend. In addition to the techniques for listening in general, there are special techniques involved in listening effectively in lectures.

- *Tune in.* Prepare yourself for what is to be said. Good professors will help you in this step by telling you what they are going to talk about. Preview any material about the lecture so that you have some foundation on which to build the new information. You will then be more able to absorb the lecture content and to separate the information you need to note from background information to which you need only listen.
- *Ask questions.* The sort of questions you might ask are: "What is the specific purpose of this information?" "How does what is being said tie in with what I already know?" "What is the evidence for that particular statement?"
- *Review.* First, the review step involves going back, summarizing (mentally or in writing) what has been said, comparing it with what you thought was going to be said, and evaluating the worth of what has been said. Ask, "What did I learn?" Good speakers and professors help in this respect by giving a summary. Second, review your notes after the lecture when you have had some time to reflect but before you have forgotten what the lecture was about.

TAKING GOOD NOTES IN LECTURES

Effective listening goes hand in hand with developing note-taking skills. Few people can listen to a fifty-minute lecture and remember all the salient points. To get the most from a lecture, you need to develop an efficient technique for taking notes. You cannot hope to take down everything that is said in lectures. In fact, you should not try, as this will distract you from listening actively, and it will decrease your chances of remembering and understanding.

How many notes should you take?

There is wide variation in the notes individuals feel they need to take in lectures. You have to work out for yourself how much you need: strike a balance between mindlessly copying down every word you hear and taking down so little that you cannot work out what your notes mean. It is probably better to take more than you need until you are experienced enough to judge clearly. After the first evaluation, go back and look over your notes to determine whether you are writing down enough . . . or too much. Try to vary your method of note taking according to the purpose of the lecture.

TIP

To take good notes in lectures: be selective; consider your purpose; take down the main points; use consistent abbreviations; fill in details later.

Learning Outside the Classroom

International students or **EAL** (English as an additional language) **learners** often feel very challenged by the Canadian university system where so much depends on being able to process a great deal of written and spoken information. It is important if English is not your first language to engage in listening to (and speaking) English whenever possible. This will, necessarily, happen within the classroom, but should be augmented by taking advantage of any opportunities to listen to English that present themselves to you. To improve your listening skills,

- tune into local radio and television stations;
- join university clubs and societies;
- attend guest lectures on topics that are new and interesting to you;
- go with friends to English-language movies; and
- try not to spend all your time speaking with friends whose first language is the same as your own.

The more you listen, the better you will understand.

NAVIGATING LEARNING CHALLENGES
Using University Resources

Students who have difficulties with the processing of auditory information, short-term memory problems, ADHD (attention deficit hyperactivity disorder), or other impediments to listening and taking notes in class might want to find out if their university has a service that can provide them with scribes or transcripts of lectures. If you find it useful to have recorded lectures and your professors do not make them available as podcasts, then you must ask the permission of your professor before taping.

KEY CONCEPTS

Strategic listening

- If the lecture deals with vital information that is not easily available elsewhere, you will need to take notes that are as detailed as possible.
- If the material in the lecture is available in textbooks or posted online, you might find it more valuable to listen actively and only note the main points or parts of the topic that are difficult to understand.
- If the lecture is meant to provide background interest or context for something that is to come later, or that is dealt with elsewhere, you should listen as actively as you can to get the overall picture, and jot down only a few points as reminders.
- If the purpose of the lecture is to give a particular point of view on familiar or readily accessible material, you should be listening for, and noting, the professor's argument structure and points used as evidence without worrying about particular facts, figures, or dates, which you can look up later.

Hints for better note taking in lectures

You should always identify your notes. Head the page with the subject, title of the lecture, and the date. Number and date all the pages for each lecture. As the year progresses, you will collect pages and pages of notes, and having a quick way of identifying them will save time and endless searching.

Try to put the different sections of the lecture under headings, sub-headings, letters, or numbers. The following shows how this might look:

Example of how to set out lecture notes

Major heading:	HUMAN DEVELOPMENT
First major point:	Heredity vs. Environment
	(a) heredity
	(b) environment
	(c) interactions of h and e
Second major point:	Continuity vs. Discontinuity
	(a) continuity
	(b) discontinuity

Some professors will provide a structure like this for you on a PowerPoint slide or online lecture notes. If they do, try to use the given structure for your own notes. Try to distinguish between the substance of the lecture material and illustrative examples. You could bracket examples so that you can see the difference clearly. If you are taking notes longhand, you should underline headings or important words or points. Use different types of underlining for different phrases. If you are taking notes on a laptop, tablet, or netbook, you should decide what method of indicating the most important material (underlining, italicizing, and so on) is best for you. Following are some tips on devising a note-taking shorthand of your own:

- You need not bother about taking down complete sentences. Key phrases are most important.
- Use as many abbreviations as you can and develop your own form of shorthand. For example, use **&** for *and*; **w** for *with*; **c** for *about*; **–>** for *led to, caused*, or *was followed by*; and **C19** for *nineteenth century*.
- Insert abbreviations as the lecture progresses. In a statistics lecture the word "probability" might occur a number of times. You might abbreviate it to pro or pb or even p if the meaning is quite clear.

EXERCISE

USING ABBREVIATIONS

On a lined piece of paper or a new blank document on your computer, practise using abbreviations by turning the following sentences into your own unique "shorthand."

1. The Canadian university in the twenty-first century has been transformed by the almost universal introduction of new technologies: laptops, netbooks, iPads, PowerPoint slides, podcasts, and online communities.
2. The introduction of these technologies has led to a number of transformations in the way that professors think about assignment design and marking criteria.

NAVIGATING LEARNING CHALLENGES
Dyslexia

Students with dyslexia should use as few words as possible, keeping as much space as they can on the page. Make good use of abbreviations (but be sure that you will know what they represent when you look at them a week or two months from now). Write on every second line, leaving room to fill in more information later.

(http://www.dyslexia-college.com/notes.html)

- Most words are easily identified by using just the key letters (which must include the first and last letter). For example, mst ppl hv lttl trbl rdg ths.

Use pen, not pencil, for all your handwritten notes. Pencil is too difficult to read, especially after a lapse of time. Make sure that you have a wide margin, and write only on one side of the page. Use the opposite page for additions to your notes, amplifications, or summaries. Take notes on a laptop or netbook only if you are comfortable typing at a good speed. If you miss a point, there is no need to panic. Leave a space and ask a friend, the **teaching assistant**, or the professor later.

Group your handwritten or computerized notes in divided three-ring binders or virtual titled folders, respectively, so you can find them easily later.

Editing your notes

Remember, you want a set of notes to be a useful reference, so you should check to see that your notes are legible, clear, and complete. You will improve the effectiveness of your notes if you

- read your notes over on the same day as you take them to make sure you will be able to understand them later on—this also improves retention;
- write out in full any words that you have abbreviated for the first time or that are hard to understand;
- correct misspelled words and inaccurate information;
- add any new words or phrases for greater clarity, or for the purpose of filling in a detail or example;
- tie several points together or change the order so as to better organize your notes;
- underline or highlight some points emphasized by the professor; and
- consult some of the references mentioned in the lecture or your text-books in order to develop some of the points in your notes further.

Sharing notes

Cooperating with others can make note taking easier. You can compare notes with friends after a lecture to make sure that yours are accurate or to fill in gaps in your notes or understanding. Another way of making the task easier is to cooperate with someone else in the lecture. You can arrange with a friend to take notes for half the lecture each. In this way you can listen to half the lecture without writing anything down, and it will be easier to maintain concentration. Be careful, however. Not everyone is a good note taker, and sometimes individuals hear completely different messages from the same lecture. Try this method once with a friend, and only persist if you find it useful. Sometimes the very fact that there is a difference between your perception and that of somebody else can be illuminating.

Recording lectures

Some professors record their lectures and post the lectures online for any students who cannot be at the lecture. Listening to a podcast of a lecture is a very good way of hearing it without distractions and at your own speed. If your lectures are not recorded, you can ask your professor if you can record the lectures yourself. Many professors are happy to allow this. Remember that you will still have to make your own notes, and make sure that you have understood the main points. Owning a recording of a lecture does not, in itself, automatically transfer the lecture's contents into your brain.

Using lecture handouts

Remember that handouts and lecture notes provided online are usually only outlines or summaries. They are meant to supplement a lecture or make it easier to follow. Such supplements are helpful, but they are not intended to be substitutes for attending the lecture and taking your own notes. If you want to understand and recall what is in a lecture, you must listen to or read the whole text of the lecture and take your own notes.

LEARNING IN TUTORIALS, SEMINARS, AND WORKSHOPS

Tutorials and seminars, like lectures, might be new teaching and learning situations for you. Tutorial and seminar groups are small, interactive groups that meet regularly throughout the semester to complement the lectures. They are intended primarily to provide you with the opportunity to express opinions, ask questions, and discuss course content with both your peers and your teaching assistant. The size of each group depends on the number of students in the course as a whole, but is usually between ten and twenty-five students. In most courses, the teaching assistant who takes your group will also act as your main contact with the department that runs the course. Your teaching assistant will try to get to know everyone in the group and will often be responsible for marking your assignments.

What is the difference between a tutorial and a seminar?

In practice, the distinction between tutorials and seminars is blurred, and people tend to use the terms interchangeably to mean any small, informal class in which discussion takes place between teacher and students. Sometimes, however, "seminar" refers to a more formal group in which students are expected to give talks on a chosen topic, whereas "tutorial" implies an informal teaching session that complements a lecture and usually is led by a teaching assistant.

Tutorial and seminar groups provide opportunities for

- clarifying ideas covered in lectures;
- exploring some aspects of lecture material in greater depth;
- practising speaking and active listening skills;
- debating ideas with others;
- developing independent thinking skills;
- getting to know a group of students in your course; and
- getting to know at least one member of the teaching staff who will also know you and give advice and help when you need them.

Getting the most out of tutorials and seminars

To get the most out of tutorials or seminars, you must be able to join in the discussion. The responsibility for successful learning in a small group is

TIP

Attend classes regularly; prepare thoroughly; ask questions; volunteer your own ideas; encourage others to speak; listen carefully to all contributions.

shared between students and teaching assistants. If you are poorly prepared or reluctant to speak, the teaching assistant might feel obliged to fill the silence, and instead of a discussion you will have yet another lecture. The alternatives might be total silence or a dialogue between the teaching assistant and perhaps one student. Always try to have a question to ask or an idea to offer in a small group. Your teaching assistant will be grateful for any contribution, and you will feel a greater involvement with what is happening.

For a successful tutorial or seminar, you need to

- attend regularly so that you get to know people quickly and learn to work with others;
- prepare by doing the appropriate reading or any other course work;
- check through the relevant lecture notes for any difficulties or suggestions you would like to raise;
- ask questions—if there is something you don't understand, there are probably others who don't understand either;
- ask for examples or evidence to explain difficult or controversial ideas;
- put forward your own ideas, especially if they are different from the ones you have heard in lectures;
- challenge the ideas of others, but do it politely;
- encourage others to speak; and
- listen actively and attentively.

Remember that the responsibility for a successful small group is shared by all the participants.

What is a workshop?

Workshops provide another form of small group learning and teaching. They differ from tutorials and seminars in that they are "doing" sessions rather than "discussion" sessions. Workshops are directed towards practising skills and usually involve the whole class in planned activities of different kinds. To get the most out of workshops, it is vital to prepare so that you can attempt the tasks set and complete them during class time. Workshops are usually at least two hours in duration. They form an important element of skills-based subjects, and attendance is usually compulsory. An important learning task in workshops is working with others.

Joining facilitated study groups

Some universities offer facilitated study groups or supplemental instruction for their larger classes. These study groups are small (often no more than half a dozen students) and are usually led by peer mentors who have some expertise in the subject matter being taught. Participation in them is generally voluntary. The purpose of these groups is not to duplicate what is being done in tutorials but to allow students to talk about questions that they might have about how best to succeed in the course. Questions that are raised might include

- how best to approach course readings;
- what material should be recorded in class notes;
- how to approach assignments; and
- how to prepare for class tests and quizzes.

CLASSROOM ETIQUETTE

Attending lectures and participating in tutorials and seminars can provide you with information, ideas, and a wide variety of viewpoints, but only if you listen respectfully to what your professors, teaching assistants, and colleagues are saying and make sure they have a chance to speak without distractions or interruptions.

- *Turn off cell phones.* There are few things more distracting than the sound of a cell phone ringing during a lecture or class discussion. There is simply no excuse for this happening. If, for some reason, you must be prepared to take an important call, put your phone on "meeting" mode and sit near the classroom door so that you can leave the room to answer it.
- *Do not send text messages, participate in online chats, or check emails while in class.* When you engage in online conversations during a class, it is distracting for you, for other students, and sometimes even for your professor.
- *Avoid having private conversations with friends during class.* There is nothing so important that it cannot wait another thirty or forty minutes until class is over.
- *Come to class prepared.* Be sure to bring adequate supplies of paper and pens to class. If you use a laptop, know that the battery is charged or sit near a power outlet. Leave time to use the washroom before class begins.
- *Let your professor know at the start of class if you must leave early.* If you know that you have to leave early, sit near the doorway to create as little disruption as possible when you leave. If you had to come to class late, sit where you will minimize disruption to the class; if possible, stay after class to apologize and explain your tardiness to your professor.

LEARNING AND LISTENING

In all the new situations you encounter at university, active learning is the key to success, and effective listening is a crucial part of active learning and clear communication. You can practise your listening skills in all the formal teaching situations that are part of your course, and this will help you to learn more easily.

Walt Whitman has pointed out that "to have great poets, there must be great audiences too." If you think that a lecture or a small group discussion is boring, or you feel as though you have not learned anything, ask yourself whether you have been hearing without listening. If the answer is "yes," then the problem is at least partly your fault, and you can do something about it.

GLOSSARY

discipline   Field of study.

EAL learner   Someone for whom English is an additional language (also sometimes called ESL, English as a second language, or L2).

motivation   The impulse toward action: in university, usually this action involves reading course material, attending classes, writing essays, working on assignments, or studying for tests and exams.

seminar   A somewhat formal group in which students are expected to give talks on a chosen topic.

teaching assistant   Someone, usually a graduate student, who works with a professor in meeting with students individually, delivering small tutorial sessions, setting quizzes, or grading essays, problem sets, and exams.

transferable learning   Learning that is not restricted to content but, rather, addresses skills that are essential in life as well as university studies.

tutorial   An informal teaching session that complements a lecture and usually is led by a teaching assistant.

SUGGESTED FURTHER READING

Carter, Carol, Bishop, Joyce, & Kravits, Sarah L. (2008). *Keys to success: Building analytical, creative, and practical skills.* Toronto, ON: Prentice Hall.

Fleet, Joan, Goodchild, Fiona, & Zajchowski, Richard. (2006). *Learning for success.* Toronto, ON: Thomson Nelson.

Pauk, Walter. (1984). *How to study in college.* Boston, MA: Houghton Mifflin.

Vogel, Susan A. (1990). *College students with learning disabilities: A handbook.* DeKalb, IL: Northern Illinois University Press.

RELATED WEBSITES

www.ucc.vt.edu/stdysk/cornell.html
Academic Success Centre, George Washington University. "Learn the Cornell method of note taking."

www.ucc.vt.edu/stdysk/cornell.html
Cook Counseling Center, Virginia Tech. "The Cornell system."

www.adm.uwaterloo.ca/infocs/study/listening.html
Counselling Services, University of Waterloo. "Listening and note-taking."

www.dyslexia-college.com/notes.html
Dyslexia at College. "Taking notes from books and at lectures."

ANSWER KEY TO EXERCISE

Using Abbreviations
1. c21 Cdn univ = trnsfrmd by almst unvrsl intro of new tech: lptps, netbks, ipads, ppts, pdcasts, & online communities.
2. intro of techs –> # trnsfrmtions in way profs thnk abt assign design & mrkng crit.

Clocking In:
Managing Your Time

An unhurried sense of time is in itself a form of wealth.
Bonnie Friedman, 1999

One of the great advantages of university over school or work is that it leaves you free to organize your own life. A number of you will find that you do not have many formal class times, and the rest of your week can be spent as you like. Or can it? You have books to read, labs to prepare, essays to write, and exams to study for. Nobody will tell you when or how to do these things, but they will expect them to be done on time and to a high standard. If you want to enjoy yourself and do well at your studies, you will need to organize your time so that you can meet all your deadlines, read widely, and still have time to enjoy leisure activities. This chapter offers advice on organizing your time, setting priorities, and managing procrastination.

STUDYING OUTSIDE FORMAL CLASSES

University, more than anything else, is about independent learning. You will need to spend more study time outside the class than in it. Most university professors expect that their full-time students will spend the equivalent of a normal working week, each week, on their studies. The amount of work given to students doing a full-time course is based on the assumption that the students will work at their studies for about 40 hours each week. Most students have about 15 hours of formal classes each week of the semester. This leaves them 25 hours of independent study time to organize for themselves. Some students, usually those in the professional faculties, have as many as 25 hours of formal classes each week. This still leaves at least 15 hours of independent

NAVIGATING LEARNING CHALLENGES
Anticipate Possible Difficulties

It is a fact of life for students with ADHD (attention deficit hyperactivity disorder) or LD (learning disabilities) that you will have to dedicate more time and energy to your studies than many other students do. Don't set yourself up for frustration and disappointment. Rather than expecting yourself to do well with only one hour out of class spent studying for each hour spent in the classroom, you might find that a more realistic estimate would be two and a half hours of study time for each hour spent in class. This will allow sufficient time for much-needed breaks. In many cases, this means taking a reduced course load or participating in fewer co-curricular activities.

Be sure to allow ten or fifteen minutes each day to make a daily schedule of all your activities. Good organization and planning are essential (Nadeau, 1994, p. 34).

---

study time; in especially demanding programs, a student might need to put in more time, expecting to study at least one hour out of class for every hour spent in class. You will do much of that study by yourself at home or in residence, in the library, on the bus or subway, in the doctor's waiting room, in the cafeteria or café, and anywhere else that you can catch a few quiet moments.

There is a lot of evidence to suggest that students who are able to organize their time effectively do better than those who are not. When you realize just how much of your study time you have to organize for yourself, this is not surprising. So, how do you start planning your study for the year? The best way is to make up your own personal study timetable for each week and each semester and then stick to it.

> **TIP**
>
> Be realistic in organizing your time: take account of leisure, family, and work commitments. Fit them around your study time rather than vice versa.

Planning your study time

Individuals learn at different rates and have different lifestyles. Before you plan a personal timetable, you must have an idea of how you usually spend your time so that you know what you need to cut out and what it is important for you to retain. Your study timetable must reflect your usual pattern of life, or it will not be successful for your new tasks. Before you start to make a timetable, make sure you can answer the following questions:

- *How much leisure time do you need each day?* Be honest with yourself about this. Some leisure time is essential (all work and no play . . .," as the saying goes), but you must be realistic.
- *When is it best for you to take it?* You might find, for example, if you like jogging, that this exercise suits you at a particular time of the day; if

watching television is your relaxation, you should be honest about it and allow some time for that in the evening. It is no use planning to watch your favourite television show at seven in the morning so that your evenings will be free for study (unless, of course, you have made arrangements to record or download the show in order to watch it at your own convenience).

- *How long can you concentrate without your attention wandering?* Some people like to study in large blocks of, say, three hours so that they can really come to grips with any particular topic. Others like to timetable one hour at a time and to change their activities, or at least their topic, every hour. Some studies suggest that taking a very short break after only 25 minutes will allow you to work for longer blocks of time.

NAVIGATING LEARNING CHALLENGES
Between-Class Study Periods

It is particularly important for students with ADD (attention deficit disorder) or ADHD (attention deficit hyperactivity disorder) to work for shorter periods of time (approximately 15 minutes) followed by short breaks (no more than 5 minutes) to help with concentration. Setting alarms on watches, cell phones, or laptops can help you stay on track. Take advantage of the time between classes that is often wasted: this is frequently an ideal amount of time for short, focused study sessions. (Nadeau, p. 31).

- *What are the periods in the day when you feel most alert?* If you are a morning person, you might find it very productive to get started early. If you are a night owl, it is no use timetabling blocks of study starting at five in the morning.
- *Where are the places, on and off campus, that you can study best?* Ideally, study areas should be quiet, well lit, private, and comfortable. If you have children, siblings, or housemates sharing your private space at home, or if you live in a noisy residence, you might have to compromise about your study area. A quiet part of the library might be a good substitute for a private study or dorm room.
- *Does your concentration span vary according to what you are doing?* Do you find it easier to study subjects you are interested in? Most people do. If you have to study something you do not find very interesting, it might be best to work on it at your most productive time of day, rather than leaving it until the end of your study session.

- *How long do you need to spend to get certain tasks done?* Are you a fast reader? How many drafts will you need for an assignment? You need to be honest with yourself about this. You cannot expect yourself to write a 2,000-word essay in one day or night.

If you can answer all these questions easily, you are ready to start planning your weekly and semester timetables. If you cannot, you need to start with a monitoring week to observe your own activities and find out the answers.

Monitoring yourself

Try keeping a detailed diary of your activities every day for a week. This might seem rather tedious, but the result should enable you to get an overview of your usual pattern of life. You can use this pattern to decide how, when, and where study is likely to be most effective for you. Realistic study planning should be designed to match your personality and life-style. On the one hand, making general resolutions, such as "I will study x number of hours per day or week," usually does not work and can make you feel frustrated, guilty, and inadequate. On the other hand, if your social life or television watching uses up your whole week, you will have to decide what to cut out—or at least what to cut down on.

EXERCISE

MONITORING YOUR TIME

Make a monitoring timetable, like the one in Table 2.1, or use an online time-tracker or app, and during the next week, record within each slot your lectures, tutorials, labs, travelling times, meals, study times, and leisure activities. It is important to note everything you do, even for short periods. You might be surprised at how some things add up. You need to record everything that might influence how, where, and when you study best and worst. All the following points might be important.

- Note your study times, which subjects you are studying, and specify whether you are reading, writing, problem solving, note taking, or memorizing.
- Note where you are studying. Be specific. If you are in the library, what part are you in?
- Note how you are feeling at particular times of the day. For example, at four in the afternoon, are you feeling tired, anxious, relaxed, depressed, happy?

- Note the times when you have concentrated effectively and the time span for which you maintained it. Was it early in the day or late, after a meal or before one, when you were under pressure, alone, or with a friend, after physical exercise?
- Note distractions through the day, either distractions within yourself or from the environment. These might include arguments with other people, expectations and demands made on you by family and friends, health concerns, or anything that upsets you.
- Try out different places rather than studying in the same place all the time. Note how you respond to different environments.
- Note anything that was especially successful or unsuccessful.

When your monitoring week is over, you might be able to look at your timetable and see a pattern that will help you to plan the weeks ahead. Plan to maintain the factors that have helped you to study and to manage or change the ones that have distracted you. Once you know your pattern, you can use the same kind of timetable to draw up daily and weekly study goals according to semester deadlines.

Table 2.1   Monitoring timetable for planning personal study

Times	Mon	Tues	Wed	Thurs	Fri	Sat	Sun
8–9							
9–10							
10–11							
11–12							
12–1							
1–2							
2–3							
3–4							
4–5							
5–6							
6–7							
7–8							
8–9							
9–10							
10–11							

Drawing up a personal study timetable

If you want to make the most of your study time, you will need two timetables. The first is a timetable for the whole semester, listing target dates for tests, class presentations, essays, problem sets, labs, and required reading. Be clear about your short- and long-term goals for managing course readings, handing in work, and preparing for tests and exams.

Planning your semester

Sometimes students make the mistake of jotting down the dates when essays or lab reports are due but neglecting to note what percentage of their final grade these assignments are worth. It is important not to lose sight of the relative value of various assignments and tests; otherwise, you can get caught up in things that *feel* urgent at the expense of doing things that *are* important. Often students take more time preparing for quizzes, labs, and class presentations than they need to because there is an urgency about these things: these are all activities that take place within a limited period of time. With labs and class presentations, moreover, there is the additional fear of looking, or feeling, foolish in front of peers if things do not go well. An essay or project for a course that is being taken to fulfill a distribution requirement, though, feels as if it can easily be neglected until the last minute. At that point, however, necessary research materials may no longer be available and you simply will not have enough time to do a good job; these larger research projects, too, frequently are worth a substantial portion of the final grade.

- An assignment that is worth 5 per cent of your final grade should be given 5 per cent of your time; an assignment that is worth 50 per cent of your final grade should be given 50 per cent of your time.
- Planning a whole **semester**, rather than just a week, at a time allows you to identify **"crunch" periods**, those few weeks each term when most of your assignments at least *seem* to all be due at once.
- Once you have identified crunch periods, plan around them: get **seminar presentations**, major research for final papers, course readings, and time-consuming group projects out of the way as early in the term as you can.
- Whenever possible, plan your personal life around crunch periods, too. If you intend to take a short vacation, entertain a friend from out of town, or have your wisdom teeth out, try to schedule these things before or after the mid-term crunch.

Chunking

Looking at the due dates for all your assignments, quizzes, and class presentations on a single one-semester calendar allows you to think intentionally and realistically about ways to "**chunk**" the work that you have to do. Chunking involves dividing large tasks into smaller, more manageable parts: for instance, you might divide a fifty-page chapter that has been assigned into five ten-page units, reading one unit a night for a week; you could chunk a 1,500-word essay into an introduction, a conclusion, and three main points, all of which are approximately 300 words in length; or you might divide a group project into four distinct stages, planning separate sessions for **brainstorming**, researching, writing, and editing.

- Chunking helps you stay on track with assignments; it is also a good technique to keep you from feeling overwhelmed: for most of us, it is much easier, and less stressful, to imagine ourselves tackling small, concrete tasks than it is to picture ourselves initiating large, multi-staged projects.

Back-planning

Chunking also makes it easier to **back-plan**. Back-planning entails identifying a goal; then listing all the logical steps that you must take in order to reach that goal; and, finally, developing a reasonable schedule for tackling each of the different steps. If you have already broken a larger task into discrete chunks, then all that is left for you to do is ensure that you have enough time to get everything done. If you figure that it will take you three hours to write 300 words, then you know, for instance, that it will take you 15 hours to write a 1,500-word essay. If you know, too, that you cannot write more than 300 words a day, then you will need five days to write the essay, breaking it into chunks. You might add to that a day for planning, five days for research, a day for organizing your resources and documentation, and a day for a final editing. The total number of days, using a back-planning model, would be 13 with an extra day added in case something goes wrong. If you know that you have an essay due on the last day of November, then you must start working on it no later than the 15th of the month.

- Do not forget to factor in the unexpected when back-planning: things like seasonal flu and unanticipated social invitations can undermine even the best-laid, and best-intentioned, plans.
- It is usually possible, and often necessary, to back-plan several activities at the same time. For any given week, you might simultaneously be working on a group project, writing an essay, keeping up with course readings, and studying for a test.

EXERCISE

BACK-PLANNING

Imagine that you have two weeks to accomplish the following:

1. Read a 42 page chapter, divided into six subsections, in your psychology textbook.
2. Read a 56 page chapter, divided into eight subsections, in your biology textbook.
3. Write a short (three-page) essay for anthropology in response to a five-page article that your professor has posted online.

Back-plan the three assignments:

- List the various steps involved (chunk the tasks) in each of the three assignments.
- Make a two-week schedule: plan to accomplish each of the component tasks, completing all three assignments within 14 days.

JUGGLING COMPETING DEMANDS

Setting priorities

In addition to juggling competing academic obligations, most students have to balance their schoolwork with the demands of busy personal lives. A number of studies have shown that students who engage in co-curricular activities perform better academically than those who spend their time doing nothing but studying; it is frequently essential, though, for students to make difficult decisions about how much time to dedicate to part-time jobs, volunteer activities, athletics, student clubs, and leadership opportunities. The decision about whether to spend an afternoon studying chemistry, volunteering at a hospital, or working in a local pharmacy should, whenever possible, be made intentionally, after weighing a number of considerations: How well are you doing in the course? What kind of experience are you getting from your volunteer activity? How badly do you need the money that you make at your part-time job?

- When you must choose between several competing activities, be sure to think about your overarching priorities: Are you most concerned with having a 4.0 **GPA** (grade point average)? Is making a contribution to society most important to you, both personally and professionally? Is your foremost consideration paying the rent? Maybe spending time with friends and family, or becoming a varsity athlete, or taking a leadership role on campus is what you most want to accomplish. Unless you have taken the time to identify your key priorities, it will be difficult to choose how best to spend your time.

EXERCISE

SETTING PRIORITIES

Take a few moments to list three activities or goals that are important to you. Rank them (1 = most important; 2 = less important; 3 = least important) in order of importance. Refer to this list when trying to make decisions about how best to use your time.

Co-curricular activities

If your foremost priority is achieving a high GPA, do not assume that spending all your time studying is the single key to success. What many students do not realize is that most **co-curricular activities** actually foster important competencies to help you succeed academically, personally, and professionally. For instance, working collaboratively with others is a skill that you will need in order to excel in laboratory and field work, various performance art programs, designing engineering projects, and so on. You might find that, rather than distracting you from your studies, joining a campus choral group, film society, or dragon boat team can actually make you *more* successful in your academic pursuits: while planning the program for your film society's fall festival, you will probably develop skills in organization, negotiation, project management, and communication—in short, in all the competencies that will help you succeed in *any* group enterprise that you engage in.

• How much time you allocate for individual academic and social activities should depend, in part, on the degree to which they will help you achieve your larger, overarching goals.

Planning your week

Once you have these goals clearly set out, you can make another table, based on your monitoring table and the deadlines set in your semester table. This is a timetable for the coming week. Keep in mind some of the following suggestions when developing your study plan.

• Determine which tasks will take a lot of concentration and which will take little effort.
• Allot your difficult tasks (for example, reading challenging course materials or solving complex equations) to the periods in the day when your concentration is best.
• Place the tasks that require less concentration, like rewriting or reviewing notes or making **flash cards**, at times you are aware that your concentrating ability is low.

When you feel that you do not have enough time to get everything done, even though it looks in your schedule as if there is plenty of time, it is usually because you are trying to tackle the wrong task at the wrong time. Most often, there is a temptation to fill available time in your schedule with tasks that take a lot of time but are not overly difficult; these are sometimes called **time-intensive** tasks. If you have a research paper to write, for example, you might spend a weekend in the library going through books and articles and taking notes. There is nothing wrong with this; in fact, it is what you should be doing. It becomes a problem, though, when you have done enough preliminary research and could (or should) start writing your paper, but instead you head back to the library to do more research. This is a very common pattern. It happens for two reasons: Reading through books and articles for a research paper is usually not a very intellectually challenging exercise. It takes a lot of time, but does not necessarily present any real difficulty. If you dedicate time to it, you will see results. It is also "safe"; no one is going to evaluate you on how many notes you take or how well you take them.

Actually writing your paper, though, can be an altogether different matter. For many students, writing a paper can be a demanding task, requiring concentration and intellectual effort: it is a **mind-intensive** activity. When you finally decide that it is time to start writing, moreover, there is no guarantee that you will be able to do so. You might sit . . . and sit . . . and sit . . . and not think of a single idea to write down. The fact that your professor will be evaluating you on what you write does not make matters easier. The result is that students often put off writing until the last minute. By then, they have too many notes to sift through, too little time to do a thorough job, and too much pressure to be able to think and write clearly.

- Be careful not to fill your weekly schedule with only time-intensive activities; be sure to allow enough time for mind-intensive activities so that you do not leave them until the last minute.
- Avoid the tendency, too, to concentrate on tasks or subjects that are easier or more interesting than others. It all has to be done sometime.

EXERCISE

TIME-INTENSIVE VS. MIND-INTENSIVE ACTIVITIES

Take a few moments to think about all the activities that you have to do every day.

- List three activities that you find mind-intensive.
- List three activities that you find time-intensive.

Refer back to these lists when planning how to use your time.

TIP

Use small blocks of time for "busy" tasks like photocopying or sorting out lecture notes. You can use even fifteen minutes productively for tasks like this.

Another way to use time more effectively is to take advantage of periods during your day that might otherwise be wasted. Most students have thirty or forty minutes between classes that get spent texting friends or standing in line at coffee kiosks. Start thinking of ways to take advantage of these brief periods to do small tasks that might otherwise start to add up and leave you feeling overwhelmed.

Finding time for yourself

When you are planning your weekly schedule, be sure to make time for the things that you find personally fulfilling. Students sometimes decide to eliminate from their schedules things that they think should not really have a place in their busy lives anymore. If you have been following a weekly television show, or have always had Friday or Sunday dinner with your family, or like to play pickup hockey on weekends, or are used to taking time every day to look at friends' social networking pages, it is probably not a good idea to try to completely eliminate these things from your schedule. When you do not make time in your daily life for the things that are important to you, no matter how trivial they might seem, you will probably end up wasting time on things that are much less satisfying. If, for instance, you decide that you will not let yourself tune in to a television show that you usually watch, in all likelihood you will spend the hour (and often significantly more time than that) aimlessly searching websites, chatting with friends online, sorting clothing, or reading magazines and fan fiction; in short, you will not get your academic work done *and* you will have missed out on something that you enjoy.

> **TIP**
>
> Make room in your schedule for the things that are important to you. Just be sure to set a reasonable time limit for them (and stick to it!).

- Include specific time for meals, leisure, and recreational activities. This is essential.

Give yourself a break

Although it might seem counterintuitive, taking time away from your studies, in the form of short breaks, can actually help you study in a more sustained and focused way. Pushing yourself to stay with a long assigned reading, especially an informationally dense textbook, is not a strategy that will help you learn. At some point, your brain simply shuts down and stops processing information. Try getting into the habit of taking a short break before brain fog settles in.

> **TIP**
>
> Set a timer for your study periods (25 minutes) so you don't have to keep watching the clock. This method is sometimes called the **Pomodoro Technique**. It was popularized by Francesco Cirillo, who was inspired by an egg timer in the shape of a tomato!

There is an additional problem in studying without taking breaks: if you do not give your mind time to make meaning of what you have been studying, then you run the risk of not being able to retrieve the material when you are under pressure. Have you ever had the experience of putting in long hours studying for a test, limiting the number of breaks that you take because you are afraid that you simply cannot afford to take any time away from your studying, and then, when you are actually writing the test, going blank when you look at a question? You know that you have encountered the material before; you can even picture the textbook page in your mind, but you just cannot recall the electron-dot structure for formaldehyde, the role of agribusiness in NAFTA, or the difference between synecdoche and metonymy. The experience of going blank most often happens when you study for too long without taking a break. Although you might not realize it, when you are stretching, getting a glass of water, or making notes to yourself about things you need to do, your brain is actually processing, or making meaning of, the information you have been studying. In a sense, it is filing the information so that the material can readily be retrieved. If you do not give your mind time to do this, then sometimes it becomes difficult to find the material that you are looking for because it has not been "sorted" and "filed" for easy retrieval.

Long- vs. short-distance studying

Just as there are some athletes who are better suited to long- than they are to short-distance running, so there are some students who work best when they have long, unbroken blocks of time (except for five-minute breaks!) available to them; other students get tired after just an hour. It is useful, in planning your weekly schedule, to identify which one of these models best describes how you work. If you know that you need long periods of time to settle into your work—perhaps starting a study period with some typical "distractions" (checking your email and friends' social networking pages or making yourself a snack) but then working without interruption for whole days at a time—then you need to guard against the impulse to book noon-hour writing centre appointments, arrange to meet friends for lunch, or agree to take a shift at work in the middle of the day. You will feel that you have just barely started (if, in fact, you start at all, knowing that you will be interrupting yourself in a short while) when it is time to pack up your things and leave. It is best to use the available shorter periods of time in your schedule for getting things done, and to keep whole days or nights unbroken by other responsibilities. If, by contrast, you are someone who gets bored and distracted after working for short periods of time, then be sure to break up long, empty days with other activities: you will not work for a full day without interrupting your studies, anyway, so prepare to work for only short periods of time to avoid frustration and disappointment in yourself.

- Decide whether you prefer large blocks of concentrated study or shorter periods alternating with other activities.
- Once you have decided on a schedule that seems to work for you, let other people know when you are free to do things with them, and when you have to spend time doing your work.

Watch out for procrastination

Procrastination is a more common problem among university students than you might imagine. A surprisingly large number of bright students did well in high school without actually working very hard. They realized at some point that if they put a lot of work into an assignment they did well, but if they put very little work into an assignment, pulling it together at the last minute, they might also have done well; as a result, they came to university having learned that there is no particular benefit in putting time or effort into something. For most students, though, this "strategy" simply does not work in a university setting: the standards are much higher than they were in high school and the competition is too intense. It becomes necessary to break the habit of doing things at the last minute, but, like most bad habits, procrastination is a difficult behavioural pattern to break.

If you find yourself putting off doing something, ask yourself the following questions:

- *Is there something about the task that I do not understand?* We frequently procrastinate when there is something about a task that we find confusing. If you do not know what an **annotated bibliography** is, then it is very likely that you will not know how to start writing one. If you are confused about how to initiate something, get help.

- *Am I waiting until the "right" moment to begin working on something?* The right moment is . . . now. Sometimes you just have to sit down and start working. Thinking can be a bit like turning on a water tap that has not been used for a long time: the water will run rusty before it runs clear. Sometimes you simply have to stay with a task until your mind rids itself of mental "rust" (thoughts, worries, daydreams, and so on) before you can focus. Remember, too, that thinking takes time. This seems obvious, but it is something that we often forget. You cannot force an idea into your head; you have to wait patiently for it to arrive.

- *Do I have trouble deciding what task to do first?* Be specific in your schedule about what you will study in each time slot. Instead of writing "English" in a timeslot, for example, write "read two chapters of *The Stone Angel*." If you cannot do everything you wanted in the time you have set yourself, you will know to set a smaller task for your next study block.

- *Do I frequently find myself thinking, "I really have to start that essay about Margaret Atwood now" or "I ought to be working on my math assignment"?* Every time you say to yourself "I must," "I should," or "I ought to" do something, give yourself a little mental shake; rephrase what you have been thinking: "I *want* to get going on that English assignment about dystopia in *The Handmaid's Tale*" or "I would *like* to see if I can figure out the solution to that problem we were working on in calculus." Sometimes you have to remind yourself that you are actually interested in literature, geology, psychology, or physics. That is why you came to university in the first place. And if you do not ever get *any* pleasure out of doing your schoolwork, then maybe it would be a good idea to arrange to meet with your registrar or someone in a career counselling service.

TIP

Set short-term goals for each evening's study. Make sure that your goals are not too ambitious. Combine some routine tasks with more challenging study.

- *Do I feel that there is so much work to do that there is no point in even trying to get it done?* When you are feeling overwhelmed by how much work you have, remember chunking. Breaking assignments into smaller components (reading chapters, not textbooks; writing paragraphs, not essays) can make seemingly insurmountable tasks less daunting.

- *Do I feel that studying takes up all my time, that I never have time to spend with my friends?* Finding friends with whom you can prepare for exams or review a day's lectures can turn studying into a social occasion; it can also foster active learning and improve your communication skills.

- *Do I delay starting because there is a part of me that figures that whatever I do will never be good enough?* Perfectionism keeps many students from working on assignments. If you feel that nothing you do will meet your own (often impossibly high!) standards, then there can seem to be no point in even starting. Remind yourself that you do not have to compromise your standards. You can still try to do the very best that you can, even if the time that you have—whether it is a month, a week, or an hour—seems ridiculously short. If you suspect that you are a perfectionist, put strategies in place to prevent giving up before you even begin; for example, learn to narrow down research essay topics so that you really can cover all the available material relating to your topic in a reasonable amount of time.

- *Am I usually disappointed in myself for failing to follow the schedules that I make?* Setting unrealistic expectations for yourself can also make you feel inadequate. It is another way that perfectionism manifests itself. Be flexible about your schedule and feel happy about changing it to meet unforeseen circumstances, changing moods, or health needs. Being too rigid is as unproductive as being disorganized.

> **TIP**
>
> Leave some time free for unexpected difficulties, distractions, and fun.

EXERCISE

IDENTIFYING PROCRASTINATION POTHOLES

If you are someone who tends to procrastinate, take a few moments to think about the last time you put off doing something. Now try to figure out why you procrastinated.

- Did you feel overwhelmed?
- Did you feel resentful?
- Were you uncertain about how to begin?
- Did you feel that it just wouldn't be good enough?

Often, identifying the source of your procrastination is the first step toward moving forward.

STUDYING AT NIGHT

Studying at night is a necessary but daunting part of university study unless you are one of those dedicated and super-organized people who can keep to a regular nine to five study program five days a week, every week. How can you make it easier?

Studying productively at night

- Try to beat fatigue with gentle exercise: skip, run, swim, or jog for a short session after you finish your day's work but before you start your evening study.

- Start the night's program with a short period of quiet planning to set realistic goals for the evening. You will feel better if you have goals, and better still if you achieve them. To stimulate energy, it is useful to start with material that is fresh, like reviewing lecture notes for the day. Go back and date and title the notes. Underline points that you remember the professor emphasizing. Fill in any words that you missed.

- Check whether there is anything that needs to be done urgently. If there is, you might need to change your timetable, but you will be glad you checked.

- Understand your own feelings. If you are feeling tense, worried, or depressed, can you trace the cause? There are usually some options to explore to dissipate the feelings. If you cannot see where to start or where to go next, talk to someone about it. Your ability to study will be very strongly influenced by the way you feel, so never ignore your feelings; however, you probably cannot afford the time wasted using them as an excuse to do nothing.

GLOSSARY

annotated bibliography Alphabetically ordered list of works (for example, papers or books) on a given topic, which summarizes and assesses each item.

back-planning A scheduling technique that starts with identifying a goal, then listing all the steps that must be taken to reach that goal, and then developing a plan for tackling each of the different steps.

brainstorming Jotting down all the ideas that come into your head as a prelude to writing an essay or other assignment.

chunking Dividing large tasks into smaller, more manageable units.

co-curricular activities Activities on campus (leadership, athletics, clubs, student societies) that are not part of the academic curriculum but that often support or enhance academic programming.

"crunch" periods Several weeks in the academic term (usually the middle and the end of each term) when many assignments are due and tests or exams are written.

flash cards   Index cards on which key information is noted, with terms and concepts written on one side of the card and definitions, examples, references on the other.

GPA   Grade point average: a measure of a student's academic achievement; usually both a sessional and a cumulative GPA are tracked.

mind-intensive activity   An activity that requires concentration and, usually, a distraction-free environment.

Pomodoro Technique   A technique based on using an egg timer to maintain short study periods, popularized by Francesco Cirillo.

procrastination   Putting things off until tomorrow that you can do today, usually resulting in anxiety and, often, work that does not reflect a student's true knowledge and ability.

semester   Originally referring to one of the two periods of an academic year; generally used less literally now, with many universities now having three terms per year.

seminar presentations   An in-class presentation taking the form of a prepared essay that is read aloud in class or, more frequently, an informal talk or PowerPoint presentation on a given subject.

time-intensive activity   An activity like making flash cards or rewriting notes that takes quite a bit of time but does not require much effort or attention.

SUGGESTED FURTHER READING

Carter, Carol, Bishop, Joyce, & Kravits, Sarah L. (2008). *Keys to success: Building analytical, creative, and practical skills*. Toronto, ON: Prentice Hall.

Cirillo, Francesco. (2009). *The pomodoro technique*. Retrieved from Lulu.com

Fleet, Joan, Goodchild, Fiona, & Zajchowski, Richard. (1988). *Successful learning*. London, ON: University of Western Ontario.

Hallowell, Edward M., & Ratey, John J. (2005). *Delivered from distraction: Getting the most out of life with attention deficit disorder*. New York: Random House.

University of Victoria. (1996). *Strategies for studying*. Victoria, BC: Orca.

Walter, Tim, & Siebert, Al. (1987). *Student success*. New York: Rinehart and Winston.

RELATED WEBSITES

www.asc.utoronto.ca/Publications/Time-Management.htm
Academic Success Centre, University of Toronto. "Time management."

http://ADHD-world.blogspot.com/
Conners, C. Keith. "ADHD World."

www.ucc.vt.edu/stdysk/htimesug.html
Cook Counseling Center, Virginia Tech. "Time scheduling suggestions."

www.learningcommons.uoguelph.ca/guides/time_management/html/ analyze_need_for_structure.html
Learning Services, University of Guelph. "A guide to time management: Analyzing your need for structure."

Reading Up:
Strategic Reading

The more that you read, The more things you will know.
Theodor [Dr. Seuss] Geisel, 1978

APPROACHES TO READING

Imagine that you want to order a vegetarian takeout dinner from a local Indian restaurant. When you open their menu, you probably do not begin at "starters" and then work your way through the entire menu, reading the ingredients of each soup, kebab, tandoori, beef, lamb, chicken, rice, and vegetable dish. You might select an order of mixed vegetable fritters and then go to the vegetarian listing. Once there, you probably do not read every detail about every dish, but skim the section for something with ingredients that you especially like—say, chickpeas and potatoes. You carefully read the descriptions of a few dishes, then find one that has chickpeas cooked with potatoes, onions, and aromatic spices. That's the one you want. You choose some rice and roti to have with it and place your order.

When mechanics check their manuals to find how big a spark-plug gap should be, or when bakers check their recipes to find how much coconut to use in a Nanaimo bar, they take control. They skim the material and then focus on what they want to know.

Reading for work is often like this. Reading for pleasure can be, too. Confident readers skim the beginnings of novels and reject ones that do not appeal to them. They might skim over a book of poems before deciding which ones they will read more carefully. To be an efficient reader, you need to know why you are reading and what you are looking for.

Putting yourself in control as a reader is essential for success in university. Being in control of your own reading means that you have to decide what to read and how to read it. You also have to take risks by leaving some books, articles, or sections of books or articles, unread. You cannot read everything, and you cannot read everything in the same way. You must match your method of reading to your purpose for reading. Authors write in many different ways depending on their subject areas, their purpose for writing, and the audience they are writing for. You need to be flexible and to use an approach that is suitable for your own purpose and the kind of book or article you are reading.

PRACTISING READING

You can increase your reading speed and understanding of language by practising your reading. Like any other skill, reading comes more easily if you do it often. Just as your driving improves as you become more familiar with the steering, the gear shift, the brakes, and the roads, and just as you learn to bake good bread by trying different techniques on many occasions, you become a good reader by reading a lot and by trying different ways of getting the most out of your reading. One good way to practise your reading is to read articles from a newspaper like the *Globe and Mail, La Presse,* the *Financial Post*, the *Ottawa Citizen*, the *Gazette*, the *Calgary Herald*, or the *Windsor Star*, and better-quality magazines like the *Walrus, Scientific American, National Geographic, Rolling Stone Magazine*, the *Economist, Brick*, the *New Statesman*, or similar publications.

Reading these publications will have three benefits. First, it will improve your reading speed and comprehension. Second, it will accustom you to reading in different subject areas on topics that interest a wide range of educated people and, thus, it will familiarize you with the vocabularies and writing styles of those subjects. Finally, it will give you examples of professional writers producing information and opinions for the kinds of readers you will be writing for. Reading the major political, economic, and scientific articles (not just the entertainment and the sports sections) in one newspaper each day and one magazine each week will help with your communication skills at several levels. You can legitimately count time spent in this way as study time.

Be wary of courses that promise glib ways of improving your reading speed. These are a bit like the advertisements that promise to remove all the unsightly fat from your thighs in three weeks, or to give you pectoral

Improving language acquisition
Students for whom English is an additional language (EAL) will find it especially useful to read well-written English language newspapers and magazines extensively. Try to keep flash cards containing words that, although new to you, appear frequently in these sources.

muscles like Arnold Schwarzenegger's in six days without any diets or exercise. Most people read at a speed that allows them to comprehend what they are reading. Improving your speed is no use if you do not at the same time improve your comprehension. The more you read, the more easily you will understand, but you must be reading at the right level and in areas where the style and level of understanding required are relevant to your studies. Reading celebrity and entertainment magazines will not help you read and understand physics textbooks more easily, and flipping through clothing catalogues will probably not help you read law journals. Novels, biographies, and books of popular science, as well as current affairs magazines and newspapers, will help to extend your vocabulary and feeling for the structures of professional writing.

Improving reading speed

Underlying the technique known as **speed-reading**, though, is one very important idea: if you really focus your attention (and your eyes!) on what you are reading, you will probably find that you can read faster than you think you can. Most of us read inefficiently, bringing to the task no sense of urgency. This happens, in part, because much of the reading that we do—at least, until we go to university—is done purely for pleasure; it is something to occupy us on a rainy day at the cottage or to help us fall asleep at night. As a consequence, if you sit down to read a chapter of your psychology or chemistry textbook after dinner tonight, there is a good chance that you will still be reading that chapter long after you should be getting ready for bed. If you do not intentionally think about reading quickly, you will probably find that reading will fill any amount of time that you give to it.

> **TIP**
>
> Although there are a number of speed-reading systems, the most important thing to remember is to stay on task: read actively; read attentively.

You *can* train yourself to read faster, however. Find a book that is not particularly challenging: often a current bestseller is a good choice. Read it before turning in for the night, timing yourself to see how many pages you get read in ten minutes. If you read five pages in that time, then in a few days, see if you can read six pages in ten minutes. If that works, without your sacrificing any comprehension, then in a few days, try for seven. Keep up this pattern until you reach the point where you simply are not understanding and retaining new material. Backtrack until you are reading for maximum speed, comprehension, and retention. Keep reading each night at this new increased reading speed. For many of us, reading faster is a question of making the effort to read at an increased rate combined with developing the eye muscles that allow our eyes to quickly scan a page without getting tired. In all likelihood, you will find that as your reading speed improves when you read for pleasure, it will also improve when you are reading assigned texts.

EXERCISE

READING SPEED

- Pick out a book to read and decide on a consistent way to track your reading speed. You might want to use the reading log in Figure 3.1 below.

Figure 3.1   Reading log

Book Title		
Date	# Minutes	# Pages

- Read for ten minutes. Note how many pages you read.
- Do this for three days.
- On the fourth day, try to read one more page in the same time period (ten minutes).
- Do this for three days.
- On the eighth day, try to read one more page in the same time period (ten minutes).
- Repeat this pattern.
- Stop trying to increase your speed when you have reached a speed at which you no longer understand or remember what you read.
- Go back to reading at your new "best" speed.
- Try to maintain this as your new reading speed.

Skimming texts

Learning to effectively skim or scan a text is essential to managing your course work at university. Not every word in every assigned text is going to be important, and it is critical that you develop strategies to help you figure out what you need to read carefully and what might at some point be important but does not have to be read carefully right now.

NAVIGATING LEARNING CHALLENGES
Using Modified Speed-Reading

Some studies indicate that students with ADHD (attention deficit hyperactivity disorder) might benefit from using a modified speed-reading method. Just as reading too quickly can affect your ability to focus on what you are reading, reading too slowly can inhibit concentration and impede your ability to process information.

(http://www.cusu.cam.ac.uk/academic/exams/speedreading.html)

- Have a question in mind before you open up your textbook or journal article; you might want to know, "What are the key ideas being presented in this chapter?" or "Is the material covered in this article going to be relevant to the essay I am writing?"
- When you are skimming a text, do not bother trying to take notes.
- Remember—you can probably read faster than you think you can.
- Do not get bogged down by words or concepts that are unfamiliar. The point of the exercise is not to understand or retain what you skim; the point is simply to get an overview of what is there.

EXERCISE

SKIMMING

Skim the text in Figure 3.2. Try to catch the general idea without worrying too much about details.

Figure 3.2   Skimming a text

> **Reading for Pleasure vs. Reading for Speed**
> Students often feel that they must choose between reading for pleasure and reading for speed. The best reading, though, propels us forward, urging us to turn the pages of a book at an ever-increasing pace simply because we want to know what will happen next. This is the urgency that most of us feel when we are reading a murder mystery or a thriller. The *Twilight* series of books, for instance, frequently has this effect on people: what kind of trouble, we wonder, will Bella and Edward find themselves in next? Just imagine, though, feeling the same sense of urgency when reading a cellular systems or sociology textbook. The trick to becoming a successful student is to generate within yourself just as much curiosity and excitement when you read a textbook as you experience when you read a best-selling novel.
>
> **Source:** Nellie Perret

Now answer the following question: what was the central idea in this passage?

Skimming allows us to pick up key ideas without getting caught up in details.

Reading for different purposes

There are many reasons for reading and as many ways of approaching reading.

- To evaluate a resource book, you might use the contents' page or index to decide which sections you need to consult.
- To locate specific information, you might skim over most things very quickly until you find what you are looking for. For example, in reading a newspaper, people usually leave out more than they read. You do not read the world news if you want the local curling results.
- To understand reasons and facts, and to remember them, you might need to read slowly and deliberately and make notes in your own words as you read.
- To enjoy words and descriptions, for example, in poetry and some prose, several readings might be necessary in order to get the feel of the language or to picture a scene.
- To read creative literature, you would read the whole work, following the structure created by the author, since the structure and the order in which the piece is written might be essential to its overall meaning.
- When you read for leisure or entertainment, you might drift with the book, allowing the writer to control the extent and pace of your reading, or you might dip in and out, skipping the boring bits and re-reading the good bits.

Getting started on your reading

You might need to spend some time developing a basic understanding of a new subject area before you read in depth. Before you start consciously trying to learn new information, make sure that you have some background knowledge and some sort of framework in which to place the new information you are learning. There are several strategies you can try if you are having difficulty understanding the reading set for your course.

- Begin with a general introduction, such as a reliable online encyclopedia or a very general textbook, and read slowly.
- Keep a dictionary handy to look up unfamiliar words. If the same unfamiliar words occur a number of times, you should note them for easy reference, perhaps in a "dictionary" of your own. You can adapt a small address book for this purpose and keep it with you. Review unfamiliar words in the bus or while you are waiting in line. Writing explanations for unfamiliar terms in your own words will help you to remember what they mean.

- Ask questions: "What is the author saying?" "How can I use this information?" "How does this information relate to my experience?" Try to write down the answers to these questions.
- Prepare for your reading by referring to any lecture or tutorial notes on the same subject to gain an overview of your topic or areas of study.
- Break the reading into small sections, and make notes on one section at a time.
- If its language or style makes a book or article too difficult for you, ask your professor or teaching assistant to suggest an alternative text or online resource that is more accessible.

Reading to find information

To take full control of any reading task that involves searching for information, you need to gain a general overview of the book or article you are consulting. You can use the layout of the text as a guide to make your reading easier. Before you begin to read any textbook or article in detail, follow the preview set out below in order to decide what to read.

Once you have an overview, you will be in a position to make important decisions. You might decide that a chapter or article is not worth reading in detail, or that the book does not deal with what you want to know. You might decide that only part of a book or chapter is relevant to your present purpose. You might decide that the whole is so important that it is worth careful reading.

Whatever your decision, the quick survey is an essential first step. You should never embark on careful reading until you have looked ahead and decided what you need to do.

> **TIP**
>
> When you encounter an unfamiliar word, make a note of it, but do not immediately look it up in a dictionary. It is best to first try to figure out its meaning by considering its context. Once you think you know what it means, look it up to see if you are right.

KEY CONCEPTS

Tips for previewing a book
- Glance at the title of the book and think about what it means. Academic texts, unlike many works of popular journalism or fiction, usually have descriptive titles that give you an idea of what the book's contents will be.
- Look at the information about the author or authors of the text and the date when the book was first published. This might help you to understand the authors' point of view and where their work fits in with other publications in the same field.
- Scan the contents page of a book before you begin reading. It will give you an overview of what the book covers and of where the authors have placed their emphasis.
- Look at the book's index to see whether the book covers the particular topics that interest you, and how much space is devoted to them.
- Read the first paragraph or so of each chapter.

KEY CONCEPTS

Tips for previewing a chapter or article
- Check the beginning and the end of any article or chapter of a book for an abstract, summary, or synopsis. Often this will make it unnecessary to read anything else.
- Skim the pages looking for subheadings that indicate content.
- Check the end of the chapter for a glossary. Looking over key words and their definitions before you read can save you time and trouble later.
- Look at illustrations, diagrams, and graphs, and read their captions to get further clues to content.
- Read the first sentence of each paragraph.

Reading to remember

Most people learn best by interpreting new information in terms of what they already know. A major step in reading, too, is to learn to recall what is familiar about a topic. With what you know in the forefront of your mind, you can begin to make predictions about what the writer will say, or you can think of questions that you would like the book or article to answer.

It is common for students to spend many hours reading a chapter in a textbook and then, after putting the book away for the night, realizing that they do not remember very much of what they read. This does not mean that they are not intelligent enough to understand the material or they are daydreaming instead of paying attention to the text. There is something a little illogical about expecting ourselves to remember information that is written down. Some archaeologists believe that writing was developed in order to keep track of chattel when humans started amassing more than they could "warehouse" in their memories. We write information down when it is no longer efficient—or, sometimes, even possible—to store it in our memory. When we read, then, we generally read for comprehension, not retention: we do not need to remember that Uruk was first investigated by William Loftus in the 19th century; all we need to know is that there is a detailed entry containing this information listed under "U" in the *Concise Oxford Dictionary of Archaeology*. Retaining the information that you read does not just happen; you have to read attentively and purposefully in order to remember.

There is more to learning, though, than just memorizing lumps of information that you do not understand. In fact, most people find it almost impossible to retain information they do not understand. Once again, the reader needs to take control and decide the purpose of storing information. Decisions about why you need to retain information affect decisions about what information you store. Is all or only part of a particular set of information worth committing to memory? Is the overall framework of the topic important or are only a few details?

The SQ3R reading method

The **SQ3R** reading method is a structured approach to reading that can be very helpful for learning (that is, both understanding *and* retaining material) or revision.

- *Survey*. Scan the material you want to learn to get a picture of the overall argument or the area covered by the book or article you are reading. Be sure to take a moment to consider the title: What do you already know about the subject? What are you interested in learning?
- *Question*. Ask questions of the text. Turn any headings or subheadings into questions, and then try to answer them in your own words. It does not matter if you ask the "right" question; often when you take the next step and start to read, you discover that the text is "answering" an altogether different "question." The important thing is to be actively looking, rather than passively waiting, for answers.
- *Read*. Go through the text in the light of the question you have asked, and take notes at your own pace and in your own words.
- *Recall*. Close the book or cover with a piece of paper the section you have been reading; try to remember what you have read. Write down what you remember in your own words or say it aloud. (Some people call this second "r" *recite*.) Only by testing your recall will you know how successful your learning has been.
- *Review*. Later, go back over all your notes to make sure you don't forget and to see how what you have learned relates to the course as a whole and your other readings, and to get a sense of what you still need to study.

> **TIP**
> Use the SQ3R reading method: Survey; Question; Read; Recall; Review.

> **TIP**
> Students who have trouble concentrating while they're reading will find the SQ3R method, because it promotes *active learning*, especially useful.
> (Nadeau, 1994, p. 32)

Taking notes to help you to remember

Learning by heart, or memorizing, should make up only a small part of your learning, but, when it is necessary, you need to do it efficiently. To do this, you must read systematically and make notes in your own words. Photocopied or printed material you have taken from books and articles, or lectures printed from the course websites can give you a false sense of security about what you know. To be sure you really understand something and can remember it, you must be sure that you can explain it in your own words. Being able to highlight or underline important points with coloured markers is no guarantee that you can explain them to someone else. *When in doubt, write it out.* If you can do that, you will soon know it. Below are some guidelines for taking notes that will help you to learn new material.

- Note only the important points. Leave out most examples and small details.
- Write notes in everyday language, using consistent abbreviations where you can. (See the sections on taking notes in lectures in chapter 1.)

EXERCISE

SQ3R

Practise the SQ3R method with the third chapter of John Steckley and Guy Kirby Letts's *Elements of Sociology: A Critical Canadian Introduction*, entitled "Culture," in Figure 3.3.

1. *Survey the chapter.*
   You might ask yourself the following:
   - What do I think is meant by the term "culture"?
   - What do I already know about culture, particularly as it might relate to contemporary Canadian society?
   - Can I think of any ways in which different sorts of culture (popular culture, counterculture, high culture) are related?
   - Looking at the subtitles, can I see any common threads?
   - What do the illustrations tell me about the chapter content?
   - After reading the chapter's stated "learning outcomes" and its summary or conclusion, can I identify any key themes that I should be looking for as I read?
2. *Transform headings and subheadings into questions.*
   - "Mass Culture and Popular Culture" might become "What is the difference between 'mass' and 'popular' cultures?" or "Why is it important to distinguish between 'mass' and 'popular' cultures?"
   - "Symbols of Ethnic Identity" might become "Why might cultures develop symbols of ethnic identity?" or "Do symbols of ethnic identity differ from other kinds of cultural symbols?"
   - "Norms" might become, simply, "What is meant by the term 'norm'?"

Figure 3.3   Sample textbook page

Norms

Norms are rules or standards of behaviour that are expected of a group, society, or culture. There isn't always consensus concerning these standards: norms may be contested along the sociological lines of ethnicity, race, gender, and age. Norms are expressed in a culture through various means, from ceremonies that reflect cultural mores to symbolic articles of dress. In the following sections, we'll have a look at the different ways in which norms are expressed or enforced.

Sanction

People react to how others follow or do not follow the norms of their culture or subculture. If the reaction is one that supports the behaviour, it is called a **positive sanction**. It is a reward for 'doing the right thing'. Positive sanctions can be small things such as smiles, a high five, or a supportive comment, or they can be larger material rewards, such as a bonus for hard work on the job or a plaque for being the 'Innovator of the Year' at college. A hockey player who gets into a fight is positively sanctioned by teammates at the bench banging their sticks against the boards, or by the standing, cheering crowd.

The opposite of a positive sanction is a **negative sanction**. It is a reaction designed to tell offenders they have violated a norm. It could be anything from a 'look' with rolling eyes or a mild joke (like when I hear 'Who are you—Santa Claus?' directed towards me, a middle-aged, well-proportioned sociologist with a big beard) to a nasty note left on the windshield of a car taking up two parking spaces on a crowded street, to the fine you pay at the library for an overdue book.

Folkways, Mores, and Taboos

William Graham Sumner (1840–1910) distinguished three kinds of norms that differ in terms of how seriously they are respected and sanctioned.

3. *Read actively, searching for the answers to the questions you have posed.*
    - If you read this passage actively, you will find, for example, the answer to the question, "What is meant by the term 'norm'?": "norms are rules or standards of behaviour that are expected of a group, society, or culture" (Steckley & Letts, p. 75). Through the process of searching, though, you will also glean other important facts (for instance, that norms tend to be protean, shifting from one group or culture to another). The trick is not necessarily to ask the "right" question; it is simply to ask a question and then to read the text, *actively* searching for an answer.

4. *Now, try to recall what you have read.*
    - Keep a piece of paper handy to cover up the text you have read. Usually, it is a good idea to formulate a question. You might ask yourself, for instance, "What does 'norm' mean?" "What are four possible divergent groups that might define their own norms?" "How might norms express themselves in a culture?" Then read and try to recall a small section, or even just a paragraph, at a time.
    - This kind of self-testing helps process the information into your long-term memory.

5. *Review the information, actively testing your recall.*
    - Leave ten or fifteen minutes at the end of your study session to go back over what you have read, covering it with a piece of paper and testing yourself to see how much you remember.
    - If you have taken notes, periodically test yourself on them, as well, to keep the material at the forefront of your memory, asking yourself, "What does 'norm' mean?" and so on.

- Reduce the number of main points to what is absolutely essential.
- Link each point to a sequence of very familiar things so that when you think of the sequence, you will recall all the points.
- Use diagrams, sketches, and graphs to help give you a picture of the information. Many people, particularly those with a strong visual modality, find it easier to remember pictures than words.
- Read over your own notes several times. Keep coming back to them at regular intervals.
- Test yourself from time to time.
- Learn the whole rather than parts. For example, you should learn a poem by reading it through as a whole many times rather than just memorizing bits. If you need to learn a list of definitions or other items, relate them to each other or to something you know rather than trying to learn the list by heart.
- Use different methods for learning the same information. Read your notes, write them out again, say them out loud, and draw diagrams that show relationships between different points.

TIP

A recent study has shown that putting notes into larger font sizes probably does little to enhance memorization, but using a font style that is both unfamiliar and difficult to read might help you remember.
(http://www.nytimes.com/2011/04/19/health/19mind.html?pagewanted=1&_r=1&smid=fb-nytimes)

- Practise using the information, or discuss it with others and write about it.
- Make up your own examples to help you understand and remember.

Taking reading notes for tests and exams

In some courses, you will be expected to remember a great deal of information. Really understanding the course material is essential to your mastery of a subject; however, in some courses, particularly those using objective forms of evaluation such as multiple-choice or true/false tests, you will also need to recall a great deal of very specific information: names, dates, terms and definitions, formulae, geographical locations, chemical reactions, and so on. It is necessary to have some strategies for taking notes on this kind of material, as well. The three best techniques for taking this type of notes are Marginal Notes, the Cornell Note-Taking System, and Flash Cards. Which of these techniques you decide to use for taking notes on material requiring the memorization of detailed information depends on your own learning style, the layout of the textbook you are using, and your need for notes that are easy to carry around with you and review.

Marginal notes

To take marginal notes, use the SQ3R system, but after you have formulated "questions" and read the text to find the "answers," take a few moments to write key words or questions in the margin of your textbook and to underline or highlight the key information. An example of marginal notes is in Figure 3.4.

You can then test your memory of information at a later date by covering up the text, looking at your marginal "questions," and trying to recall the correct "answers." There is no point in simply duplicating the material from the textbook in your marginal notes, as in the example below:

Cornell note-taking system

The **Cornell note-taking system** (see example in Figure 3.6) was popularized by Prof. Walter Pauk at Cornell University. With this system—which was originally developed for taking notes on paper, although students have been adapting the system for taking notes on laptops, netbooks, and tablets—you take separate notes on your readings, using a sheet of standard three-ring binder paper that you have divided into three sections:

1. Draw a vertical line down the page, six centimetres from the left side of the paper. The section to the left of the vertical line will be used for marginal notes, including key words and "questions."

TIP

A number of PDF annotators (iAnnotate, Jarnal, PDF Annotator) are available for introducing highlighting and underlining, and making marginal notes into PDF files. Some textbook publishers, too, are working on developing apps that will make it possible to make—and share!—marginal notes in ebooks.

(http://chronicle.com/blogs/wiredcampus/textbook-publisher-announces-'app'-approach-to-learning-materials/30090)

Example of marginal notes

Figure 3.4   Sample marginal notes

3 | CULTURE   75

Norms

Norms | **Norms** are <u>rules or standards of behaviour</u> that are <u>expected of a group, society or culture</u>. There isn't always consensus concerning these standards: norms may be contested along the sociological lines of ethnicity, race, gender, and age. Norms are expressed in a culture through various means, from ceremonies that reflect cultural mores to symbolic articles of dress. In the following sections, we'll have a look at the different ways in which norms are expressed or enforced.

Sanction

Positive sanction | People react to how others follow or do not follow the norms of their culture or subculture. If the <u>reaction is one that supports the behaviour</u>, it is called a **positive sanction**. It is a reward for 'doing the right thing'. Positive sanctions can be small things such as <u>smiles</u>, a <u>high five</u>, or a <u>supportive comment</u>, or they can be larger material rewards, such as a bonus for

hard work on the job or a <u>plaque for being the 'innovator of the Year'</u> at college. A <u>hockey player who gets into a fight is positively sanctioned by teammates at the bench banging their sticks against the boards</u>, or by the <u>standing, cheering crowd</u>.

The opposite of a positive sanction is a **negative sanction**. <u>It is a reaction designed to tell offenders they have violated a norm</u>. It could be anything from <u>a 'look' with rolling</u> eyes or <u>a mild joke</u> (like when I hear 'Who are you Santa Claus?' directed towards me, a middle-aged, well-proportioned sociologist with a big beard) to <u>a nasty note</u> left on the windshield of a car taking up two parking spaces on a crowded street, to <u>the fine you pay at the library for an overdue book</u>. | Negative sanction

Folkways, Mores, and Taboos

William Graham Sumner (1840–1910) distinguished three kinds of norms that differ in terms of how seriously they are respected and sanctioned.

EXERCISE

MARGINAL NOTES

Write marginal notes, highlight or underline the central information in the following passage. Keep in mind that the purpose of marginal notes is to turn the text into a tool for self-testing.

Figure 3.5   Exercise: Marginal notes

Ethnocentrism

Ethnocentrism occurs when someone holds up one culture (usually, but not always, the culture of the ethnocentric individual) as the standard by which all cultures are to be judged. It follows a simple formula: "All cultures like the gold-standard culture (usually but not always the one 'I' belong to), are good, praiseworthy, beautiful, moral, and modern. Those that are not are bad, ugly, immoral, and primitive." Ethnocentrism can manifest itself in many forms. It can entail saying that business should be run in only one way—the way of the cultural model—that policing should take only one form, or that progressive policies should concentrate only on certain ideas.

Source: Steckley & Letts, 2010, p. 82

Example of inefficient marginal notes

norm=rule/stand. behav. expect.< grp, soc. or cult.

"Norms are rules or standards of behaviour that are expected of a group, society, or culture."

Example of Cornell note-taking system

Figure 3.6   Sample Cornell note-taking system

Culture	-Steckley & Letts, cdn. Soc

P.75
Norm =
	Rules or standards of behaviour expected of
	   1) group
	   2) Society
	   3) Culture

Positive Sanction = (ex.)	Reaction that supports certain behaviour - smile - high 5 - supportive comment - bonus @ wrk - team banging sticks for hockey fight - cheering crowd
Negative Sanction = (ex.)	Reaction to tell offenders they've violated norm - 'look' (rolling eyes) - 'mild joke' (Santa Claus) - nasty note - Parking fine
	Norms, rules or standards of behaviour expected from a group, society, or culture, are upheld by the application of positive and negative sanctions.

2. The section to the right of the vertical line will be used for jotting down important information (the "answers" to the "questions" that you write in the left-hand margin).

3. Draw a horizontal line on the page, five centimetres from the bottom of the paper. The section beneath the line will be used to summarize the information that you have written in the right-hand column.

Writing a summary at the bottom of the page accomplishes several things. You will need to

1. look over your notes. Looking over your notes the same day you write them will increase your retention by as much as 60 per cent;
2. synthesize the information, asking yourself what the key points of the reading were (this fosters critical thinking, as discussed in chapter 4); and
3. express the ideas contained in the text in one or two complete sentences. This gives you invaluable practice putting your ideas down coherently in writing. You will probably find that at university a great deal of time will be spent learning new facts and concepts, but there will be little opportunity to think about how to express this information in your own words—without the pressure of a looming essay deadline or the ticking of a clock in an exam room. Taking half an hour each day to practise writing complete, well-crafted sentences will make writing under pressure, when you do have to do it, less onerous.

Like Marginal Notes, the Cornell Note-Taking System lends itself well to self-testing. You can cover up the text in the right column and try to remember the "answer" to the "question" you have posed in the left one.

> **TIP**
>
> There are a number of useful online templates for producing Cornell Notes sheets.
> (http://wiki.43folders. com/index.php/Cornell_ Notes)

Flash cards

Many students find using flash cards for material that they need to memorize a particularly good way to take notes. This is an especially useful technique for anyone who spends time each day commuting or riding on public transportation: the cards have the advantage of being very portable and easy to use when space and time are limited.

You can easily make flash cards whenever you have small blocks of time or if you are too tired or distracted to work on something requiring more concentration. As you are reading your textbook, indicate material that you think you might be responsible for knowing. It is easiest to put a sticky note or draw a faint pencil line next to the text. Keep some standard index cards handy. Write key words or concepts on one side of the card, indicating the source and page number (or, if it is from a lecture, the date); on the reverse side of the card, put definitions, examples, and any other material that you think you might need to know. Do not write too much!

Once you have made the flash cards, you can take them with you anywhere, reviewing as you stand in line, wait for a class to start, or have lunch. Sometimes you might look at the front side of the card and try to recall the material that is written on the reverse side; at other times you might look at the back side of the card and try to recall the key term or concept to which it refers.

EXERCISE

THE CORNELL NOTE-TAKING SYSTEM

Use the sample Cornell note-taking sheet (see Figure 3.7) to take notes on the passage in Figure 3.5.

Figure 3.7   Exercise: Cornell note-taking system

> **TIP**
>
> Using a note-taking system that allows for easy self-testing is a great way to be sure that you are studying for recall and not just recognition.

Reading for assignments

You might need to read a number of books and articles in preparing to write an essay even though you might not, in the end, use everything you read. It is as important to have a plan for your reading as it is to have a plan for your assignment. You can waste a lot of time unless you think carefully about what you are reading and why you are reading it.

Improving pronunciation

Students whose first language is not English might find it useful to put the pronunciation of the key word in square brackets on the front side of the card. Figure 3.8 shows an example of a flash card.

Example of a flash card

Figure 3.8   Sample flash card

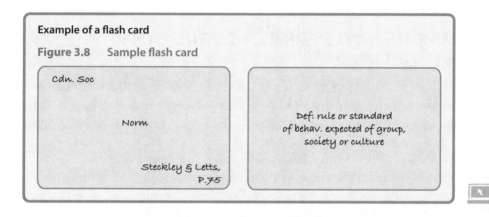

Cdn. Soc

Norm

Steckley & Letts, p. 75

Def: rule or standard of behav. expected of group, society or culture

EXERCISE

FLASH CARDS

Use the sample flash card template in Figure 3.9 to take notes on the passage in Figure 3.5.

Figure 3.9   Exercise: Flash cards

TIP

Students who have trouble concentrating for long periods of time find flash cards a great way to learn: they present material in a compressed format and promote active studying.

- Begin with a book or article from the reading list that gives an overview of the topic. Leave more specialized publications until you have an idea of what is important to the topic as a whole.
- Ask yourself what you need to find out. Write down your own questions as a guide to your reading and note the answers (and where they come from) as you go.

- Check the authors, publication date, contents page, and index of each item before you start reading to see if the material is relevant to your needs.
- Skim-read the relevant sections and compare them with other material before you start to take notes. You might need to skim through several books or articles before deciding what you want from each.

MAKING NOTES FOR ESSAYS AND OTHER ASSIGNMENTS

Although it is necessary to make notes in order to conduct research for an assignment, you need to be as selective in your note taking as you are in your reading. Analyze your assignment topic before you begin. Think about your purpose for making notes. You are rarely set an assignment that says, "Write down everything you know about x." Usually you will be trying to show that you can interpret and use information to answer a specific question. You will save a lot of time if your research is directed, from the beginning, to the task you have been set or you have set yourself.

Always photocopy relevant material or take notes from any books and journals you have borrowed from the library. If possible, print out Internet materials. You might never get your hands on them again. If you rely on your memory, on being able to borrow the book just when you want it, or on finding that elusive website, you might find yourself without some vital link in the awesome essay you were planning.

Some practical suggestions for making and storing research notes

- Use either index cards or three-ring binder paper, and write on one side only. You might also use a netbook, laptop, or tablet, but be sure to develop a consistent method for naming your documents.
- Record full bibliographical details at the top of the page when you start using each new text so that you can cite your sources fully and correctly in your assignment. (See chapter 14 for information on how to acknowledge your sources.) For example,
  » Steckley, John and Guy Kirby Letts. (2010). *Elements of sociology: A critical Canadian introduction* (2nd ed.). Toronto: OUP.
  » pp. 75–6   Wm. Graham Sumner: 3 norms
                       1) folkways 2) mores 3) taboos
  » p. 80   Cdn vs. US values (M. Adams)
  » p. 83   Potlatch Act (1884)

- Store any photocopied material with your own notes. Make sure that each photocopy is labelled clearly with its title, date of publication, author, and any other necessary bibliographic information.
- Record the page numbers of what you have read with any notes you take as you go along.
- Record chapter headings and page numbers in the margin of your notes as you move through a text so that you will know exactly where each piece of information came from.
- Number the pages of your notes so that if you drop them, or the dog eats a few pages, it will not cause major delays.
- Leave a wide margin and plenty of space on each page so that you can add comments or additional information later. (You might want to use the Cornell Note-Taking System.)
- Use headings and subheadings for all the notes you make to help you find and assemble the information in a different order if you decide to later.
- Use your own words in making notes to make sure you understand what you read.
- Identify and acknowledge all quotations you use in your assignments. (See chapters 13 and 14 for information on how to use quotations.)
- Write legibly. You must be able to read—and understand!—your notes weeks, or even months, from when you write them down. If you take notes on a laptop or netbook, be sure that you are consistent about formatting.
- Avoid over-using highlighters when reading photocopied material. Too much "colour-coding" can make your text confusing. Brief notes in your own words are more useful, and writing them will help to fix the information in your mind. These notes can be made in the margin of photocopied material.
- Organize and file your notes under subject and topic headings. You can do this alphabetically by authors or subjects, with a colour-coding system, in labelled folders, or by using any other system that works for you. If you are working with note files, be sure that you are consistent in how you name these and where you save them.

As a university student, you will spend a lot of time reading and studying independently. The reading will take less time if you do it efficiently, will be more enjoyable if you can do it easily, and will stay with you if you make your own notes. You might never feel quite like Logan Pearsall Smith, who wrote in 1931: "People say that life is the thing, but I prefer reading." However, you might be surprised to find how much reading can enhance your life.

TIP

If you want to use an exact quotation, copy it down accurately. Make sure that spelling and punctuation are accurate. Distinguish direct quotations by using quotation marks or writing them in a different-coloured pen. Use "[sic]" in your notes to indicate material that is in some way flawed or incorrect in the original.

TIP

If your university makes a bibliographic management program available to you, it is definitely worth the time and trouble it will take to learn to use it!

TIP

Store your notes carefully. If you take online notes, be sure to give them names you'll remember and to back them up frequently. Losing them could mean disaster.

GLOSSARY

Cornell note-taking system   System for taking reading and lecture notes, popularized by Walter Pauk at Cornell University.

sic   Latin term for "so" or "thus," inserted into text in square brackets to mean that unusual or incorrect textual material has been reproduced precisely as it was in the original.

speed-reading   Technique using skimming and scanning strategies, developed to maximize rate at which you read.

SQ3R   Reading system based on surveying, questioning, reading, recalling (or reciting), and reviewing, developed to promote active reading and increase retention.

SUGGESTED FURTHER READING

Darvill, Timothy. (2010). *The concise Oxford dictionary of archaeology*. New York: Oxford University Press.

Ellis, David B. (2007). *Becoming a master student*. Boston, MA: Houghton Mifflin.

Fry, Ron. (2004). *How to study*. Clifton Park, NY: Delmar Cengage Learning.

Pauk, Walter. (1984). *How to study in college*. Boston, MA: Houghton Mifflin Company.

RELATED WEBSITES

www.asc.utoronto.ca/Publications/Reading-and-Note-taking.htm
Academic Success Centre, University of Toronto. "Reading and note-taking."

www.cusu.cam.ac.uk/academic/exams/speedreading.html
Cambridge University Students' Union. "Academic speed reading."

www.nytimes.com/2011/04/19/health/19mind.html?pagewanted=1&_r=1&smid=fb-nytimes
Carey, Benedict. "Come on, I thought I knew that!"

http://lsc.sas.cornell.edu/Sidebars/Study_Skills_Resources/cornellsystem.pdf
Center for Teaching and Learning, Cornell University. "Cornell notetaking system."

http://lsc.sas.cornell.edu/Sidebars/Study_Skills_Resources/readingspeed.pdf
Center for Teaching and Learning, Cornell University. "Rapid reading."

http://lsc.sas.cornell.edu/Sidebars/Study_Skills_Resources/readingsystem.pdf
Center for Teaching and Learning, Cornell University. "Textbook reading systems."

http://elawstudentguide.wordpress.com/2011/03/03/cornell-notes-in-the-ipad/
Elawstudentguide. "Cornell notes in the iPad."

http://wiki.43folders.com/index.php/Cornell_Notes
43 Folders. "Cornell notes."

http://leap.ubc.ca/get-teched-up/apps-to-help-you-get-your-study-on/note-taking-templates/
University of British Columbia. "Note taking templates."

http://learningcommons.ubc.ca/get-started/study-toolkits/textbook-reading-toolkit/

University of British Columbia. "Web research & reading toolkit."

www.lib.uoguelph.ca/assistance/learning_services/handouts/learning_from_texts.cfm

University of Guelph. "Learning from textbooks."

www.lib.uoguelph.ca/assistance/learning_services/handouts/reading_and_the_web. cfm

University of Guelph. "Reading and the web."

www.writing.utoronto.ca/images/stories/Documents/notes-from-research.pdf

University of Toronto. "Taking notes from research reading."

http://chronicle.com/blogs/wiredcampus/textbook-publisher-announces-'app'-approach-to-learning-materials/30090

Young, Jeff. "Textbook publisher announces 'app' approach to learning materials."

ANSWER KEY TO EXERCISES

Skimming

The central idea in this passage is that we should learn to read course material with as much interest and engagement as we do with books that we read for pleasure.

Marginal Notes

See Figure 3.10 for the answer to the exercise on writing marginal notes.

Figure 3.10   Answer key to exercise: Marginal notes

> **Ethnocentrism**
> **Ethnocentrism** occurs when someone holds up one culture (usually, but not always, the culture of the ethnocentric individual) as the standard by which all cultures are to be judged. It follows a simple formula: "All cultures like the gold-standard culture (usually but not always the one 'I' belong to), are good, praiseworthy, beautiful, moral, and modern. Those that are not are bad, ugly, immoral, and primitive." Ethnocentrism can manifest itelf in many forms. It can entail saying that business should be run in only one way—the way of the cultural model—that policing should take only one form, or that progressive policies should concentrate only on certain ideas.
>
> **Source:** Steckley & Letts, 2010, p. 82

Cornell Note-Taking System

Figure 3.11 provides the answer to the exercise on the Cornell note-taking system.

Figure 3.11   Answer key to exercise: Cornell note-taking system

Cornell Note-Taking

	Steckley & Letts, 82
Ethnocentrism	Occurs when some one holds up 1 culture
	(usually, domin. 'gold standard' ['gs'] one)
	as standard by which others are judged
characteristics 'gs' cult	- cultures like 'gs' =
	good, praiseworthy, beautiful, moral, modern
	- cultures not like 'gs' =
characteristics non 'gs' cult	bad, ugly, immoral, primitive
Manifested:	- buisiness should conform to 'gs' model
	- policies take 1 form ('gs' model)
	- policing " "
	- policies concentrate on ctn. ideas
	Ethnocentrism occurs when one culture is held up as a 'gold standard' against which others are measured: the dominance of one culture (thought to be good, beautiful, moral, etc.) over other 'lesser' cultures (thought to be bad, ugly, immoral, etc.) is reflected in business practices, policies, and policing.

Flash Cards

See Figure 3.12 for the answer to the flash cards exercise.

Figure 3.12   Answer key to exercise: Flash cards

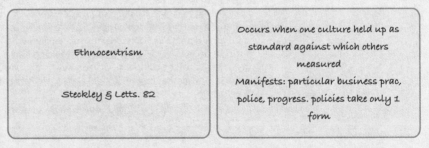

Thinking Through: Critical Thinking

The important thing is not to stop questioning.

WHAT IS CRITICAL THINKING?

Usually, if someone tells you that you are being critical, they mean that you have formed or are expressing a negative opinion about something; for instance, a friend might tell you that you are being "too critical" of another friend's clothing or personality, of a movie you just went to together, a meal you just ate, or a lecture you attended. In this context, your being critical is not perceived as an indication of your measured judgment and discernment; instead, it is seen as a personality flaw or perhaps a manifestation of your having "gotten up on the wrong side of the bed" this morning. This common understanding of what it is to be critical can cause quite a bit of confusion for many university students because when a professor asks you to write a "critical analysis" or to "critically evaluate" an assigned article, he or she has something very different in mind.

At university, being critical rarely means deciding that you like or dislike something. Instead, it involves understanding *why* someone presented information in a certain way and *how* an argument is constructed, as well as determining whether the evidence used to support the argument is reliable, logically presented, and compelling. To think critically means to think carefully, reasonably, and logically. In practice, it means not accepting something as well reasoned or true just because you read it in a book, a newspaper, or on a website, or you heard someone say it on the radio, television, or even in a classroom.

Critical thinking

Critical thinking usually starts with asking questions:

- What is the purpose of the lecture or text (to educate, to explain, to convince)?
- What is the background (discipline or education) of its author?
- Who is the implied audience?
- What is the central claim or thesis?
- What evidence is used to support it?
- Where does the evidence come from?
- How reliable is it?
- How relevant is it?
- How current is it?
- Are there implicit biases in the selection or omission of evidence?
- What theoretical approaches are invoked?
- How well is the argument structured (see chapters 8 and 9)?
- Are there gaps, leaps in logic, or fallacies in the argument?
- Are the conclusions supported by the evidence and arguments presented?

(Adapted from Knott, "Critical reading towards critical writing")

Putting information in context

When you are a student, it is very easy to get caught up in amassing information, but thinking critically requires that you always consider the context in which you find that information. Imagine, for example, that you are attending a lecture on offshore oil drilling. How different will that lecture be, both in content and intent, if it is delivered by a geologist, an economist, an environmentalist, or a political scientist? It is likely that each discipline will have a unique perspective on the topic. Even within the same discipline, there will be divergent ideas, assessments, and opinions, and sometimes even discrepant "facts"—or, at the very least, contradictory interpretations of the same facts. It is not that one speaker is right while the others are wrong, but simply that the strength of the overall thesis or argument and the validity of the evidence used to support it cannot fairly be assessed apart from the context in which they are found.

Determining purpose

You can improve your understanding of a complex argument by first asking yourself what its purpose is. When you attend a lecture, read a textbook or article, or listen to people engaging in a classroom discussion, ask yourself what the speaker or author's intention seems to be.

Students at university sometimes make the mistake of finding fault with an argument by using criteria that best apply to something else: they criticize a raven for not being a writing desk. If someone sets out to do no

TIP

Thinking critically requires you to see the whole picture; that is why it is so important to skim notes before a lecture or do a quick survey before reading a chapter.

TIP

Identify the intentions of authors or professors (the implicit purpose behind their enterprise) before evaluating the relative strengths and weaknesses of their work.

Determining purpose

- Is it an **argument**? Is someone taking a clear stand and supporting it with evidence?
- Is it an **analysis**? Is someone examining the relationship between the parts and the whole or determining how or why something works in a particular way?
- Is it a **critique**? Is it someone's evidence-based critical appraisal or evaluation of something, often a work of art?
- Is it a **narrative**? Is someone simply telling a story?
- Is it an **exposition**? Is someone delineating a process or exploring a cause-and-effect relation between things?
- Is it a **description**? Is someone, drawing on the evidence of the five senses, using precise imagery to convey what something is like?

(Procter, "Understanding essay topics")

more than describe a process, then it is important not to blame them for failing to present competing accounts or perspectives or for providing little in the way of analysis.

Look who's talking

You probably would not pay too much attention to your younger sibling's suggestions about how best to write an essay on "Blindness and Sight in *King Lear*" for your Shakespeare course, and you would not ask your English professor for advice on what to wear if you were going to meet some friends at a movie or a pub. Without consciously thinking about it, you make judgments every day regarding how reliable or unreliable, how appropriate or inappropriate your sources of ideas and information are. In your daily life, you innately use certain criteria to determine whether a person's information or analysis should or could wisely be considered in a given situation.

- How well do you know the person?
- How reliable is he or she?
- How good is his or her judgment?
- What expertise does he or she have on the matter in question?

The same criteria are relevant when assessing the validity of a spoken or written source at university: as a student, you are not always in the position to know how accurate "factual" material really is, but you *can* consider the credentials of the person presenting that material and the suitability of that particular expertise in examining the topic at hand. You can, as well, evaluate the logic and coherence of the presentation itself.

Knowing something about the source of your information also sheds some light on the best way to approach the topic itself. If you were to

KEY CONCEPTS

Reliability

Developing the ability to determine the reliability of a source has become especially important as we move to an increased democratization of "expertise." The Internet has become a virtual podium from which just about anyone can broadcast opinions and support them with what is all too frequently questionable "evidence." Learning to think critically about sources has become an essential skill, both at university and in the world outside the classroom.

TIP

As a student, you will want to pay attention to the ways of thinking that are unique to the disciplines that you are studying as well as to the content itself.

consider the hypothetical lecture on offshore oil drilling, you could anticipate differences in the kinds of information presented and the approaches taken to the subject depending on the academic background of the lecturer: the geologist might concentrate on land formations, stratigraphic records, or geologic assessment units; the economist might consider production costs, employment rates, or domestic economic gains; the environmentalist might discuss ecosystems, conservation, and pollution; and the political scientist might be interested in energy and climate legislation, campaign strategies, and oil self-sufficiency. Each discipline has its own approach to material and its own way of thinking, talking, and writing that is appropriate to it.

The implied audience

Another important question to ask yourself when listening to university lectures or reading scholarly texts is what audience they were intended for. Knowing this can help you listen or read more critically: a lecture intended for first-year undergraduates is probably going to be quite different from an academic paper that a university professor delivers to an audience made up mostly of peers. In both cases, there will be assumptions made about the breadth and depth of the audience's knowledge. Something intended for undergraduates will, in all likelihood, be fairly general, defining terms and concepts; it will primarily be expository, presenting information in as clear and straightforward a way as possible. Something intended for an audience of senior academics will, by contrast, be concerned with a particular and usually a new or unique area of academic exploration and will be based on the assumption that the audience has a reasonably sophisticated knowledge of discipline-specific language and concepts; it will, most often, be analytical and framed as an argument.

TIP

Knowing what to look or listen for when reading assigned texts or attending lectures, respectively, can be a real challenge at university. You will probably find that taking a few minutes to determine what kind of audience a speaker or writer had in mind can help you anticipate what type of information and what modes of reasoning you will be most likely to encounter.

Identifying the thesis

One of the first things to do when listening or reading critically is to identify the central claim or thesis of the material you are studying. Students sometimes mistakenly think that a thesis has to be a direct, sweeping (often so over-simplified as to be meaningless) observation or statement of intent: "In this paper, I will prove that contemporary Canadian culture and identity are more than just a pale reflection of American popular culture" or "Today I will be looking at Michael Ondaatje's masterful use of figurative language." Usually, an argument's thesis both indicates its primary focus or theoretical foundation and suggests the general direction in which its supporting evidence will lead us (Procter, "Using thesis statements"). "By comparing *American Idol* to its Canadian counterpart, we can see how the fundamental historical and ideological differences between the two countries have informed their popular cultures and identities" or "Today I will consider Michael Ondaatje's assertion that his use of the imagery of burying and unearthing is 'forensic' in *Anil's Ghost*, while in *Handwriting* it is 'archaeological.'"

If you get into the habit of underlining or highlighting the author's central argument when you are doing assigned readings or looking over your lecture notes, you will find that it soon becomes easier to identify the main argument of a text or discussion. Again, critical thinking is fostered by purposefully asking questions. In this case, you want to always ask yourself, "What is the central claim or thesis of this argument?"

> ## TIP
> Use highlighting or underlining to help you find the thesis in your readings or lecture notes.

CONSIDERING THE EVIDENCE

When you are reading texts or listening to lectures, pay attention not only to the author's central claim but also to the evidence that he or she uses to support that claim. Many of us have had moments in our daily lives when we have questioned a friend's interpretation of an event because the "evidence" that he or she has used to support the claim hasn't been very convincing: "She's selfish," one friend says of another, "because she won't let me borrow her new shoes." We can all see the possible flaw in this logic. There might be very good reasons—none of which has anything to do with selfishness—why one friend might not want to lend another a pair of new shoes. It is also true when assessing scholarly arguments that you must be very careful to assess *all* the evidence presented before determining whether an author or lecturer's central claim is both well founded and adequately supported.

We have already considered the importance of assessing the authority, reliability, and suitability of the person making a claim. We must use these criteria, as well, in assessing the evidence that he or she presents to support that claim.

Where does the evidence come from?

It is always important to consider the source of evidence when evaluating how useful it is in supporting (or refuting) a thesis or claim. Often, an argument relies on the authority of an expert, someone who is "more knowledgeable in a particular subject area or field than most others are" (Vaughn & MacDonald, 2007, p. 128). In general, Vaughn and MacDonald observe, experts are more likely to be correct—when providing evidence on their field of specialization—than the average person in the street (or student in the classroom!) for two reasons: they have freer access to material in their area and they are better prepared to evaluate that material. "Experts," they note, "are familiar with the established facts and existing **data** in their field and know how to properly evaluate that information" (p. 128). It is worth noting, then, whether an author or professor's claim is well supported by *appropriate* expert evidence.

Problems arise, though, when we discover that the experts on a certain subject are not in agreement (as is the case more often than you might imagine). In this instance, we have to weigh one expert's opinion against that of another. We must also watch out for arguments that are supported by the evidence of someone who is an expert in his or her own field but has no particular expertise in the area in question. This is something that we see all too frequently in advertising when a celebrity, who might know a great deal about camera angles, character research, or contract negotiations, is touted as an expert on the best watches to buy, the finest wine to drink, or the most effective weight-loss plan.

KEY CONCEPTS

Four criteria for evaluating expertise

Vaughn and MacDonald propose that we use four criteria when evaluating someone's expertise in a given area:

- education/training in the relevant area
- experience in examining and making judgments in the relevant area
- established reputation with peers as an authority in the relevant area
- "professional accomplishments" (awards, academic honours) in the relevant area

(Vaughn & MacDonald, p. 130)

How reliable is the evidence?

When evaluating the reliability of someone's evidence, considering the expertise of its source is certainly important. In the sciences and social sciences, though, the reliability of evidence (or data) also depends on an experiment's repeatability and consistency:

- How many times was the experiment performed?
- And how carefully was it performed?

We need to be able to trust that the methods and materials used in one execution of the experiment were pretty much the same as those used the previous time and the time before that. Imagine, for instance, that you are trying out a recipe for baking brownies.

- How many times would you have to prepare the brownies using that recipe in order to say that the recipe is a reliable one: Once? Twice? Twenty times?
- How reliable would your assessment be if you used dark chocolate one time, milk chocolate the next, and cocoa powder the third time?

Or suppose that a friend tells you that one of your professors "never gives extensions on essays." Before accepting this as true, you might ask yourself the following:

- On what evidence is your friend basing this conclusion?
- Was he or she the only student in the class to ask the professor for an extension, or did three students . . . or half the class ask?
- Were their excuses for needing the extension all the same and all equally valid?
- Were all their requests refused?

When evaluating the reliability of a source, be sure to consider whether or not it is based on evidence that is both *replicable* and *consistent*.

How relevant is the evidence?

As a critical thinker, if you have determined that the evidence presented is reliable, you must also assess whether or not it is actually relevant to the central claim or thesis being argued. If, for example, you have concluded that the brownie recipe, which you have now used 30 times without alteration, can be trusted, this knowledge is of no particular value to you if you decide that what you really want to do is bake sugar pie. If you are reading an essay about childhood obesity in Canada and discover that much of the supporting data come from Statistics Canada but are derived from studies that pertain to Canadians aged 18 and older, or come from the American Heart Association, then it is probably wise to question the validity of the research for supporting the topic in question and, ultimately, the credibility of the author's conclusions. While there is no reason to distrust the sources, the data are not applicable to a study of obesity in Canadian children.

TIP

Evidence must be both *reliable* and *relevant*.

How current is the evidence?

Having the most up-to-date research or evidence tends to be less important in some fields (the humanities) than it is in others (the life, physical, and social sciences). This is why priority is placed on the date of published research in certain citation systems but not in others (see chapter 14). If you think, for example, about how rapidly our understanding of immunology is changing or how much the environment has been altered over the past 50 years, then it is clear that scientific data that predate the first known case of AIDS will not be especially useful to support a study of epidemiology in the modern world. A paper on the environmental impact of offshore oil drilling that draws exclusively on research published prior to 2008—or on the impact of natural disasters on nuclear power plants that draws exclusively on research published prior to the 2011 crisis at Fukushima Daichi—will also be presenting outdated (and therefore potentially flawed) evidence. Even in the humanities, there are sometimes important reasons to pay attention to the publication dates of all sources. For instance, a research paper examining the nature of the protagonist in the novels of Jane Urquhart that makes reference to no work of her fiction written after 1997 will have a very limited perspective on character development in the oeuvres of that author. When you are reading research papers or attending lectures (especially, but not exclusively, in the sciences and social sciences), pay attention to the publication date of the evidence that is being used to support the central argument.

Is there enough evidence to support the claim?

It is difficult—maybe even impossible—to say precisely how much evidence is needed to make a compelling case. Some evidence is irrefutable and is sufficient in itself. This conclusive evidence is sometimes called **"smoking gun" evidence**, making reference to the murderer who is caught standing over a dead body, holding a recently fired gun in his or her hands. Most supporting material used for research papers or lectures, though, does not fall into this category. When critically evaluating an argument, read or listen carefully to determine whether enough supporting evidence has been provided to make a solid case. Imagine yourself sitting in class listening to a history professor who, after arguing that the First World War was the result of miscalculations and misunderstandings, offers just one example to support her claim. Although the thesis might be valid, without the support of adequate evidence, it is difficult to determine whether or not her claim is justified. While there is no definitive number of examples

> **TIP**
>
> When assessing the credibility of an argument, pay attention to whether the person making the claim has provided adequate supporting evidence.

that she would have to provide in order for her case to be compelling, giving more than one example would be a good start!

Are there biases in the selection (or omission) of evidence?

When thinking critically about an argument, it is also important to consider any possible biases that might be in play in the author or lecturer's decisions about what evidence to include and what evidence to omit. Suppose you are reading a chapter in your sociology textbook comparing American and Canadian social values: the author argues that the social values of the two nations have become increasingly divergent over the past 20 years. You might, after looking at the data (taken from questionnaires administered in 1990, 2000, and 2010) presented in support of this claim, notice that the author selected only those responses relating to one field of inquiry—say, Americans' and Canadians' respective attitudes toward public health care—to support his assertion. Tracking down the original study, you discover that this was just one field out of twenty-five that were surveyed. It is certainly possible that questions relating to other values (attitudes toward the environment or the importance of universal funding for education) might indicate that American and Canadian social values aren't nearly as divergent as the author would have us believe.

TIP

Watch out for possible biases in the selection of supporting evidence!

EXERCISE

ASSESSING EVIDENCE

Imagine that you are reading a research paper about adolescents and literacy in Canada since 2007. You look at the list of references and see a single source: an article reviewing the "Canadian Adult and Life Skills Survey" (2003), in which the state of literacy in 16- to 65-year-olds in Canada and six other countries is examined. Why might you question the conclusions of the paper?

Conflicting and confirming evidence: watch out for your *own* biases!

As a critical thinker, you must be alert, too, to your own tendency toward bias: it is human nature to embrace evidence that confirms our own values and beliefs and to reject evidence that denies them:

"We ignore evidence, deny it, manipulate it, and distort it. Somehow there is very little comfort in knowing that everyone occasionally does this dance."

(Vaughn & MacDonald, p. 140)

When you are reading an article or listening to someone lecture, be particularly vigilant if the central claim is something that you feel very strongly about. If someone frames an argument that confirms our own deeply held beliefs, we tend to accept the evidence provided without carefully appraising how reliable, relevant, current, and complete it is. By contrast, if someone challenges our beliefs, presenting evidence that conflicts with our point of view, we tend to be especially harsh in our appraisal of the evidence provided. Thinking critically means trying (with the understanding that none of us is completely without bias!) as hard as we can to be dispassionate in evaluating both the thesis or argument and the evidence put forward in support of it.

LOOKING AT THE ARGUMENT

Having looked at the importance of evidence in supporting an argument, it is also worth taking some time to consider the primacy of the argument itself. The necessary steps involved in carefully formulating and intentionally structuring a written argument are explored in depth in chapter 9. As a critical thinker, it is necessary for you to pay attention to both the theory that might inform an argument and the logical structure that supports it.

Thinking about theory

Not every argument is constructed on a scaffolding of theory, but it is important, nevertheless, to be alert to the possibility of an author or speaker's invoking a certain theoretical approach. If you recognize that an argument derives from a particular theoretical perspective (structuralism, post-structuralism, functionalism, feminism, and so on), then you can safely make certain assumptions about the basic premises that inform the argument and the logical course of its development: in writing an essay on the social organization of the university, for example, a functionalist might examine how each of the various groups within the university (faculty, staff, administration, and students) function together to support the larger social structure, while a feminist might explore how gender difference creates power imbalance throughout the institution as a whole.

Structuring the argument

Chapter 9 will look carefully at the importance of structure in developing an argument. Arguments can be organized in any number of ways, although **deductive** and **inductive** reasoning are two of the most commonly discussed in studies of rhetoric and critical thinking.

Arguments: deductive vs. inductive

- A deductive argument follows a line of reasoning to a seemingly rational (but not always correct!) conclusion:
- "Zaihra likes novels. *Such a Long Journey* is a novel. Therefore, Zaihra will like *Such a Long Journey*."
- The **fallacy** here is clear: the fact that Zaihra likes novels does not necessarily mean that she will like *all* novels.
- Inductive reasoning starts with a **premise** that is thought to be true and then builds an argument based on that premise.
- An inductive argument can be problematic when the premise that it is founded on is incorrect:
- "The Earth is flat. If we travel too far in any direction, we will fall off and drift into space."

GLOSSARY

analysis An examination of the relationship between the parts and the whole.

argument A clear stand supported with evidence.

critique Evidence-based critical appraisal or evaluation.

data Facts, statistics, or other information, often used as supporting evidence.

deductive argument A form of argument in which no evidence is needed because you argue from premises that are known to be true to a conclusion that necessarily follows from those premises.

description An account drawing on the evidence of the five senses, using precise imagery to convey what something is like.

exposition Delineation of a process or exploration of a cause-and-effect relation between things.

fallacy An error in reasoning.

inductive argument A form of argument in which you reason from premises that are known to be true to come to a conclusion that is probably, but not certainly, true.

narrative A story.

premise Supporting statement.

smoking gun evidence Irrefutable evidence.

SUGGESTED FURTHER READING

Browne, Neil, & Keeley, Stuart F. (2006). *Asking the right questions: A guide to critical thinking*. Upper Saddle River, NJ: Prentice Hall.

Cottrell, Stella. (2005). *Critical thinking skills: Developing effective analysis and argument*. Basingstoke, UK: Palgrave Macmillan.

Fisher, Alec. (2002). *Critical thinking: An introduction*. West Nyack, NY: Cambridge University Press.

Rudinow, Joel, & Barry, Vincent E. (2004). *Invitation to critical thinking*. Belmont, CA: Wadsworth/Thomson Learning.

Tufte, Edward. (2006). *Beautiful evidence*. Cheshire, CN: Graphics Press.

RELATED WEBSITES

www.dartmouth.edu/~writing/materials/faculty/pedagogies/argument.shtml
Gocsik, Karen. (2004). Dartmouth College. "Teaching argument."

http://writing.utoronto.ca/advice/reading-and-researching/critical-reading
Knott, Deborah. University of Toronto. "Critical reading towards critical writing."

ANSWER KEY TO EXERCISE

Assessing Evidence

Although the source of the evidence seems reliable, it is not relevant: it is considering the wrong age group (16–65; the paper claims to be about adolescents) and the wrong time period (2003; the paper claims to be considering literacy since 2007). There is only one source used, which is not sufficient.

Teaming Up:
Working in Groups

Please accept my resignation. I don't care to belong to any club that will have me as a member.

Groucho Marx, 1959

As part of your university study, you will almost certainly be asked to complete group projects of one kind or another. Most university courses incorporate group work as part of the learning process for students. Most group projects have a dual aim: (1) for the group of students to complete a piece of work that could not be completed in the available time by an individual working alone, and (2) for individual students to learn and practise the skills needed for working with others in an organized, cooperative process.

This chapter considers why group work is important, suggests some strategies for successful team building, and offers some advice about writing group projects and preparing group oral presentations.

Group work skills are highly valued by employers of graduates. You need only look at any job postings to see that "ability to work as part of a team" is an essential criterion for almost every field of graduate employment. In introducing group work projects into the curriculum, universities are preparing undergraduates to deal with the situations they will find in the workplace.

Group work should be an enjoyable and effective part of your learning experience. It can, however, be difficult and frustrating if you do not expect and anticipate difficulties and have the strategies to overcome them. The difficulties of working as part of a group are no more challenging than the difficulties of working alone, but they are different. You and your group members need to be aware of potential problems and how to deal with them if you are to get the most out of any group work project.

What is a group?

A group in the context of university study is two or more people who

- come together to work with a common goal or purpose;
- use agreed and accepted rules and procedures for working together;
- share a commitment to accomplishing the goals of the group; and
- are accountable for achieving the goals of the group within a set time frame.

WHY USE GROUPS FOR STUDY AND IN THE WORKPLACE?

Groups are often more effective than individuals in accomplishing tasks, making decisions, and solving problems because

- groups have access to more information than individuals and are less likely to miss something of importance about a given topic;
- groups can accomplish more than an individual within a given time frame, particularly in the area of research;
- group members can check each other's work and help to reduce mistakes; and
- groups can think of more ideas, suggestions, and alternatives than individuals working alone.

WHAT DOES GROUP WORK OFFER INDIVIDUALS?

Most people enjoy working as part of a group. After all, sports teams and social and recreational groups exist in almost every aspect of society. They offer individuals a structured way of interacting with others while undertaking a specific challenge or activity. Group work at university has the same advantages as teamwork in the community or specific sporting activities and allows you to develop many skills. Groups

- give individuals a sense of belonging and ownership;
- allow individuals to develop **interpersonal skills**;
- provide scope for individuals to use a full range of abilities in any task;
- allow students to prepare for the complex nature of many tasks in research and business; and
- reinforce the need for a specific aim and time frame for any task.

Work in Groups
Students whose first language is not English often find working in groups a challenge. Look at group work as a wonderful opportunity to work on your communication skills!

WHAT KINDS OF TASKS ARE APPROPRIATE FOR GROUPS RATHER THAN INDIVIDUALS?

It's important that group projects be taken on with the understanding that the task at hand can best be accomplished by a group rather than a single student.

KEY CONCEPTS

When are groups effective?

Groups are effective when

- the problem is complex and one person is not likely to have all the relevant information;
- there is a large amount of information to collect and **analyze** in order to arrive at a decision or solution;
- there are several possible solutions or ways of doing something, and no single best solution or method is known to exist;
- there is sufficient time for the group to meet, explore, discuss, and make decisions; and
- the group members are the ones to be affected by, or to implement, the decision, policy, or solution to the problem.

Sometimes, though, tasks can more efficiently be handled by a student working on his or her own.

KEY CONCEPTS

When are individuals effective?

Individuals are more effective than groups when

- there is a best solution or policy and a person with relevant expertise who is recognized as the best qualified to implement or decide on the policy or solution; and
- conditions are changing rapidly, and decisions must be made and implemented quickly and clearly.

(Adapted from Galanes & Brilhart, 2000, p. 10.)

WHAT MAKES A GROUP EFFECTIVE?

The characteristics of an effective group are set out below.

> **TIP**
>
> Effective groups are the result of group members being committed to the goals of the group and to understanding and cooperating with each other.

- Group members share a common goal, are committed to achieving it, and are prepared to work with others to do so.
- Group members set their own rules for how the group will work, review those rules periodically, and stick to them.
- Members listen to each other, help each other to clarify ideas, explore options, and show interest in each other.
- The group focuses on problem solving and creative development of ideas. Members encourage differences of opinion and do not allow themselves to be distracted by interpersonal issues or internal competition.
- The group identifies its own resources and uses them in the most productive way, allowing group members freedom to use individual skills for the benefit of the group.
- Group members are prepared to deal openly with conflict or disagreement and to resolve or manage it in a way that does not isolate individuals.
- Work within the group is balanced and shared both to complete tasks successfully and to promote cohesion and trust within the group. If the group is attractive to its members, a successful achievement of its goals is much more likely.

HOW CAN YOU MAKE YOUR GROUP EFFECTIVE?

Time spent on developing an effective group is as important as actually working on your project, and you should allow time for it when you are organizing your timetable for the project.

> **TIP**
>
> You have to work at making your group effective.

Group development

You need to understand how a group develops. Just because you have formed (or been allocated to) a group, you will not automatically and instantaneously turn into a cohesive team. Most groups need to go through four stages of development before the group is a working entity. It helps if you recognize the stages and can act to move the group on to the next development rather than worrying that you are not progressing or that your group is somehow different from others.

Getting acquainted

You should take some time to get to know each other. At your first meeting, introduce yourselves, talk about the task, have coffee together, and discuss your feelings about group work in general and the project you are working

KEY CONCEPTS

The stages of group development

There are four stages of group development.

- *Forming*: At this stage, the group is getting together, and members are finding out about each other and trying to establish guidelines and shared expectations. Individuals tend to be polite and tentative and to defer to each other. There is a lot of confusion about what to do and how to do it, and it might seem as if no real work is being done.
- *Storming*: By this time, individuals are getting to know each other and are starting to assert themselves. There are arguments about who is doing what, who is in charge, and differences in values and ways of doing things. Personality clashes might emerge, and still the work progresses slowly.
- *Norming*: At this stage, people are starting to settle down and to work out ways of cooperating, what the group's ground rules need to be, and what the group's goals are and how to achieve them. Progress on the work is speeding up as well.
- *Performing*: When the group gets to this stage, it is ready to focus entirely on the task and to concentrate on doing the work it was created for. Progress is swift.

(Adapted from Dwyer, 1993, pp. 524–6)

on in particular. Such time is not wasted. It is an important first step in turning a group of individuals into a team.

Understanding the project

You must make sure that you all understand what the project is about right from your first meeting and that you all have the same frame of reference for it. As a group, it is useful to be in agreement about various aspects of the project.

If you cannot answer any of these questions or if people have different ideas about them, designate one or two members of the group to talk to your professor or teaching assistant, get the answers, and report back to the group.

> **TIP**
>
> Make sure that everyone has a list of correct names, contact phone numbers or email addresses, and appropriate contact times for every member of the group. Some professors will establish online communities for students working together on a class project.

KEY CONCEPTS

Establishing a frame of reference

As a group, try to answer the following questions:

- What is the purpose of the project? Why have you been asked to complete it?
- Who is the intended audience? For whom should you be writing or presenting?
- What exactly should the project consist of? How long is it? How should you present it? What should it look or sound like?
- What are the assessment criteria? Are they clearly set out?
- What deadlines are involved? What is the final completion date?

Allocating roles

You should allocate roles to different group members at your first or second meeting. At the very least, you will need a chairperson to direct your meetings and keep you focused on the task, and a secretary or note taker who will record decisions taken and tasks to be done along with their deadlines. You might wish to allocate other roles as well on a permanent or week-by-week basis. It might be a good idea, for example, to have someone act as timekeeper to make sure that your discussions on specific topics do not spill over and take up the whole meeting. You might also want someone to act as progress-chaser to contact people whose contributions are not on time, to check that everyone is available for the set meeting time, or to coordinate activities by individual members.

Organizing your time

You must organize your time right from the beginning. Have regular, structured meetings with an agenda, fixed starting and ending times, and recorded notes or minutes of what took place. Set deadlines for stages of your project and for group members to complete allotted tasks. Draw up a timetable for the whole project and work to it. Of all the strategies for completing a successful project, the organization of time is the most important and, for many people, the most problematic.

KEY CONCEPTS

The group nobody needed

A group of students had four members: Everybody, Somebody, Anybody, and Nobody.

There was an important job to be done.

Everybody was sure that Somebody would do it. Anybody could have done it, but Nobody did it. Somebody got angry about that because it was Everybody's job. Everybody thought that Anybody could do it, but Nobody realized that Everybody wouldn't do it.

It ended up that Everybody blamed Somebody when Nobody did what Anybody could have done.

(Gibbs, 1994, p. 7)

MAINTAINING AN EFFECTIVE GROUP

In a group, members consistently perform at least two different roles that contribute to reaching the objectives set by and for the group. These different roles are called **task roles** and **maintenance roles**. For a successful group, you should think about how the group can use different talents, rather than trying to get everyone to be the same and to do the same kinds of tasks. Some people's strengths might lie in their contribution to the task. Others might excel in maintaining an atmosphere that ensures the long-term viability of the group. An individual who is an innovator, for example, might be a great ideas person but might need an investigator to put his or her ideas into practice and a group worker to keep him or her working well within the group environment.

Some typical group roles are set out below. Use the table to think about who in your group could play which group role. You do not need to fill every role.

> **TIP**
>
> Remember that the main strength of a group lies in the fact that it brings together different people with diverse strengths.

Group roles

Role	Who is like this?	Who is not like this?
Innovator Produces ideas, imaginative, unorthodox, radical, clever, uninhibited. Can be over-sensitive, prickly. May need careful handling.		
Investigator Finds things out, always knows someone who . . . , brings information back to the group, enthusiastic, gregarious. Can be lazy and complacent.		
Chairperson Self-confident, commands respect, good speaker, thinks positively, good at guiding the group. Can be domineering, bossy.		
Shaper Energetic, drives everyone along, needs to succeed, makes things happen. Can be disruptive and argumentative, impatient, and a problem if things don't go his or her own way.		
Evaluator Careful, makes intelligent judgments, tests out ideas, evaluates proposals, helps the group avoid mistakes. Can become isolated and aloof, pessimistic, or overly critical.		
Group worker Sympathetic, understanding, sensitive, shows a strong concern for social interaction, leads from behind. Places the group above personal concerns. May be indecisive.		
Organizer (secretary, note taker) Methodical, hard-working, reliable, orthodox, turns ideas into feasible plans and gets down to tasks that need doing. Can be inflexible and uninspiring.		
Finisher (progress-chaser) Painstaking, conscientious, follows through and works hard to finish things properly. Meets deadlines and pays attention to detail. Can be over-anxious and perfectionist.		

Source: (Adapted from Gibbs, p. 4)

SUPPORTIVE BEHAVIOUR WITHIN THE GROUP

Groups work best when members use interpersonal skills to create an atmosphere of trust and cohesion within the group. This involves listening and speaking to other group members in a way that encourages them to contribute and to value the experience of being in the group. If members do not feel comfortable, divisions can grow and defensiveness can build up, and a poor project is usually the result. Galanes, Adams, and Brilhart (p. 154) describe supportive behaviour in the following way:

- *Supportive behaviour*: desiring to understand the other's point of view; describing your own feelings and beliefs without making the other person wrong: "Tell me more about how your idea would work."
- *Problem orientation*: trying to search honestly for the best solution without having a predetermined idea of what the solution *should* be: "What ideas do you all have about how we might solve this?"
- *Spontaneity*: reacting honestly, openly, and freely: "I really like that, and here's what else we could do . . . "
- *Empathy*: showing by your words and actions that you care about the other group members: "You had a car accident on the way here? Are you okay? Is there anything we can do to help?"
- *Equality*: minimizing status differences; treating every member of the group as an equally valued contributor: "I know I'm the chair, but the solution belongs to the whole committee, so don't give my ideas any more weight than anyone else's."
- *Provisionalism*: being tentative in expressing your opinions; being open to considering others' suggestions fairly: "I have an idea I think might work."

TIP

Before you begin a group project, you should be aware of potential problems and put strategies in place to deal with them.

PROBLEMS WITH WORKING IN GROUPS

There are some difficulties with working as part of a group. You will probably encounter at least some of the following problems in working on any group project.

- Groups take longer than individuals to make decisions. Work on a group project seems to go slowly at first while members get used to working with each other, discuss alternative approaches, and sort out who is doing what. Once things are under way, however, tasks can be done quickly. If there is a tendency for the group's meetings to degenerate into idle chat, the chairperson needs to take control and to allow some time for diversion before reminding everyone of the timelines for the meeting and for the task as a whole.

- Groups are made up of individuals. You might find that some people do not talk enough and some people talk too much. Again, it is the chairperson's responsibility to draw out the quiet people by asking them questions: "What do you think about . . . ?" Sometimes shy people respond well to specific questions. It is also the chairperson's responsibility to prevent one person from dominating: "That's interesting, but it would be useful to get some other points of view in the limited time we have . . . "

- Groups might lose key people while a task is in progress. People might get sick, have personal difficulties, or drop out of the course. You must allow for this possibility in your time management and have an alternative plan to fill gaps if necessary.

- Groups might have problems with individuals who do not do their assigned part of the work. You must decide early on a mechanism for dealing with this problem. You must be prepared to confront the individual concerned and have firm rules in place to deal with those who do not pull their weight. If everyone knows in advance what the process is for dealing with the problem, the problem is less likely to occur. In particular, it is a good idea to have a written statement of each person's tasks and responsibilities and to check on individuals' progress at each meeting.

- Groups might find that allocating responsibility for decisions is difficult. The answer here is to keep notes of group meetings and to record all group decisions so there can be no doubt about how decisions were arrived at. Groups might choose an easy way out to avoid conflict or additional discussion. Once again, it is important to confront difficulties, ask for suggestions, deliberately discuss alternatives, and record decisions. You must also build an environment in the group in which people feel free to express their opinions and to disagree on issues without the discussion becoming personal or individuals being isolated from the rest of the group.

- Assessment of group projects at university can cause problems, especially if some students are perceived by their group members to be shirking their part of the work. The answer to this lies in the assessment process. Ask the professor what he or she intends to do about people who do not pull their weight, and ask for some ideas about what you can do. Once you have agreed on a system, it is up to you to make sure that it works. Learning to do this is part of learning to work in a group.

TIP

You should go through the project's assessment criteria with the professor in charge of your project before you begin, and make sure that all group members are happy with it and understand it.

NAVIGATING LEARNING CHALLENGES
Using Your Strengths

Students with Asperger syndrome often find working in groups especially challenging. Find a way to use your strengths: your ability to focus and a direct, logical, and hard-working approach to the task at hand.

(http://www.bournemouth.ac.uk/disability_support/staff/asperger.html)

COLLABORATIVE WRITING OF A GROUP PROJECT

Once the research is done and the group is ready to write up or present the project, there are at least two ways you can go about it. For a written project, one of the following is the most common method.

- The group can plan the project and divide up the material so that different individuals write separate sections. Individuals then circulate their sections for comment, and the whole group meets to revise the document. This is the most common way for student groups to proceed. If you work this way, you will probably need to have one person do the final collating and proofreading. That person would normally have a smaller part in the original writing process to compensate for doing more work at the end. It would be a good idea to have another person do a final check and perhaps be responsible for the printing, binding, title page, table of contents, and references.
- If the group has one member who is a particularly good writer, you might decide to give that person less of the research to do and ask him or her to write up the project once all the material is ready. The group would meet to discuss that person's draft, and the writer would do the necessary revisions. The editing and proofreading would then be done by the group, with the writer making any final decisions. Once again, you would choose someone who is good at layout and design to prepare the packaging for your project.

Whichever method you use to write up the project, plan the organization, format, and style of the document in advance so that you can more easily put sections together in a consistent style. You should also have clear agreement on the purpose and audience for your document and the length of each section, so that everyone is approaching the material in the same way.

Remember that it is vital to check your document for clear writing, logical development, and consistency in spelling, punctuation, and grammar.

Leave yourself time for this editing process. It is one of the most important stages in producing a professional document.

MAKING A GROUP PRESENTATION

In preparing to present your project as an oral presentation, remember that you have choices and, within the guidelines you have been given for the assignment, can determine the method of presentation according to the resources of your group. You will need to sit down as a group, review the material that your research or fieldwork has uncovered, and plan what to say and how to say it. You can divide up the presentation among the group members, do something creative, or, if one of your members is a talented speaker, ask him or her to carry the main responsibility. It will take time to do this, and you will need to review the finished product as a group before you make a final decision about how to present it. Once you have decided, all the usual rules for oral presentations apply. (See chapter 15 for advice on oral presentations.) You must check with your professor before you decide to use any unconventional presentation methods.

If you are presenting different sections as individuals, make sure that all group members look alert and interested while other members are doing their parts. If you show that you are not involved in your own presentation, the audience certainly will not be!

Successful group work involves many skills and allows participants to learn more about their university course, their colleagues, and themselves. Whatever groups mean to you, you will have to work with others throughout your life, so make the most of the opportunity to begin learning the academic and life skills for your future career.

> **TIP**
>
> Some people work better alone than in groups, and some people blossom in a group situation. You will not know which category you belong to unless you have tried group work.

GLOSSARY

analyze Divide something into smaller units in order to attain a better understanding of it.

interpersonal skills The ability to employ effective communication (speaking and listening skills), empathy, tact, patience, and good humour when working with others.

maintenance roles Group roles that focus on keeping the project moving and the group working together smoothly: for example, note taking, timekeeping, and organizing group sessions.

task roles Group roles that focus on the actual work at hand: for example, planning, researching, writing, and editing.

SUGGESTED FURTHER READING

Leavin, Peter. (2004). *Successful teamwork*. Columbus, OH: McGraw-Hill Education.

Surowieki, James. (2004). *The wisdom of crowds*. New York: Doubleday.

RELATED WEBSITES

www.canberra.edu.au/studyskills/learning/groups
Academic Skills Program, University of Canberra. "Working in groups."

www.bournemouth.ac.uk/disability_support/staff/asperger.html
Bournemouth University. "Supporting students with Asperger syndrome."

www.lib.uoguelph.ca/assistance/learning_services/handouts/group_work.cfm
Learning Services, University of Guelph. "Handouts: Group work."

http://leap.ubc.ca/get-started/study-toolkits/online-groupwork/
University of British Columbia. "Online groupwork."

www.kent.ac.uk/careers/sk/teamwork.htm
University of Kent. "Teamwork skills."

Facing Up:
Coping with Tests and Exams

Examinations are formidable even to the best prepared, for the greatest fool may ask more than the wisest man can answer.

Charles Caleb Colton, 1820

Some people flourish in tests and exams, completing their best work under conditions that others may find highly stressful. In part, good performance may be a consequence of a person's particular response to stress, but it is more likely the result of good exam technique. This chapter discusses tests and exams, their types, and strategies for test success.

WHY HAVE EXAMS?

Tests and exams serve three main educational purposes. These are to test

- your level of factual knowledge;
- your ability to synthesize material learned throughout a teaching term; and
- your ability to explain and justify your informed opinion on some specific topic.

These reasons give some indication of the sorts of things an examiner is likely to be looking for when marking a test. Some tests may seek fulfillment of only one of these objectives (for example, some short-answer and multiple-choice tests may only be examining your ability to recall information), while others will be looking for all of them (for example, essay questions or oral examination of a thesis).

TYPES OF EXAMS

Four basic forms of tests and exams exist: **closed book** (or "no aids"), **open book**, **oral**, and **online exam**.

The closed-book exam is one for which you are allowed to bring no aids (books, notes, "cheat sheets") into the examination room. It can be structured as

- **multiple-choice**;
- **short answer**; or
- **essay**.

It requires that you answer questions on the strength of your wits and ability to recall information, since you are not allowed to consult any information in the exam room other than that provided by the examiner for the purposes of the test.

TIPS for EAL LEARNERS

Closed-Book Exams

EAL (English as an Additional Language) students often find this kind of test especially intimidating; be sure to consult any old tests and exams that are available to you, and try to familiarize yourself with any new vocabulary. Watch out for Canadian terms, idioms, and cultural references that might be unfamiliar but that are not relevant to the actual content area that you are being tested on.

- If you encounter an expression that you don't know—a question on an exam refers to a "double-double coffee to go," "frosh week," or "pickup hockey"—don't panic: look for the core content that you are being examined on, highlight or underline it, and just concentrate on the material that is most relevant.

TIP

All students should plan carefully for open-book exams: familiarize yourself with the textbook and, if allowed, use sticky notes to indicate sections or passages that you think you might want to consult. Finding information in a text often takes more time than you might realize.

The open-book exam (or "aids permitted") can be set as

- exam room; or
- **take-home**.

In open-book exams, you are allowed to consult reference materials such as lecture notes, textbooks, and single-page summaries or "cheat sheets." Sometimes the range of texts you may consult will be limited by your examiner.

Oral exams (**viva voce**) are used most commonly as a supplement to written exams or to explore issues emerging from an honours, masters, or PhD thesis. They may require you to give a brief presentation and then engage in a critical but congenial discussion with examiners about the content of your written work. Oral exams are also used in foreign language subjects where they are intended to test your ability to understand and speak the language.

Online tests and exams are still relatively uncommon but are used increasingly in distance education and "flexible" delivery. They embrace each of the exam types set out above, with the exception of the viva voce (although, with more universities all the time using video conferencing and Skype, it is just a matter of time before online oral exams are routinely administered). Online exams require that you complete (and submit) your test or exam while working at a computer.

Of these four types of exams, the closed-book model is most common, so the discussion of exam preparation and exam techniques will focus on that model. Nevertheless, a good deal of the general advice will apply to the other exam types. Some specific guidance on other exam forms is given at the end of the chapter.

An important component of success in tests and exams is good "exam technique." Technique can be broken into two parts:

- preparation
- writing the exam

PREPARING FOR AN EXAM

Review throughout the term

This is perhaps one of the most difficult things for most people to do in preparation for any test or exam. It is also very important. Try to review course material as the teaching term progresses, beginning with the very first day of classes. You might review by rewriting lecture notes or keeping up to date with notes from assigned readings. Not only will this help you remember material when the time comes to write the exam, but it will also make it easier to understand lecture material as it is presented throughout the teaching term. That can be a major benefit when it is time to complete the exam.

Find out about the exam

Ask your professor or teaching assistant to let you know what you can expect in the test or exam in terms of the types of questions you may be asked, the time allowed, the materials needed, and so forth. Ask, too, if you will be examined on material *not* covered in lectures and tutorials. Seek some direction about how you might focus your supplementary reading. Listen for clues from your professor about content. Sometimes professors will give thinly disguised hints about the content of an exam. ("I can promise you that you will be encountering this material again in the very near future," they might say, a day or two before a test or exam.)

> **TIP**
>
> Hermann Ebbinghaus, a German psychologist who did pioneering work in the field of memory, wrote about the **Curve of Forgetting**: essentially, if you do *not* engage in a regular review of material throughout the term, you will forget much of what you have learned. If you *do* review in a regularly scheduled way (10 minutes within the first 24 hours; 5 minutes at the end of the first week; and 2–4 minutes at the end of the first month), you will retain most of what you learned.
>
> (http://www.adm.uwaterloo.ca/infocs/study/curve.html)

If past exam papers are available to you, look at them to get a sense of the likely format of the exam you will sit and the main topics it might cover. Be aware, however, that the style and content of exams may change from year to year.

Friedman and Steinberg (1989, p. 175) suggest that you should try to anticipate questions and areas that might be in the exam. Although this can be helpful, it can also be a dangerous game for the inexperienced. It is usually better to have a good overview of all the material covered in a class. Broad comprehension means that you should be able to tackle competently any question you encounter. If you narrow the scope of your revisions, you are gambling with your grade. (It is, though, always a good idea to dedicate some of your review time to material that you already know fairly well since you have a good chance to "ace" this on tests.)

Be quite sure that you know exactly *when* and *where* the exam is to be held. This is your responsibility and not that of your professor or teaching assistant.

Find a suitable study space

Arrange some comfortable, quiet, and well-lit place where you can study undisturbed. If possible, make sure it is a place where you can lay out papers and books without the risk of their being moved. If you live with your family or share a house with other students, try to avoid studying at the dining-room table unless everyone plans to eat from plates balanced on their knees during the weeks you are studying. Avoid studying in bed: you run the risk of having trouble getting to sleep when it is time to turn in for the night or trouble staying awake when it is time to study!

Keep to a study schedule

Once you have found out the dates and times of your exams, prepare a study calendar. This calendar should allocate specific days to the revision of each topic. To do this, you may find it helpful to read the material on study timetables and the best time of day to study outlined in chapter 1. An example of an exam study calendar is shown in Table 6.1. In the example, the fortunate student has only two exams. Each exam contributes the same proportion to the final grade in a subject, and the student is performing equally well in both subjects. Reflecting this balance, the student has allocated twelve study periods to psychology and eleven to geography. Some blocks of time for relaxation, exercise, and other day-to-day activities are also set aside. In your own timetable, you might also find it helpful to schedule a break every one or two hours. During these times

TIP

Reduce anxiety by finding out as much as possible about the test or exam beforehand.

TIP

Revising for a limited range of topics covered in a class is a risky business.

you can make coffee, listen to a piece of music, or do something else that refreshes you for the next study period.

Think, too, about where you want to study. Sometimes it is a good idea to study in a different location for each of the subjects you are studying. This provides you with a break as you move from one place to another, makes the process of studying feel less confining, and sometimes even gives you some help with memorization (you can associate each physical environment with the concepts you are trying to remember).

If the exams outlined in Table 6.1 were weighted differently from one another or if the student were performing better in one topic than another, it would be advisable to devote extra time to specific topics as appropriate. Be sure to stick to your revision schedule.

EXERCISE

MAKING A STUDY SCHEDULE

Look at the schedule in Table 6.1:

1. How might you adjust it if the geography exam is worth 25 per cent and psychology exam is worth 50 per cent?
2. How might you adjust it if both exams were weighted equally, but you had a 60 per cent average in geography and an 80 per cent average in psychology?
3. How might you adjust it if the geography exam is worth 25 per cent and the psychology exam is worth 50 per cent, AND you have a 60 per cent average in geography and an 80 average in psychology?

TIP

Make a personal study timetable and keep to it.

Table 6.1 Example of an exam study calendar

Date (Nov.)	Morning activity	Afternoon activity	Evening
20	End of classes	Relax, buy groceries etc.	Get notes in order
21	Get notes in order	Psychology	Psychology (play squash)
22	Psychology	Psychology	Psychology
23	Geography	Geography	Relax (swim)
24	Geography	Geography	Geography
25	Psychology (yoga)	Psychology	Psychology
26	Psychology	Psychology (run)	Psychology
27	Psychology	Psychology exam	Relax
28	Geography	Geography	Geography (play squash)
29	Geography	Geography (swim)	Geography
30	Geography exam	Celebrate!	Continue celebrating!

Get started and maintain a positive attitude

Once you have prepared a timetable and found a place to study, do not procrastinate. Get started. There is no doubt that studying is hard work, but the longer you avoid preparing for an exam, the more difficult the task becomes. Do not delay your start because of doubts about your ability to complete the exam. Instead, be positive and have faith in your ability to plan, manage, and produce your own success.

Concentrate on understanding, not memorizing

In most written exams, you will need to demonstrate your understanding of the subject material rather than regurgitate recalled information. In consequence, revision should focus on comprehension first and facts second. Be sure you understand what the course was about and the relationships between content and overall objectives. When you have a grasp of course objectives, you will be in a better position to make sense of content. Possession of a "conceptual framework" on which you can hang substantive material will also allow you to respond in a critical and informed manner to exam questions. To develop this understanding, check course syllabuses, lecture notes, essay questions, practical exercises, and textbooks. Draw a concept map that indicates the key ideas of a topic and the relationship between them. You may also find it helpful to condense your notes from, say, thirty pages to six pages and then to one page. Then expand them out again without referring to the original notes. This process of condensing and elaborating on material should help you to develop a good understanding of the subject matter.

Vary your revision practices

To add depth and to consolidate your understanding of course material, use various means of studying for a topic (Barass, 1984, p. 147). Set yourself questions, solve problems, organize material, make notes, prepare simple summary diagrams, and read notes thoughtfully. Once you have engaged in preliminary review, studying in a group allows you to check your understanding of the material against that of others, identify areas that you need to review some more, and get practice in applying concepts you have learned to unique scenarios or case studies that your peers might bring to the study session.

TIPs
for EAL
LEARNERS

Studying with Others
Students for whom English is not their first language can find studying with others particularly useful: it provides them with an opportunity to ask questions about unfamiliar idioms and vocabulary.

Practise answering exam questions

Have a go at answering past exam questions under exam conditions. Be sure you understand some of the key phrases and instructions that might appear (for example, **discuss critically**, **evaluate**, **compare** and **contrast**). The glossary at the end of this chapter may help you to clarify some of these terms. You may also find it helpful to take your trial exam answers to your professor or teaching assistant to confirm that you are on the right track.

One good reason for practising exams under exam conditions has to do with changing technology. You probably do most of your writing on a computer. In an exam, you are likely to be asked to write manually for three hours. Can you do that? What happens to your fingers? Further, computers allow you to move paragraphs around and make revisions quickly. Paper and pen do not offer that liberty, and you have to plan your writing much more carefully. Get used to using **correction tape** if it's something you haven't worked with before.

It is especially important to practise if you are preparing for an oral language or other similar exam. Practise with a friend or family member who is well versed or fluent in the topic of the exam. Try to think of the sorts of things the examiner might ask you to demonstrate, and practise some brief, clear answers. You may discover areas that need revision when you have to try to make concepts and arguments clear to someone else.

Seek help if you need it

If there is topic matter you do not understand, ask your professor or teaching assistant. If you are experiencing emotional or other difficulties that affect your study, speak to the professor, your registrar, a don, or someone in a university health or counselling service. You will not be the only person facing such problems.

Maintain regular patterns

Do not make the mistake of suddenly taking caffeine tablets with highly caffeinated cola and staying up into the early hours of the morning cramming information into your overtired brain. You run the risk of falling asleep during the exam. Radical changes to your lifestyle are likely to increase levels of stress and may adversely affect your exam performance. If you are in the habit of exercising regularly, keep doing that. Most people find that exercise perks them up, reduces stress, makes learning easier, and enhances exam performance. Exercise a little common sense too. Do not make test and exam revision time the same time that you shock your body with a conversion from couch potato to trainee marathon runner.

TIP

Good exam preparation includes looking after yourself.

You might also consider telling your partner, friends, and family that you may be a little more difficult to live with while you are studying!

Watch what you eat!

On the day of your exam—if the exam is in the morning—it is vital that you consume something to raise blood-sugar levels. If you do not think you can eat, try drinking a regular or soy latte, fruit juice, or something similar. It is better that you try to eat something like muesli that is slowly digested than something that will give you a momentary buzz (e.g., a double-chocolate doughnut) before dumping you on a post-sugar low. If you do not think you can eat anything substantial, try several small, healthy snacks (e.g., dried fruit and nuts). Do not face an exam on an empty stomach.

Dress appropriately

For a typical closed-book exam in a lecture hall or university gymnasium, the key is to dress comfortably. Be sure that you will be warm enough or cool enough to function at your optimum level. Feel good about how you look. Your performance may match that feeling.

Pack your bag

Make sure you have your student identification card (in most universities you are required to present your ID in order to write the exam), pencils/pens, ruler, paper, eraser, watch, lucky charms, a functioning **clicker** (classroom response system), and a calculator (if required). Exam booklets and scribbling paper (sometimes in the form of the inside cover of the exam booklet) will usually be provided. If the weather is hot, you might also want to pack a drink. This is particularly important for summer exams in poorly insulated exam venues. Take extra warm clothing if it is possible that the exam venue will be cold.

Be sure that you are familiar with what aids you are—and are NOT!—permitted in an examination room. Many students are surprised to discover that simply having a cell phone on their person during an exam is considered an infraction by most universities: know the rules and obey them!

Get to the right exam in the right place at the right time

Be sure that you know whether the exam is held in the morning, afternoon, or evening. You should also double-check the location of the exam. Every year, some people turn up in the evening for a morning exam or arrive at the wrong place. If you do miss the exam for some reason, *see your professor, teaching assistant, or registrar immediately*. You will often find your professor in his or her office or the examination room for the duration of the exam.

Arrive in good time—not too early, not too late. When you are planning your departure for the exam, allow for the possibility of traffic delays, late buses, and bad weather.

NAVIGATING LEARNING CHALLENGES
Accommodations and Obligations

If you have made arrangements with your university's accessibility services, be sure that you understand what your obligations are and be sure, as well, that you meet them (e.g., are you responsible for letting the office know the dates and times of all your examinations so that the service has sufficient time to arrange alternate accommodations for you?).

Most university accessibility services will provide a range of supports to assist students in writing exams. If you require some kind of accommodation, it is best to figure out with your counsellor or case manager what will be most useful for you. If you have heard, for instance, that a friend received additional time on a test, don't just assume that this is what will be most beneficial for you. Typical accommodations might include

- extra time because assistive devices sometimes require additional time to operate;
- extra time for rest breaks;
- extra time for processing information due to a disability;
- special assistive devices available in an exam centre; and
- use of a scribe.

(http://www.accessibility.utoronto.ca/staff/accomstrat/Test---Exam-Accommodation.htm)

WRITING EXAMS: A GUIDE

Before an exam, almost everyone feels tense and keyed up. However, if you have studied effectively and know about the type of exam you will be sitting, the anxiety you feel will probably help you perform at a higher level than if you were quite matter-of-fact about the whole affair. Breathe deeply and enter the exam room with a sense of purpose. You know your subject, and you know what the course was about. Here is the opportunity to prove it!

Check that you have all pages, questions, and answer sheets

On rare occasions, printing or instructional errors may occur. Confirm with the **invigilator** that you have all the materials you need to complete the exam. Check the reverse side of every page of the exam to see if there are extra questions hiding there.

> **TIP**
> If you are anxious about writing a test or exam, sit down beforehand and put all your worries and concerns down on paper for 10 minutes. A recent study shows that this can greatly improve your performance.
> (Ramirez & Beilock, 211–13)

> **TIP**
> Always make sure you have the entire exam.

Read the instructions carefully before beginning

Check to see how long you have to complete the exam, which questions need to be answered, and the mark value of each question. It is wise to *repeat* this process after answering the first question (or several, in the case of a multiple-choice/short-answer exam) to confirm that you are doing things correctly. Professors find it most disheartening to mark an exam paper by a capable student who has not followed the instructions. It is even more upsetting to be that student.

Work out a timetable

Calculate the amount of time you should devote to each question, as in Example A. Time allocations can be calculated on the basis of marks per question. If you are well informed about the exam well before you start studying, then you already have calculated how much time you will have for each question.

Example A: Three-hour exam (that is, 180 minutes)		
Question 1	10 %	18 minutes
Question 2	15 %	27 minutes
Question 3	25 %	45 minutes
Question 4	50 %	90 minutes
Total	100 %	180 minutes

Such a time budget could be modified usefully by allowing time for reading over and planning the order in which you will be answering the

EXERCISE

MAKING AN EXAM TIMETABLE

Fill in the table below to plan how you would use your time if you were writing a two-hour test.

Questions 1–10 (multiple-choice)	2 % each (20 %)	__minutes
Question 11 (short answer)	20 %	__ minutes
Question 12 (short answer)	20 %	__minutes
Question 13 (short essay)	40 %	__minutes
Total	100 %	120 minutes

questions and how much time should be allocated to each question at the start of the exam (say, 5–10 minutes), and some additional time (another 5–10 minutes) at the end of the exam to proofread answers. Indeed, both planning and proofreading time can be most valuable.

Example B: Two-day take-home exam (that is, about 16 working hours)		
Question 1	12 marks	@ 2 hours
Question 2	38 marks	@ 6 hours
Question 3	50 marks	@ 8 hours
Total	100 marks	16 hours

In Example B, an eight-hour working day (for example, 8 a.m.–noon, 1 p.m.–5 p.m.) has been used to calculate the amount of time available for each question of a take-home exam. The student in this example might then add some time in the evening to proofread answers.

It is most important that you not only allocate your time carefully but that you *adhere to your timetable*. It would be stupid, for example, to spend 40 minutes on Question 1 in Example A or to spend all of the first day on Question 1 in Example B. To help with this, write down the time you need to start each question or section of the exam soon after you get into the exam room. Keep this timetable handy and stick to it. The point is obvious but worth stating: a small amount of extra time spent on any question deprives you of time on others. Time discipline may be difficult, but it is undeniably a key to exam success.

Read the questions carefully before beginning

In the case of in-class essay exams with no aids permitted, you will sometimes be given some preparatory time (commonly 10 minutes) in which to read the questions and to make notes on scrap paper. Use this time effectively. Carefully choose the questions you will answer and think critically about their meaning. Take note of significant words and phrases and underline key words. Jot down ideas that spring to mind as you look over the questions. Use the time as a brainstorming session, and record your thoughts immediately. Do not rely on your memory. After several hours of answering an exam paper, you may have completely forgotten the brilliant ideas you had for that last question. Your notes will trigger your memory. If there is no additional time allotted for planning, it is still useful to take a few minutes at the start of the exam to read over, think through, and formulate rough answers to the questions asked.

TIP

All students (but particularly those with learning or language challenges) can benefit from planning ahead for take-home exams: make sure that you have all your resources (texts and notes) at home and ready to go! This is *not* the time to discover that your printer cartridge is out of ink.

Plan your answers

Do not make the mistake of rushing into your answers like the proverbial bull at a gate. Work out a strategy for approaching your answer to each question. Once the exam has begun, use the ideas you jotted down during reading time as the basis of an essay plan for each answer. Make a rough plan consisting of main points arranged in logical order. This might all be done on separate pages in your exam answer booklet. Not only is a plan likely to give a coherent structure to your answers, but if you do run out of time, the marker may refer to the plan to gain some impression of the case you were making. However, take care to distinguish essay plans from final answers in your answer booklet (for example, a pen stroke through the plan).

If you are not given additional time to plan your exam, it is still important to dedicate some time to do this.

TIP

Plan your exam.

Begin with the answers you know best

There is usually no requirement for you to answer questions in any particular order. It is often helpful to tackle the easiest questions first to build up confidence and momentum. Further, if you have the misfortune to run out of time, you will have shown your best work.

Note that in some standardized tests that are written directly online, this is not the case: you will be expected to answer the questions in a particular order. In some instances, the difficulty of the exam (and the highest possible grade that you will be able to receive on it) is determined by the number of preliminary questions that you answer correctly.

Answer the questions asked

The most common mistake people make in exams is not answering the question that was asked, sometimes opting to write a prepared answer on a related topic (Barass, p. 156; Friedman & Steinberg, p. 175). Markers want to know what you think and what you have learned about a *specified* topic. As you will appreciate, the right answer to the wrong question will not get you very far!

When answering essay-type questions, it is important that you present your own definitions of some of the key concepts that you are being tested on. Occasionally, your understanding of a term or concept will lead you to answer the question quite differently from what the person who set the exam had in mind. If you can convince the marker that your understanding of the term or concept is founded on an intelligent and thoughtful interpretation, then you might, in fact, receive marks for an answer that might otherwise be considered incorrect.

TIP

Examiners prefer focused, concise, and careful answers—not pages of waffling and padding.

Answering exam questions

Examiners are assessing your level of understanding of particular subjects:

- Do not try to trick them.
- Do not try using the "shotgun technique," by which you tell all that you know about the topic irrespective of its relevance to the question.
- Do not try to write lots of pages in the hope that you might fool someone into believing that you know more than you do.
- Concentrate instead on producing focused, well-structured answers.

That will impress an examiner!

Attempt all required questions

It is usually easier to get the first 30–50 per cent of the marks for any written question than it is to get the last 30–50 per cent. It is, therefore, foolish to leave any questions unanswered. In the worst case, make an informed guess. If you find that you are running out of time, write an introduction, outline your argument in note form, and write a conclusion. This will give the marker some sense of your depth of understanding and may result in your being rewarded appropriately.

Grab the marker's attention

People marking written exam papers usually have many exams to assess. They do not want to see the exam question rephrased as the introduction to an essay answer. They probably do not want to read a long introduction to each answer. Instead, they want you to capture their attention with clear, concise, and coherent answers. Spare the padding. Get to the point.

Emphasize important points

Underline and highlight key points (Friedman & Steinberg, p. 176). You can do this by underlining words and by using phrases that emphasize important matters ("The most important thing to note is . . . ", "A leading cause of . . . "). In the sciences and social sciences, you might also find it useful to employ headings in essay answers to draw attention to your progression through an argument. Your examiner will certainly find headings useful. If used judiciously, bullet/numbered lists and correctly labelled diagrams can also be helpful.

Support generalizations

Use examples and other forms of evidence to support the general claims you make (Dixon, 2004, p. 161; Friedman & Steinberg, p. 177). Your answers will be more compelling and will signal your understanding of course material much more effectively if they are supported by appropriate examples drawn from lectures, reading, and your own experience than if they rest solely on bald generalizations.

Write legibly and comprehensibly

Examiners hate handwriting that is hard to read. It is very difficult to follow someone's argument if frequent pauses have to be made to decipher hieroglyphics masquerading as the conventional symbols of written English. Please try to write legibly. If you have problems writing in a form that can be easily read, write on alternate lines or print to ensure that the examiner is able to interpret your work. Express yourself clearly, too. Errors of punctuation and grammar may divert the examiner's attention from the positive qualities of your work. Many problems of expression can be overcome by using short sentences. In fact, these often have greater impact than long sentences.

TIPS for EAL LEARNERS

Keep It Simple
If English is not your first language, do not try to impress your marker by using an ornate vocabulary and complex grammatical structures: keep it simple!

Leave space for additions

Begin answers on new pages so that you can add material if time allows. This is particularly important if you have been prudent enough to leave yourself some time for proofreading. More frequently than you might imagine, people find that they recall material about one question while they are answering another. It is useful to have the time and space to add those insights.

Keep calm!

If you find that you are beginning to panic or that your memory has gone blank, stop writing, breathe deeply, and relax for a minute or two. A few moments spent this way should help to put you back on track. Do not give up in frustration and storm out of the exam room. Why run the risk of working out a way through a problem *after* you have left the exam room but while the exam is still on? If you are experiencing a panic attack and really cannot focus on the exam at all, be sure that you let the invigilator know what is happening. He or she might be able to accompany you out into the hallway, where you can walk, shake out, or get a drink of water. If you find that you need to petition to rewrite the exam, it will be essential that the invigilator was made aware of the situation.

No matter how desperate things may seem, do not cheat! Exams are carefully supervised. Copying and other forms of academic dishonesty in exams do not go unnoticed.

TIP

Don't leave a test or exam early in despair. Stay and think.

Proofread completed answers

Allow yourself time to proofread your answers. Check for grammatical errors, spelling mistakes, and unnecessary jargon. You may also find time and opportunity to add important material you missed in the first attempt at the question. Contrary to the popular opinion that people tend to become less rational as an exam progresses, changing correct to incorrect answers, some people actually think *more* clearly as they work their way through an exam, catching mistakes they had made or remembering information that they thought they had forgotten.

Sensible exam technique is crucial to success. If you follow the advice outlined above, you will have taken some major steps towards a distinguished exam performance.

SPECIFIC ADVICE FOR MULTIPLE-CHOICE EXAMS

Aside from familiarity with the tested material, good results in multiple-choice exams depend, in part, on your being conversant with some of the peculiarities of this form of exam. As the following points suggest, there is much more to success in a multiple-choice exam than simply selecting (a), (b), or (c).

*   Go quickly through the test, answering all those questions you can complete easily. If there is a question you find difficult, move on and return to it later if you have time.
*   Multiple-choice options occasionally include a number of completely unrealistic options, sometimes added by the examiner for comic relief. Delete those options that are clearly incorrect. Consider humorous responses for deletion, as they are likely to have been included as "distractors." This will help you narrow down your choices.
*   Read all the answer options before selecting one.
*   Avoid extreme answers. For example, if you were asked to state the correct population of Vancouver in 2006 and the options were (a) 525 thousand, (b) 578 thousand, (c) 478 thousand, (d) 52 million, you would be well advised to avoid option (d) as it is distinctly larger than the alternatives.
*   Avoid answers that include absolutes (Burdess, 1991, p. 57; Northey & Knight, 1992, p. 117). In the world in which we live, "never,"

TIP

Make yourself familiar with the quirks of multiple-choice exams.

"always," "no one," and "everyone" are rarely true—although this rule of thumb may be less appropriate for some science topics!

- Avoid answers that incorporate unfamiliar terms (Burdess, p. 57; Northey & Knight, p. 117). Examiners will sometimes use technical words as sirens, luring you into shallow waters. Again, however, this may be less useful in some science topics where uncommon terms are used frequently.

- Do not be intimidated or led astray by an emerging pattern of answers. If, for example, every answer in the first ten questions of the test appears to have been (b), that does not mean that the next answer "ought" to be a (b). Nor, of course, does it mean that the next answer is not (b), or that some of your previous answers are wrong.

- If there appears to be no correct answer among the options provided, choose the option you judge closest to correct.

- If in real doubt about the correct answer, select the longest option or the option with most qualifications. It is often more difficult for an examiner to express a correct idea in few words than it is to express an incorrect one.

- Unless you have been advised that penalties are imposed for giving incorrect answers, answer every question. If you do not know the answer, make an informed guess. If the question has four options, you have a 25 per cent chance of getting the answer correct.

- Do not "overanalyze" a question. If you have completed a multiple-choice test and are proofreading your answers, be cautious about revising your initial response. If you are hesitant about changing your original answer to a different response, you are advised to leave things alone. You probably got it right the first time.

- For multiple-choice exams that make use of a clicker, be sure that you have remembered to bring one that is functioning to class. Having an extra battery handy is never a bad idea. Do not allow yourself to give in to the temptation to look at the person sitting next to you to see what option he or she is selecting.

SPECIFIC ADVICE FOR ORAL EXAMS

Except in the languages and in medical disciplines, formal oral exams are quite rare. Most people do not get the opportunity to practise them as they might a written or multiple-choice test. Partly as a result of this, the oral exam, or viva voce, can be quite intimidating. But if you think carefully about it, the oral exam is simply a formalized extension of the sort of discussion you might have had with colleagues, friends, or teaching assistants about the subject you are studying. As such, it should not be too daunting a prospect. Remember, the examiners are real people, too. In some instances, they may be quite nervous about the entire process themselves and particularly about their ability to put you at ease so that a genuine, thoughtful discussion can take place.

In preparing yourself psychologically for an oral exam, think about its likely aims. If you do not know the aims of the exam, ask your professor or teaching assistant. Generally, the examiners will want you to fill in detail that you might not have had the opportunity to include in a written paper or in your thesis. The examiners may also wish to use the viva voce as a teaching and learning forum. They may want to encourage you to think about alternative ways in which you might have approached your topic and to discuss those alternatives with them. If you can, try to look forward to a viva voce as a potentially rewarding opportunity to explore a subject about which *you* may be the best informed.

In preparing and completing an oral exam, consider the following points of advice.

- If the oral exam is about a thesis or some other work you have written, read through that work, taking a few notes on its central points and otherwise refreshing your memory of it. Think about key matters from each section that you would like to discuss. You will then be better positioned to make the viva run as you would like should the opportunity arise.

- As the date of your oral exam approaches, conduct a search of recent journals to see if any relevant papers have been published. Your examiners may not yet have read those papers, and this will give you an opportunity to impress them (Beynon, 1993, p. 94) with your initiative.

- Enlist the help of a friend or family member who is well versed in the topic of the exam. Try to think of the sorts of things the examiner might ask you to demonstrate, and practise some brief, clear answers. The section below sets out some questions commonly asked in oral exams. In trying to make your answers to these questions clear to your classmate or relative, you may discover areas that need further revision.

- Present yourself in a way that is both comfortable and that suits the formality of the occasion. As a rule of thumb, think about the type of clothing your examiners are likely to be wearing and dress slightly more formally than they will.

- Try to display relaxed confidence. To do this, maintain eye contact with your examiners, sit comfortably in an alert position, and do not fidget. Remember to speak clearly. Try to formulate brief but clear answers. To this end, it is useful to have considered some of the questions you might be asked before the exam begins. A list of some common questions raised in oral exams is provided below.

- If you do not understand a question, say so. Ask to have the question rephrased. It may not be you who has the problem; it is quite possible that the question does not make sense.
- Take time to think about your answers. Do not feel obliged to rush out a response.
- To give yourself an extra few moments to think about a question, you may find it helpful to repeat the question aloud—but not every time!
- In most exams, as in a discussion, you should feel free to challenge the examiners' arguments and logic, but be prepared to give consideration to their views.
- If it appears to you that the examiners have wrongly interpreted something you have said or written, let them know precisely what you meant.

<aside>
TIP

Before an oral exam, prepare your answers to questions you are most likely to be asked.
</aside>

<aside>
KEY CONCEPTS

Common questions in oral exams

A number of questions appear often in oral exams. Give them some careful thought before the exam.

- Why did you select your research question?
- How does your work connect with existing studies? Does it say anything different? Does it confirm other work?
- What makes your thesis or report a distinguishable part of the literature in the discipline? (What makes your contribution a work of philosophy? biology? economics? or physics?)
- Why did you select your methodology? Are there any weaknesses in the approach you adopted?
- What are some of the sources of error in your data?
- What practical problems did you encounter? How did you overcome them?
- What are the particular strengths or weaknesses of your work?
- Are any of the findings unexpected?
- What avenues for future research does your thesis suggest?
- What have you learned from your research experience? What would you do differently if you had your time again?
</aside>

SPECIFIC ADVICE FOR OPEN-BOOK EXAMS

- The open-book test or exam is deceptive. At first you might think, "What could be easier than a test into which I can take the answers?" Later—perhaps as late as during the exam—you may come to realize that these exams can be more difficult than you ever could have imagined. The key lies in the fact that to deal with open-book exam questions as quickly and effectively as possible, you must know your subject. The open-book exam simply allows you access to specific examples, references, and other material that might support *your* answers to questions. You still have to interpret the question and devise an answer. *You* must produce the intellectual skeleton upon which your answer is constructed and, upon that, you must place the flesh of personal knowledge, example, and argument drawn from reference material. If you do not understand the background material from which the questions are drawn, you may not be able to perform as well as you should. You may not be able to locate the supporting material in the reference books.

> **TIP**
>
> Take-home and open-book exams require careful preparation.

KEY CONCEPTS

> **Tips for open-book exams**
>
> The following advice may be useful in preparing for an open-book exam.
> - Study as you would for a closed-book exam.
> - Prepare easily understood and accessible notes for ready reference.
> - Become familiar with the texts you are planning to use. If appropriate, mark sections of texts in a way that will allow you to identify them easily (for example, highlighter pen, sticky notes). Do not mark books belonging to other people or to libraries!

SPECIFIC ADVICE FOR TAKE-HOME EXAMS

While a take-home exam may appear to offer you the luxury of time, preparation remains a key to success. Do not make the mistake of squandering your time trying to get organized *after* you have been given the exam paper! Not only will you be "burning daylight," but the preparation is likely to be hurried and inadequate. Here are some suggestions to help you prepare for a take-home exam.

Take-home exams present opportunities and challenges. They provide an opportunity to write very good answers to questions. They also offer the challenge of knowing when to stop. It can be very tempting to spend too much time on the exam, gnawing on it as a dog would on a bone. If you have been given 48 hours in which to complete an exam, you do not have to work on the questions that long. Nor are you expected to produce some mammoth tome. Instead, you should produce concise, carefully considered, well-argued answers, supported with examples where appropriate. The time available for the exam is not intended to suggest you write endlessly. The time is given for you to think carefully and to focus clearly on the questions asked.

> **TIP**
>
> Set limits on the time and resources you will use in a take-home exam.

Tips for take-home exams

- Be sure to have at your disposal appropriate reference material with which you are familiar. In short, you should have read through, taken notes from, and highlighted a sufficiently large range of reference materials to allow you to complete the exam satisfactorily.
- Arrange all the reference material in a way that allows you to find specific items quickly (for example, alphabetically by author, under subject headings, by date of publication, or by some other useful method).
- If you will be writing the exam on a computer, be sure that there are sufficient supplies of paper, ink cartridges, or toner to allow you to print the paper when you have finished late at night and all the stores are closed!
- Keep to a timetable.

ONLINE EXAMS

Although they are still fairly uncommon, online exams seem destined to be used more widely in many fields of study. Much of the advice about preparing for and completing exams that has been set out earlier in this chapter applies to this form of exam, but there are a few peculiarities and key points that need to be considered.

- Become familiar with your computing and testing environment. As with any other exam, it is helpful to feel as comfortable as possible with the medium or context in which the exam will be conducted. An unfamiliar computing environment can distract you enough that you perform poorly in an exam. It might be argued, too, that there are more opportunities for things to go wrong in a computer-based test or exam than in other forms of exam. Although many of these are beyond your control, you can prepare yourself to respond to difficult situations. This begins by becoming familiar with the computing environment you will be using. If you are not using your own home computer, check to see if the machines you will be using are organized in ways with which you are not familiar. If they are, spend some time getting acquainted with the hardware and software. It may also be possible to find a computer in a location that is quiet enough to allow you to concentrate on the exam. If practice exams are available, try them. This experience will allow you to check and confirm your access to the machine and the exam itself. It will also help you uncover and then resolve any problems that may arise before the test or exam. If no practice exam is available, ask if one can be made available.

- Know your username and password. Most student computing facilities require that you use an account to gain access to the online exam. These accounts can be specific to each student or they can be generic, allowing each student to use the same account to log on. Be sure that you know your current and correct username and password. Do not assume that the account you used last year will work this year. Make sure it does. Make sure, too, that you enter your personal identification and password details correctly when you begin the exam. An error here might identify your answers as those of another student.

NAVIGATING LEARNING CHALLENGES
Special Accommodations

Deal with special needs. If you have any special needs, related perhaps to visual impairment, memory deficits, or seating requirements, make these known to your lecturer or tutor well before the exam. It can be very difficult, if not impossible, for staff to try to accommodate an individual's specific needs as the exam is commencing. At the very least, having these things organized ahead of time will minimize distractions and problems that might prevent you from performing well.

- Know how to deal with malfunctions. The best way to prevent a computer or software malfunction is to make sure your computer is restarted before you begin the exam. To do this, you may need to arrive at the exam room early, power down the machine, wait 30 seconds, and then restart the computer. Once the machine has started, it is best not to use the computer for anything until you are allowed to start the exam. If you experience a malfunction with software or hardware, record the time of receipt and content of any error messages you see on the screen and report the problem to the invigilator. If possible, do not dismiss the error message. Computer personnel will need to see the messages to resolve the problem.
- Read instructions carefully. It is important that you read all the instructions provided by staff and presented to you by the software. If you do not understand what something means, ask.
- Disregard your neighbour's progress. In many online exams, the order in which questions are presented to students may vary. This is sometimes used as a way to prevent cheating. Do not be discouraged, then, if any or all of your neighbours are moving much more quickly through the exam than you. It is possible that the software has

presented them with different and perhaps less difficult sections of the exam from those that you are completing.

- When answering a text-box exam (essays or short answers), and where possible, it is a good idea to compose your answer as a document, saving it on your hard disk. Then "copy and paste" answers into the exam format/software. Avoid working from a USB flash drive or Memory Stick for this purpose. Actively editing a file from a USB drive is not the most reliable method—commonly because there is not enough space on the drive for the software to store the information you want to preserve or because the Memory Stick has become corrupt. By saving your work on your hard disk or the network, you will still have a copy of the work you have completed should the exam software fail for some reason. You must also save your work frequently. Even if the computer is set up to automatically save, it is a good idea to manually save about every five minutes if you are actively working on a document. Save more often if what you are writing is complex and difficult to reproduce, less often if you are not actively writing.

TIP

Work locally. Save frequently.

- If you are required to submit your exam answers on a USB flash drive, copy them from your network or hard-disk storage space to the Memory Stick, taking care to leave a version on the network or your hard disk—even if it means emailing a copy of your answers to yourself.
- Keep records and submit your answers. It is a good idea to record the number of each question you have not answered or questions you are not sure about so that you can easily go back to them. This is particularly important in multiple-choice and true/false exams. Most students complete these exams well within the allocated time and often feel impatient about searching through each exam question looking for questions that should be checked. Most exam software allows you to edit and change answers to questions until you choose to submit them for assessment. It is not unknown for students to answer all exam questions and log off without formally submitting their answers for assessment. Make sure you submit your answers!
- When you finish your exam, be sure you have saved a copy of your answers (as noted above), get a printout of your work if possible, and receive some acknowledgement of your submission. This might take the form of a receipt. Finally, if the software provides you with a score, record it and keep it so that you can compare it with the final grade you receive.

Good luck!

GLOSSARY

clicker A classroom response system used to foster student participation in class.

closed-book exam An exam in which you are not allowed to consult any information in the exam room other than that provided by the examiner for the purposes of the test.

compare Look at similarities and differences between ideas, places, events, etc. (often used in conjunction with contrast).

contrast Give a detailed account of differences between selected phenomena (often used in conjunction with compare).

correction tape An opaque tape that can be used to cover mistakes, leaving a clean surface for writing.

Curve of Forgetting Theory developed by German psychologist Hermann Ebbinghaus examining the relation between remembering and scheduled review.

discuss critically Give strengths and weaknesses. Back your case with a discussion of the evidence. Criticizing does not necessarily require you to condemn an idea.

essay exam A subjective exam in which you answer questions by developing a thesis and supporting it using a structure that has a clearly defined beginning, middle, and end.

evaluate Appraise the worth of something and make a judgment.

invigilator A person who is responsible for administering an examination.

multiple-choice exam An objective exam in which questions are posed and several options (usually four or five) are offered as answers.

online exam An exam that requires that you complete (and submit) your exam while working at a computer.

open-book exam An exam in which you are allowed to consult reference materials, such as lecture notes, textbooks, and journals.

oral exam An exam that requires you to give a brief presentation and then engage in a critical but congenial discussion with examiners about the content of your written work.

short-answer exam An exam that requires you to give brief answers, usually in the form of defining a term or concept, contextualizing the concept within a particular discipline, and listing several specific examples.

take-home exam An exam written outside an examination hall, usually with a one- or two-day deadline.

viva voce Oral exam [medieval Latin]; see **oral exam**.

SUGGESTED FURTHER READING

Fleet, Joan, Goodchild, Fiona, & Zajchowski, Richard. (1986). *Successful learning*. London, ON: University of Western Ontario.

Hay, I. (1996a). Examinations I: Preparing for an exam. *Journal of Geography in Higher Education, 20* (1), 133–8.

———. Examinations II: Undertaking an exam. *Journal of Geography in Higher Education, 20*(3), 259–64.

Hay, I., & Bull, J. (2002). Passing online exams. *Journal of Geography in Higher Education, 26*(2), 239–44.

O'Brian, Dominic. (2007). How to pass exams: *Accelerate your learning—memorise key facts—revise effectively*. London: Duncan Baird Publishers.

Pauk, Walter. (2000). *How to study in college*. Boston: Houghton Mifflin Company.

RELATED WEBSITES

http://asc.utoronto.ca/Publications/Multiple-Choice-Tests.htm
Academic Success Centre, University of Toronto. "Multiple choice tests: Preparation strategies."

http://asc.utoronto.ca/Publications/Essay-Exam.htm
Academic Success Centre, University of Toronto. "Preparing for an essay exam."

http://asc.utoronto.ca/Publications/Writing-Exams.htm
Academic Success Centre, University of Toronto. "Writing exams."

http://asc.utoronto.ca/Publications/Multiple-Choice-Test-Writing.htm
Academic Success Centre, University of Toronto. "Writing multiple choice tests."

www.accessibility.utoronto.ca/staff/accomstrat/Test---Exam-Accommodation.htm
Accessibility Services, University of Toronto. "Test and exam accommodation."

www.adm.uwaterloo.ca/infocs/study/curve.html
Counselling Services, University of Waterloo. "Curve of forgetting."

www.sdc.uwo.ca/learning/mcwrit.html
Student Development Centre, University of Western Ontario. "Writing multiple choice tests."

http://ub-counseling.buffalo.edu/stresstestanxiety.shtml
University at Buffalo. "Test anxiety."

ANSWER KEY TO EXERCISE

Making a study schedule

Date (Nov.)	Morning activity	Afternoon activity	Evening
20	End of classes	Relax, buy groceries	Get notes in order
21	Get notes in order	Psychology	Psychology (squash)
22	Psychology	Psychology	Psychology
23	Geography	Geography	Relax (swim)
24	Psychology	Psychology	Psychology
25	Geography (yoga)	Geography	Psychology
26	Psychology	Psychology (run)	Geography
27	Psychology	Psychology	Psychology
28	Psychology	Psychology exam	Relax
29	Geography	Geography	Geography (squash)
30	Geography exam	Celebrate!	Keep celebrating!

Making an exam timetable

Questions 1–10 (multiple-choice)	2% each (20 %)	24 minutes (2–2 ½ minutes each)
Question 21 (short answer)	20 %	24 minutes
Question 22 (short answer)	20 %	24 minutes
Question 23 (short essay)	40 %	48 minutes
Total	100 %	120 minutes

Finding Out:
Becoming Well Informed[1]

Knowledge is of two kinds. We know a subject ourselves, or we know where we can find information upon it.

Samuel Johnson, 1775

Whether you are at university studying biology or psychology, education or English, one of the places on campus you will probably visit frequently is the university library. Often described as the "heart" of the university, the library certainly plays a central role in learning, scholarship, and research. For you, the student, it also offers a welcoming place where you can study in comfort and a place where you are encouraged in your search for knowledge. As a repository of the written word, it opens up to you the vast store of human intellectual achievement. You may find you go there to search for online sources or to browse through books on art. You might meet friends in a discussion area in the library to work together on an assignment, or decide to work on your essay using library computers. You may also use a computer lab or a wireless network to search online databases and catalogues. If you study off campus, you will be a frequent visitor of the virtual library. The library website is the gateway to the available electronic resources.

This chapter introduces you to the variety of resources provided by most university libraries and the skills you will need to make the most of them. Throughout your time at university, it will be important for you to be familiar with the library and its catalogue system so that you can locate material in the library and on the Web.

---

1   This chapter has been revised and updated for this edition by Gillian Eldridge, Liaison Librarian for Science and Engineering at Flinders University Library, Adelaide.

WHY ARE RESEARCH SKILLS IMPORTANT?

Imagine you have to write an essay on questions such as the following: "Will China be the next economic superpower?" "Discuss the use of brain-washing by religious sects." "Describe the evolution of the Carolinian life zone flora of Ontario."

To research these questions fully you may need to know how to

- use the catalogue effectively;
- obtain statistical information;
- search electronic databases for journal articles; and
- search for information via the Internet.

Having used these methods to find documents that deal with your subject, the next task is to evaluate them.

Being "**information-literate**" means you can find the information needed for any task or decision.

As you progress through your studies, you can expect to improve your research skills if you take advantage of the opportunities offered by the library. The skills you learn will help you in your university work, as well as being of long-term use in your career. *As society becomes increasingly information-based, your ability to find and use information may be crucial to your success.*

> **KEY CONCEPTS**
>
> **Evaluating resources**
>
> Ask yourself the following:
> - How reliable is the information?
> - How appropriate is the information?
> - How up to date is the information?

> **KEY CONCEPTS**
>
> **Information literacy**
>
> An information-literate person knows:
> - when they need information;
> - how to find information;
> - how to evaluate information; and
> - how to use information effectively.
>
> (Bundy, 2004, p. 3)

BECOMING FAMILIAR WITH THE LIBRARY

The first step in developing your research skills is to get to know the library. This can take some courage if you are one of the many new university students who suffer from what is called "library anxiety." Are you daunted by the size of the library, scared by the new technology, too embarrassed to ask for help, and unsure where to begin? If so, you are not alone. Even if you do not identify with these feelings, you will have to learn where things are located and how the library at your university operates. The browsing approach—wandering among the shelves to find a suitable book—may have been successful in a small public or school library, but it rarely works in a large academic library and may waste a great deal of time.

Begin by finding out which library you will need to use. There are often libraries that specialize in a particular area, such as medicine or law, which you may need to use as well as, or in some cases instead of, the general library. Familiarity with the library's resources is also important if you are one of the many students who undertake some or all of their course(s) online, study externally, or do not have the opportunity to come into the library regularly. Take the time to orient yourself to the online resources and find out how to get help when you need it.

How can you familiarize yourself with the arrangement of the library, its electronic resources, its services, and its policies? Librarians have developed a multitude of ways to help in the orientation process.

- *Guided and virtual tours*: At the beginning of the semester, most academic libraries offer guided tours led by library staff to show you the main areas and services of the library. You will not remember everything, but it is a good introduction and you will have the opportunity to ask questions on the way. Sometimes there is even an online tour, with photographs, screen shots, maps of the library's physical layout, and key information designed to assist you with finding out.
- *Webpages*: The library website is an excellent starting point for discovering what the library provides. Explore the website to find details of library services, to link to the catalogue, to ascertain what electronic resources are available, and to get online help.
- *Printed guides and brochures*: You will usually find booklets and brochures that provide essential information such as floor plans, opening hours, and borrowing rights. In many cases, there will be a guide to help you with the computer catalogue or information about relevant databases for your course.
- *The information desk*: The information, reference, or enquiry desk is the first place to ask for help in the library, whether your question is "Where are the photocopiers?" or "How many people earning more than $60,000 a year cycle to work in Vancouver?" The librarians at the **information desk** are there expressly to help you. You are *not* wasting their time by asking what you consider a dumb question. However, if they are besieged by enquirers or your question requires a very detailed answer, staff may refer you to another librarian or suggest you make an appointment.
- *Subject librarians*: Most academic libraries have **subject librarians** (sometimes they are called faculty librarians or liaison librarians) who can provide in-depth assistance in the subject areas they are responsible for. Often they give tutorials and training sessions on

TIP

For ease of access, you can bookmark the library homepage or place it in the Favourites folder of your Web browser.

finding information in their subject areas, and sometimes they are available to give specialized help related to a particular topic.

- *Virtual reference service*: Most universities now provide a mechanism for you to ask a query or reference question online. This is sometimes called the Virtual Reference Desk or Ask a Librarian. You submit your query in an email or an online form, and, in some cases, you may be able to chat online to a librarian.
- *Online tutorials*: Many libraries have online tutorials to assist you with how to find information, search individual databases, and locate resources. Explore these options; time spent in getting to know more about how to search a particular resource effectively will be well spent.

USING THE LIBRARY CATALOGUE

The library catalogue is the key to library resources, whether books, journals, audiovisual materials, electronic journals, or databases. It gives you information about materials available from the library and the details you need to locate them. Most Canadian university libraries have computer catalogues that you can access on campus as well as remotely, from any computer connected to the Internet.

To use the library effectively, you need to understand the catalogue system.

You will be well rewarded if you learn how to use the catalogue properly at the beginning of your academic career. The time spent will soon be recovered by turning you into a quick and efficient searcher, and you will uncover material that may otherwise have remained hidden.

KEY CONCEPTS

The catalogue system

The catalogue allows you to do a whole range of things, including

- search for an item by author, title, or key word;
- search for material on a particular subject;
- find out the **call number** (essentially the "address" on the shelves) of items in the library;
- connect to electronic journals and books as well as databases via the Web address;
- find out whether an item is out on loan, and when it is due back;
- place a hold or reserve on a book that is out on loan, so that you are notified when it is returned;
- check what books are currently on loan to you, or renew your loans; and
- connect to the library catalogues of other major libraries to see if they have material you need.

Librarians realize that the catalogue is not as simple to use as it may at first appear, and they usually provide assistance in various forms. Here are some of the options you are likely to be able to choose from:

- tutorials on using the system (often held at the beginning of the semester)
- online help screens available on most catalogue systems
- assistance at the information desk—*always* ask when you do not know how to do a search, or cannot understand the information on the screen

Remember that the computer catalogue is user-proof. You can try any of the menu options and experiment with searching without the slightest possibility of damage to the data or the terminal.

LOCATING MATERIAL IN THE LIBRARY BUILDING

Once you have used the catalogue to get information about physical items in the library and have recorded the call number of those you want, how do you then find them in the building? Many university libraries keep different types of material in separate locations. You need to become familiar with different physical collections in your library, where they are, and the system used to arrange material on the shelves.

The physical collections

(See the section on the virtual library for electronic collections.)

The common types of collections you are likely to encounter in academic libraries are listed below. The list is not exhaustive, and some libraries give their collections different names, or group them in different categories. Materials in various collections are usually designated in the catalogue by a collection or location code.

The main collection

The main, or general, collection usually consists of most of the books available for loan. The areas where they are shelved are often referred to as the "**stacks**."

The journal collection

Journals are publications that are issued at regular or irregular intervals, on an ongoing basis. They are also called magazines, periodicals, or serials. Journals are not generally for loan. Journals are useful for highly specific or up-to-date information.

The reference collection

Most reference resources (for example, dictionaries, encyclopedias, and indexes) are kept in a separate area. Because reference resources are used to look up specific information rather than for general reading, they are not normally available for loan.

The reserve collection

This is a collection of items that are in heavy demand, usually because they appear on course reading lists. In most cases, reserve material can be borrowed for short periods only, and can sometimes be used in the library only. There is a large amount of this material now available on e-reserve. See the section on the virtual library for e-reserve.

The audiovisual collection

Non-book materials such as CDs, DVDs, audiotapes, and videotapes (and even, sometimes, vinyl) are often housed in a separate area near the equipment needed to use them.

In addition to these collections, many academic libraries have other separate collections or sections: newspapers, government publications, microform, rare books, and maps are among those most commonly encountered.

Classification systems

Libraries use a classification system to arrange material on the shelves in broad subject areas. Most academic libraries use either the **Dewey Decimal Classification system** or the **Library of Congress (LC) Classification system**.

The dewey decimal classification system

The Dewey system divides human knowledge into ten main classes:

000	Generalities	500	Natural sciences and mathematics
100	Philosophy and psychology	600	Technology (applied sciences)
200	Religion	700	The arts
300	Social sciences	800	Literature and rhetoric
400	Languages	900	Geography and history

Within each main class, there is a further subdivision. For example, following are the social sciences subdivisions:

300	Social sciences	350	Public administration
310	General statistics	360	Social services, association

KEY CONCEPTS

320	Political science	370	Education
330	Economics	380	Commerce, communications, transport
340	Law	390	Customs, etiquette, folklore

Further subdivision leads to more specific numbers, with decimal points being added as required. The Dewey numbers for sociology illustrate the principle:

301	Sociology and anthropology
302	Social interaction
303	Social processes
304	Factors affecting social behaviour
305	Social groups
305.5	Social classes
305.55	Middle classes (bourgeoisie)
305.552	Intelligentsia
306	Culture and institutions
307	Communities

When material is arranged on the shelves, the numbers after the point are read as decimals:

575 comes before 575.09

575.137 comes before 575.2

KEY CONCEPTS

The library of congress classification system

In the Library of Congress system, 21 letters indicate broad subject categories:

A	General works	M	Music
B	Philosophy and religion	N	Art
C	Auxiliary sciences of history	P	Literature and language
D	History	Q	Natural sciences
E–F	America	R	Medicine
G	Anthropology and geography	S	Agriculture
H	Social sciences	T	Technology
J	Political science	U	Military science
K	Law	V	Naval science
L	Education	Z	Library science and bibliography

These broad categories are further subdivided by adding another letter. For example, following are the social sciences subdivisions:

HA	Statistics	HJ	Public finance
HB	Economic theory	HM	Sociology
HE	Transportation and communication	HN	Social history
HF	Commerce	HQ	Family, women
HG	Finance	HX	Communism, anarchism

Numbers are then added to represent specific topics:

H	Social sciences
HG	Finance
HG450	Investment

Your library may have a brochure outlining the classification system it uses and explaining its logic.

Call numbers

Each physical item in the library catalogue has a call number, which is its address in the library. Some libraries refer to call numbers as **location numbers**. The call number consists of two main parts: the classification number and usually a combination of letters and numbers, to distinguish between items about the same subject. Libraries adopt many different practices for the second part of call numbers, but often letters from the author's surname are used (see Figure 7.1). A collection code is often included in the call number to indicate which collection the item is in. Ask for assistance if you are not familiar with the system in use in your library.

FIGURE 7.1   Examples of call numbers in the Dewey and Library of Congress Classification systems

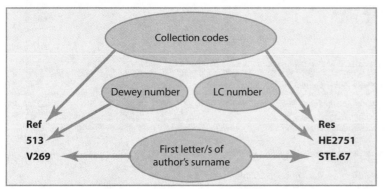

THE VIRTUAL LIBRARY: USING ELECTRONIC COLLECTIONS

Less visible than physical collections, but increasingly significant, are electronic collections, sometimes referred to as e-resources. These include databases, e-journals, e-books, and e-reserve. As with print items, details of e-resources are listed in the catalogue—in most cases you can connect to them from the catalogue screen by clicking on hypertext links or via the library website. Most e-resources can be accessed off campus if you are using a computer with an Internet connection and have a valid student login or password. You can now visit the library from your desktop at home or at work twenty-four hours a day, seven days a week. See the library website or catalogue for access details and online help.

Databases

Databases are electronic collections of information in a particular subject area. They help you find books, journal articles, newspaper articles, reports, or statistical information. While the catalogue includes titles of journals and newspapers, it does not list individual articles in those journals and newspapers. To find articles on a particular topic, you need to use databases that provide details of articles.

FIGURE 7.2   Example of screen from the full text database *Business Source Premier*

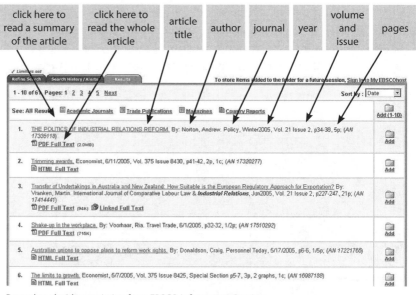

Reproduced with permission from EBSCO Information Services

FIGURE 7.3   Example of a record from the citation database
Sociological Abstracts

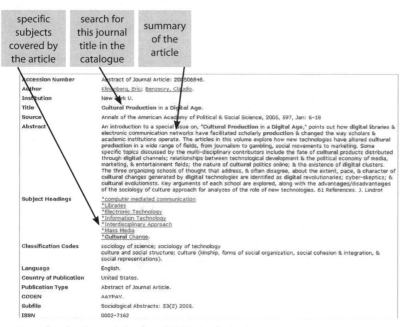

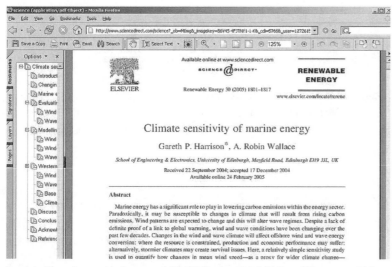

Reproduced with permission from Ovid Technologies, Inc.

FIGURE 7.4   Example of an e-journal, showing the first page of an article

Reprinted from Renewable Energy, vol. 30, G.P. Harrison & A.R. Wallace, "Climate sensitivity of marine energy" pp. 1801–17, 2005, with permission from Elsevier

Some databases are full text, which means they contain the complete document, as shown in Figure 7.2. Others databases give only the reference or citation for the item, often with a short summary or abstract of the document (see Figure 7.3). Many databases are a combination of both—that is, references for some items and full text for others.

E-journals

E-journals are the electronic equivalent of print journals. (See Figure 7.4 for an example.) In some cases you will find that the library has the same journal in both print and electronic format. Most university libraries list the titles of e-journals they subscribe to in their catalogue. Remember to check the dates that an e-journal covers—often e-journal subscriptions do not go back many years.

Libraries purchase many e-journals in bundles as part of full text databases rather than as individual titles. The advantage is that you can use the database to search for articles on the topic you want.

When using e-journals, you will find that in some cases, they do not display on screen with the same appearance as the printed version; you may get the text of the article without graphics or original formatting. PDF full text, if available, is a good choice as it looks like the printed version. To view PDF, you need Adobe Acrobat loaded on your computer.

Although e-journals are convenient, not all print journals are available electronically. Sometimes the information you need will only be available in print journals.

E-books

E-books or **e-texts** are full-length books on the Web. (An example is shown in Figure 7.5.) They can be read online or downloaded for offline reading or printing. There are two types of e-book collections: those in the public domain that are available free to anyone and those purchased, or subscribed to, by the library for university staff and students only. Some libraries purchase e-books that can be "borrowed" for a certain loan period and checked back in after use.

E-reserve

As with the traditional (physical) reserve collection, **e-reserve** consists of material recommended by your professors. These may be electronic versions of lecture notes, journal articles, chapters of books, e-books,

> **TIP**
>
> Adobe Acrobat software is readily available online for free to download, but many computers may already have Adobe Acrobat loaded.

FIGURE 7.5   Example of an e-book

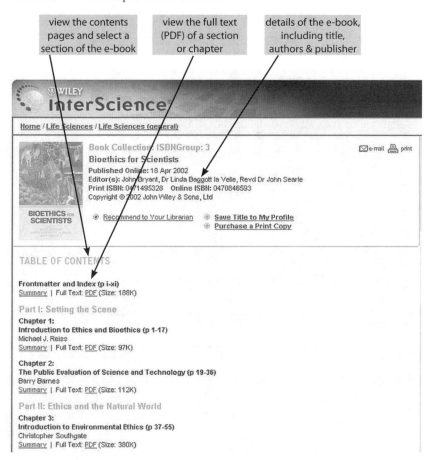

Source: Bioethics for Scientists, Bryant, J., Baggott, L., and Searle, J., 2002. Copyright John Wiley and Sons Ltd. Reproduced with permission

or exam papers. You can access e-reserve through the catalogue or library website.

Simultaneous or federated searching

Many libraries have software that searches several resources at the same time. **Federated** or **meta searching** lets you select and search a group of electronic resources, including databases, catalogues, and Web pages, simultaneously. (See Figure 7.6 for an example of a federated search screen.) This makes searching easier, but has limitations for more specialized topics.

FIGURE 7.6   Example of a federated search screen

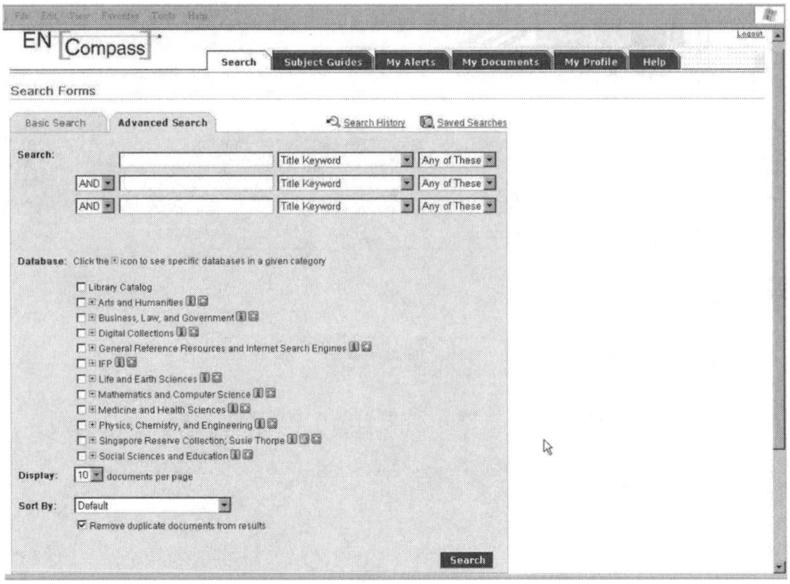

FINDING INFORMATION FOR YOUR ASSIGNMENT

When you are faced with an assignment requiring library research, the abundance of information can be overwhelming. Where do you start?

A logical approach to finding and using information is to devise a plan or search strategy. A search strategy should be tailored to the research problem, but it would usually follow the steps outlined below (and illustrated in Figure 7.7), proceeding from general sources to more specific ones.

Steps in a search strategy

Finding the appropriate resources is straightforward if you develop an effective search strategy.

KEY CONCEPTS

Understanding the topic

- Establish the precise meaning of the question and the purpose of the assignment.
- Highlight the main concepts or important words (keywords).
- Make a list of words or phrases with the same or similar meaning to the keywords. Include alternative spellings (for example, colour, color), alternative endings (for example, environment, environments, environmental), common abbreviations and acronyms (for example, AIDS for Acquired Immune Deficiency Syndrome).
- Identify the type of information you need: background information, specific facts/ statistics, theories for analysis and comparison, current research, or historical views.

Analyze the topic

One of your first tasks is to analyze the topic being discussed.

Obtain background information

- Make sure you understand the meaning of terms or concepts in the question. Refer to the appropriate chapters in recommended textbooks, as well as books and articles on your reading list.
- Consult subject-specific dictionaries and encyclopedias for any new terms, for summaries of theories, and for an overview of the topic. Remember that encyclopedias are usually a starting point, not the end point, in looking for information for assignments at university level! If the terms are still no clearer to you, consult with your professor.

Conduct a search of the catalogue

- Search the library catalogue to find out what books or e-books about your topic are readily available. Books are a fast and convenient source of information when you need a lot of information, summaries of research, or historical information. Books also help to put your assignment topic into an overall context.
- If you locate books highly relevant to your topic in the library, take note of other useful-looking references included in their bibliographies.

> **TIP**
>
> Using a keyword search, sometimes called a guided keyword search, can help when searching the catalogue.

Choose a database

If your topic is highly specific or demands current information, you will need to use an appropriate database to find journal articles or statistical information.

Following are the main points to consider in choosing the right database:

- Subject coverage: Check your library's Web pages to see which databases are recommended for your subject.
- Contents: Do you need full text or are references to articles acceptable? If the due date for your assignment is close, you may only have time for full text. Remember, however, that sometimes the information you need may only be available in print form; so restricting your search to a full text database may be unwise.

Search the database

Libraries subscribe to databases from many different suppliers who have developed different software and search interfaces. The lack of uniformity means that when you search different databases, you face a variety of appearances and features. This is where using a simultaneous or federated search may help by allowing you to search across a number of sources simultaneously. See the previous section on simultaneous or federated searching.

In order to search successfully, read the online instructions or search tips for the database you have selected.

Online help

Online help invariably covers

- how to enter search terms;
- how to combine search terms (see below);
- how to limit your results (for example, by date or language);
- how to view and select records; and
- how to save, print, or email results.

Refine your search

You may need to refine your search by

- adding more keywords;
- removing some keywords;
- using more specific terms;
- using more general terms;
- combining terms in a different way;
- limiting the results; or
- trying another database.

Databases use the connectors AND and OR to combine terms. AND is used to combine different concepts, for example, smoking and cancer. AND narrows the search results, by finding only items that contain both the terms. OR is used to combine alternative or similar words, for example, smoking or cigarettes. OR broadens the search results by finding items that contain either of the terms.

After running an initial search, review your results. Often you will find that the first results are not relevant, that there are too many references, or not enough.

Many databases provide a **search history** that gives the details of what terms or keywords you have used to search.

TIP

Print, take notes, or save to an online bibliographic management system the details of your search history so you have a record of what you have already tried or what has worked, in case you need to reproduce results or try the same search in a different database.

Locate the information

If you are using a full text database, view the article then print it, save it on a Memory Stick, or email it to yourself. If you are using your own computer to do the search, then try to save the .pdf version of the text to your own computer.

If you are using a citation database, view the references, then print, save them to an online bibliographic management system, or email them to yourself. Make sure you get the full details of each reference. If the database you are using does not automatically indicate which of these items the library holds, you will need to check the catalogue yourself for their availability. When you are searching the catalogue, remember to search for the title of the journal, not the title of the article. Not every journal indexed in the database will be available in your library. If your library does not have the journal you are after, it may be worth checking the catalogues of other major libraries in your locality.

Linking to full text

Many libraries provide a shortcut to locating the full text of an article. Alongside the reference, you will see a link, which searches across databases and checks for the full text of the article you want. It also gives you the options to search other sources, including the catalogue, to see if the full text is available electronically or in print.

Need more? Search the Web

Sometimes the information you need is most easily available from the Web. Examples are the latest news, government or company information, some scholarly research, or popular opinion.

Check your library's website for subject guides to Internet resources. These are high-quality sites selected by librarians for a particular discipline.

To find other information on the Web, use a **search engine** (a program that searches for Web documents) such as Google or Yahoo.

Read online search tips to find out how to use the search engine effectively. Search engines often have an advanced search page that gives you additional options for making your search more specific.

Evaluate the information

Make sure you evaluate the content and source of the information you are using, as it will affect the quality of your assignment. This is particularly important when you are retrieving information from the Internet. There is an abundance of information freely available on the Web, and some of this can be very useful. For instance, education (.edu) or government (.gov) sites can be an excellent source of information, especially if you are looking for some specific information (for example, a company or provincial public services website). But there is also an abundance of material that does not merit inclusion in your assignments. Here are some of the questions you should ask:

Scholarly/peer reviewed

When you are undertaking post-secondary studies, your professors will expect that the information you gather for assignments will be from high-quality, reputable sources. In particular, you may be asked to find

> **TIP**
>
> When you are searching the databases, you may see the shortcut link, which will usually have a distinctive name and icon.

> **TIP**
>
> Using the advanced search page in a search engine, you can often limit your search to education sites (.edu), government sites (.gov), or country: for example, Canada (.ca).

KEY CONCEPTS

Evaluating web resources

- Is the information found *relevant* to your topic? Does it address the topic and support the arguments?
- Is the information *current*? (This may not be important in some fields of study, such as literature, where older information may still be valid.)
- Is the information *reliable*? Was it published by a reputable publisher, such as a university press or a professional association? Generally, information from newspapers and popular magazines has less credibility than that from scholarly journals, peer-reviewed articles, and research reports.
- Does the author present facts dispassionately, or give unsupported opinions? Is the author's background and affiliation given?
- Was the information obtained from a general search of the Web? If so, look at Table 7.1, which illustrates why you should be especially wary.

Table 7.1   Comparison of the characteristics of general Web resources and library resources

Characteristics of publicly accessible Web resources	Characteristics of library resources
Anyone can publish on the Web. Webpages are not subjected to an editing or review process.	Material is usually edited and reviewed for publication. Publishers' reputations rely on accuracy.
May be inaccurate, disreputable or biased.	Librarians carefully select books, journals, databases, and websites for quality content.
Information is temporary and can disappear.	Libraries keep material permanently or until no longer required.
Quantity rather than quality.	Quality rather than quantity.
The Web is not organised or controlled by anyone. Search engines can find webpages but no one search engine covers more than a small portion of the Web.	Resources are organized and catalogued to make the search easier.
Good for public opinion, wide range of ideas, quick facts, current news, information about organisations and companies.	Good for information that is reliable, accurate, authoritative, scholarly, comprehensive, up to date as well as historical.
Mostly free, but some sites (usually the best!) charge.	Most information has been purchased.
You need to be self-sufficient.	Libraries provide trained staff to assist you.

articles from scholarly journals, peer-reviewed articles, or research articles. Regardless of whether it is stated in the assignment criteria, there will be an expectation that you are using such high-quality sources.

Scholarly journals, or academic journals, contain articles that have been written by and for academics or researchers in a particular field or subject area. One of the main characteristics that distinguishes a scholarly journal from a popular magazine is that the data has been thoroughly checked (University at Buffalo, 2005). Scholarly journals do not generally contain advertising material, and the articles often contain abstracts, research findings, data, and extensive bibliographies.

Peer-reviewed or refereed articles have been reviewed by peers or experts in the field of study before publishing. There are some resources that may help you to determine whether a journal contains peer-reviewed articles. Some libraries subscribe to *Ulrich's Periodicals Directory*, which indicates whether the journal is peer reviewed. Otherwise, you can often find this sort of detail if you visit the journal homepage on the Internet.

Research articles contain the results of research and usually contain quantitative data, analysis, methodology, and findings.

One of the benefits of using the library's resources is that material retrieved from a database search is more likely to have come from a quality source than a Web search. Some databases, such as *Scholar's Portal*, let you limit your search to peer-reviewed or refereed articles.

Using resources made available through the library will put you well on the way to finding high-quality information and higher grades for your assignments.

Consult a librarian

If you are still having trouble finding information on your topic, ask for assistance at the information desk.

Example of a search strategy

You have been given an assignment in sociology. Your topic is as follows: "The role of the media is important in informing and reflecting social life and cultural values in our contemporary world. Discuss this statement in relation to one of the following issues: genetic engineering, LGBTQ rights, national security."

This is an outline for your search strategy.

- *Analyze the topic*. You are being asked to discuss the role of the media in reflecting and shaping society. The key concepts are mass media, cultural values, or social life. You need to respond in relation to one of the issues given, for example, genetic engineering. This is an additional concept in your search strategy. You need background information on discussion of the media's role in society, genetic engineering, and research findings. Think about the key concepts and alternative keywords that you can use to search the literature. For our example, these are media or mass communication, society, culture, social life, sociology, biotechnology, and genetic engineering.
- *Obtain background information*. Look at the section about media or mass communications in the recommended sociology textbook or book of readings for your course. The particular issue you focus on can be searched later.
- Do a keyword or subject search on the catalogue on sociology, culture, or society AND media or mass communications.
- This should retrieve numerous books or e-books in the library. Those you find might find include the following:

Healey, J. (2000). *Mass media and society*. Sidney: Spinney Press.

Holtzman, L. (2000). *Media messages: What film, television, and popular music teach us about race, class, gender, and sexual orientation*. New York: M.E. Sharpe.

Munro, R., & Lee, N. (2001). *The consumption of mass*. Oxford, England: Blackwell.

FIGURE 7.7   A typical search strategy

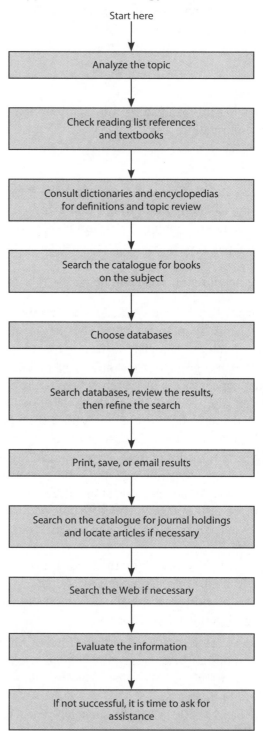

- *Choose and search a database.* For example, use a key sociology database such as *Sociological Abstracts*. The results uncover several relevant articles, including the following:

  Bauer, M.W. Public perceptions and mass media in the biotechnology controversy. *International Journal of Public Opinion Research*, 17(1), 5–22.

  Nisbet, M.C. The competition for worldviews: Values, information, and public support for stem cell research. *International Journal of Public Opinion Research*, 17(1), 90–112.

- *Locate the information.* Print, save, or email the references and any articles that are full text. Check the catalogue to see which journals are available from the library, either in print or electronic form.
- *Search the Web?* Go carefully with this topic—there is likely to beplenty of unsubstantiated and biased Web information, and the databases should provide sufficient coverage of authoritative articles.

> **TIP**
> Some assignments deal with topics that cross disciplines, so you may find helpful information under a different subject area.

SUMMING UP

The university library offers you a rich resource of information and facilities. Learning to use it effectively early in your student life is essential to successful study. The information skills you develop will continue to be invaluable to you in the emerging "knowledge economy."

This chapter has provided a basic guide to the skills you will need, including using the library catalogue, locating materials, finding journal articles, and developing a search strategy. It has emphasized, too, the importance of asking for assistance, because all libraries are *not* the same, and all are undergoing rapid change in response to advances in information technology. Librarians are your "knowledge navigators," whose primary role is to facilitate access to both printed and electronic information resources. Use their services and build on what you have learnt in this chapter to make your time using the library both enjoyable and productive.

GLOSSARY

call number A book's "address" in the library.

databases Electronic collections of information in a particular subject area.

Dewey Decimal Classification system Library system that divides human knowledge into ten main classes.

e-books Full-length online books.

e-journals The electronic equivalent of print journals.

e-reserve Resources recommended by your professors.

e-texts Online textbooks.

federated searching Makes it possible to select and search a group of electronic resources, including databases, catalogues, and Web pages, simultaneously.

information desk The information, reference, or enquiry desk is the first place to ask for help in the library.

information-literate You can find the information needed for any task or decision.

journal Publications (also called magazines, periodicals, or serials) that are issued at regular or irregular intervals, on an ongoing basis.

Library of Congress Classification system Library classification system that uses 21 letters to indicate broad subject categories.

location number See **call number**.

meta searching See **federated searching**.

search engine A program that searches for Web documents and sites.

search history Details of what terms or keywords you have used in previous searches.

stacks The areas where most of the books available for loan are shelved.

subject librarians Provide in-depth assistance in the subject areas they are responsible for.

SUGGESTED FURTHER READING

George, Mary W. (2008). *The elements of library research: What every student needs to know*. Princeton: Princeton University Press.

Heckman, Grant. (2006). *Thomson Nelson guide to web research 2005–2006*. Toronto: Thomson Nelson.

Mann, Thomas. (2005). *The Oxford guide to library research*. New York: Oxford University Press.

RELATED WEBSITES

www.adultlearn.com/elements-citation.html
Adultlearn. "The elements of citation."

www.library.cornell.edu/olinuris/ref/research/webeval.html
Cornell University Library. "Evaluating web sites: Criteria and tools."

http://libguides.uwec.edu/content.php?hs=a&pid=48748
McIntyre Library, University of Wisconsin. "Identifying scholarly or peer-reviewed articles."

http://owl.english.purdue.edu/owl/section/2/10/
Purdue Online Writing Lab. "APA Guide."

http://owl.english.purdue.edu/owl/section/2/10/
Purdue Online Writing Lab. "Chicago manual of style."

http://owl.english.purdue.edu/owl/section/2/11/
Purdue Online Writing Lab. "MLA style."

http://owl.english.purdue.edu/owl/section/2/
Purdue Online Writing Lab. "Research and citation sources."

Successful Communication

PART 2

Writing Up: Essay Writing

True ease in writing comes from art, not chance,
As those move easiest who have learned to dance.

Alexander Pope

This chapter briefly describes the purposes of academic writing before going on to discuss how to write a good essay. Most of the material in the chapter is devoted to a review of those matters your essay markers might be looking for when they are assessing your work. Much of the information and advice in the following pages is structured around the essay assessment schedule in Figure 8.1.

WHY WRITE?

Writing is an *academic and professional responsibility*. As a university graduate, you will probably be required to write—and to write well—as part of any occupation you take up. You will use writing very often to convey your ideas, arguments, and the results of any scientific enquiry to specialists in your field, the general public, clients, and your employer.

Writing is also a *generative, thought-provoking process*, as the following quotations suggest:

I write because I don't know what I think until I read what I have to say.

Flannery O'Connor

You write—and find you have something to say.

Wright Morris

But I really write to find out about something and what is known about something . . . . I write books to find out about things.

Dame Rebecca West

Writing also reveals to you how much you understand about a particular topic. By forcing you to marshal your thoughts and present them coherently to other people, writing is a *central part of the learning process*. Through writing you can also *initiate feedback on your own ideas*. Your professional reports, essays, letters to the editor, journal or magazine articles, blog entries, or tweets may spark replies that contribute to your own knowledge as well as to that of others. As such, writing (like other forms of communication) is critical to the *development and reshaping of knowledge*.

Writing is a means of *conveying and creating the ideas of new worlds*. Writing is part of the process by which you give meaning to, and make sense of, the world(s) in which you live. People who write well—for example, some journalists—influence how you think about issues. By learning to communicate effectively, you are learning to control your own destiny.

Finally, *writing can be fun*. Think of writing as an art form or as storytelling. Use your imagination. Paint the world you want with words.

HOW DO YOU WRITE A GOOD ESSAY?

During your degree program, you may write 20 to 50 **essays**, totalling about 100,000 words—many more words than there are in this book! You might as well spend a little time now ensuring that the 1,000–2,000 hours you spend writing those essays are as productive and rewarding as possible.

- *Read widely*. Reading the work of other writers in your discipline is essential. Not only will it increase your knowledge of your subject, but it will also give you a feeling of how experts write about it.
- *Devote sufficient time to research and writing*. There is no formula for calculating the amount of time you need to devote to writing essays of any particular length or "mark value." Some writers do their best work under great time pressure; others work more slowly and may require several weeks to write a short essay. However, irrespective of your writing style, doing the research for a good essay does take time. So do yourself a favour, and devote plenty of time to finding and reading books and journal articles and to consulting other sources germane to your essay.
- *Practise writing*. As with almost any art—or sport, for that matter—practice improves your ability to perform. Practice allows you to apply the "conventions" of effective writing. It also provides you with the opportunity to seek feedback on the quality of your writing.
- *Plan*. Plan your work schedule to allow time for writing and, if you can, plan your essay.

- *Write freely at first*, suspending editing until you have a substantial first draft of whatever part of your essay you are working on (Greetham, 2002, pp. 176–7).
- *Seek and apply feedback*. Rewrite and rewrite again. Writing is an individual yet *social* process. Perhaps you have an image of a good writer sitting alone at a keyboard typing an error-free, comprehensible, and publishable first draft of a manuscript. Sadly, that image is unfounded. Almost every writer produces countless drafts and seeks comment from peers and other reviewers. Listen to their comments carefully, but remember that in the end, it is *your* essay.

When you write, remember that you are writing for an audience. It is vital that you understand the ways in which an audience might react to your work. A valuable way of gaining such understanding is by allowing friends, learning skills counsellors, writing centre instructors, and others to read and comment on draft copies of your work. You might even find it useful to form a group with some friends and agree to read and respond to one another's essays critically, either in person or online. Remember, though, most universities have very strict policies on plagiarism. Be sure not to incorporate so much of someone else's feedback that the finished product is no longer exclusively your own.

> **TIP**
> Write for your audience.

WHAT ARE YOUR ESSAY MARKERS LOOKING FOR?

The answer to this question is really quite simple. The people who grade your essays want you to explain clearly what you think and what you have learned about a specific topic.

The following guidelines should help you satisfy this broad objective. They correspond to the criteria in the essay assessment schedule in Figure 8.1. These are the criteria typically used by professors when marking essays.

Quality of argument

Ensure that the essay fully addresses the question

This issue in particular is crucial to a good essay. If you do not deal specifically with the question set, the person marking your paper might assume that you do not understand the course material or that you have not bothered to read the question carefully.

- Look closely at the wording of your essay topic: for example, what does "**describe**" mean? How about "**analyze**" or "**compare** and **contrast**"? What do other key words in the assigned topic actually mean?

FIGURE 8.1   Essay assessment schedule

Student name: **Grade:**

Assessed by:

The following is an itemized rating scale for various aspects of essay assignment performance. Some aspects are more important than others, so there is no formula connecting the scatter of ticks with the final percentage for the assignment. A tick in either of the two boxes left of centre means that the statement is true to a greater (outer left) or lesser (inner left) extent. The same principle applies to the right-hand boxes.

If you have any questions about the individual scales, final comment, final grade, or any other aspects of this assignment, please see the assessor.

Quality of argument

The argument fully addresses the question	The argument fails to address the question
Logically developed argument	Writing rambles and lacks logical continuity
Writing well structured through introduction, body, and conclusion	Writing poorly structured, lacking introduction, cohesive paragraphing, and/or conclusion
Material relevant to topic	Much material is not relevant
Topic dealt with in depth	Superficial treatment of topic

Quality of evidence

Argument well supported by evidence and examples	Inadequate supporting evidence or examples
Accurate presentation of evidence and examples	Much evidence incomplete or questionable

Use of supplementary material

Effective use of figures and tables	Illustrative material not used when needed or not discussed in text
Illustrations presented correctly	Illustrations presented incorrectly

Written expression and presentation

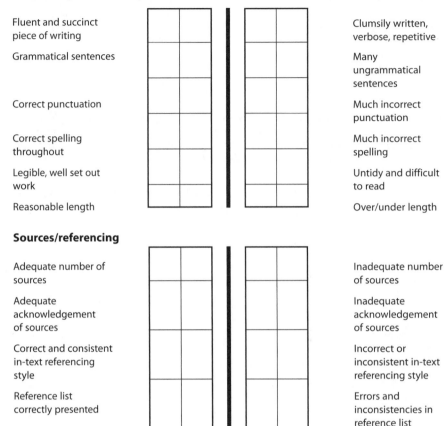

Fluent and succinct piece of writing	Clumsily written, verbose, repetitive
Grammatical sentences	Many ungrammatical sentences
Correct punctuation	Much incorrect punctuation
Correct spelling throughout	Much incorrect spelling
Legible, well set out work	Untidy and difficult to read
Reasonable length	Over/under length

Sources/referencing

Adequate number of sources	Inadequate number of sources
Adequate acknowledgement of sources	Inadequate acknowledgement of sources
Correct and consistent in-text referencing style	Incorrect or inconsistent in-text referencing style
Reference list correctly presented	Errors and inconsistencies in reference list

Assessor's comments

The difference in meaning can be crucial to the way you approach your essay. For instance, an essay in which you are asked to "critically **discuss** Elijah Harper's role in the failure to ratify the Meech Lake Accord" requires more than a description of what he did. It asks you to **evaluate** the significance of his actions. Similarly, an essay that asks you to "discuss the implications of tourism for the cultural integrity of the indigenous people of the Pacific Northwest" requires that you give central attention to the issue of cultural integrity and not that you discuss the history of tourism in British Columbia.

- Discuss the topic with other people in your class. See how your friends have interpreted the topic. Listen critically to others' views, but be prepared to stand up for your own and change it only if you are convinced you are wrong.
- Wherever necessary, clarify the meaning of an assigned topic with your professor or teaching assistant. Do this *after* you have given the

topic full thought, discussed it with friends, and established your own interpretation, but before you begin writing your paper.

- When you have finished writing, check that you have covered all the material set in the topic. The paragraph listing and rearranging technique outlined in the next section of this chapter may be helpful.

Ensure that your essay is logically developed

Nothing is more frustrating than to be lost in someone else's intellectual muddle. A paper that fails to define its purpose, that drifts from one topic to the next, that "does not seem to go anywhere," is certain to frustrate the reader. If that reader happens to be the person who is grading your paper, he or she is likely to strike back with notations scrawled in the margin criticizing the paper as "poorly organized," "incoherent," "lacking clear focus," "discursive," "muddled," or the like. Most professors have developed a formidable arsenal of terms that express their frustration at having to wade through papers that . . . are poorly conceived or disorganized.

(Friedman & Steinberg, 1989, p. 53)

In assessing an essay, markers will usually look for a coherent framework of thought underpinning your work. That is, they are trying to uncover the conceptual skeleton on which you have hung your examples and discussion. Once they have uncovered that skeleton, they will look to see if it is arranged correctly. Is it logical and coherent? Throughout the essay, you should remind readers of the connections between your discussion and this framework. Make clear the relationship between the point being made and any argument you are advancing.

> **TIP**
> Plan your essay.

For some people and for some topics—but not all—formulation of an essay framework can begin with an **essay plan** or **sketch diagram** before you start writing. In other situations, the essay takes shape as it is being written, through **freewriting**.

When you have written the first draft of your essay, check the structure. You can do this quite easily.

You might find that the summary of headings you have prepared supplies a framework on which you can base an informative introduction or abstract. A reader, provided with a sense of direction early in the paper, should find your work easy to follow.

Ensure the writing is well structured through introduction, body, and conclusion

In almost all cases, good academic writing will have an introduction, a discussion, and a conclusion. You might combine this structure with the image of an essay taking the form of an hourglass. The introduction provides a broad outline, setting the topic in its context. The central discussion

> **TIP**
> Some students, especially those who are kinesthetic learners, find putting ideas on separate sticky notes and then arranging the notes into a diagram—using an empty wall, the floor, the refrigerator, a table—a good way to do this.

KEY CONCEPTS

Working out a structure for your essay

Essay plan: If you can, try to set out an essay plan before you begin writing. That is, work out a series of broad headings that will form the framework on which your essay will be constructed. Then add increasingly detailed material under those headings until your essay is written. As you proceed, you may find it necessary to make changes to the overall structure of the essay. See Figure 8.2 for an example of a draft essay plan.

Sketch diagrams of the subject matter are also a good way of working out the structure of your essay. Write down key words associated with the material you will discuss, and draw out a sketch of the ways in which those points are connected to one another. Rearrange the diagram until you have formulated an outline. This sketch diagram can then be used in much the same way as an essay plan. There is some quite good sketch diagram and mind-mapping software on the market to help you with this process.

Freewriting: If you encounter "writer's block" or are writing on a topic that does not lend itself to use of an essay plan, brainstorm and without hesitation write anything related to the topic until you have some paragraphs on the screen or page in front of you. Then remove what you don't like and organize the material into some coherent package. To be effective, this writing style requires good background knowledge of the material to be discussed. Freewriting can be a good way of making connections between elements of the material you have read about. It is not an easy option for people who don't have a clue about their essay topic.

TIP

Students interested in learning more about freewriting might want to consult the work of Peter Elbow.

KEY CONCEPTS

Structuring your essay

- *Go through* the document, giving each **paragraph** or section a heading that summarizes that section's content.
- *Write out* the headings on a separate sheet of paper or on cards. Read through the headings. Are they in a logical order? Do they address the assigned topic in a coherent fashion?
- *Rearrange* the headings, if necessary, until they do make sense.
- *Add* new headings, if it seems appropriate, that might be necessary to cover the topic. If additional headings are required, you will also have to write some new sections of your paper. Of course, you may also find that you can remove some sections.
- *Make your amendments* and then go through this process of assigning and arranging headings again until you are satisfied that the essay follows a logical progression.
- Then, *rearrange* the written material according to the new sequence of headings.

TIP

Make sure your essay structure is *clear* and *coherent*.

TIP

Imagine your essay has an hourglass structure.

FIGURE 8.2   Example of a draft essay plan

Topic: Discuss the [advantages] and [disadvantages]
of returning to study as a mature age
student

Taskword: discuss

Content words: returning to study

Organisation: advantages and disadvantages

Plan:

Introduction
- define mature age student
  - Typical characteristics
  - differences from school leavers
- general statement of adv. & disadv.

Advantages
- maturity
- sense of purpose; dedication
- experience - life & work
- self-confidence in approaching staff
  - asking questions
  - speaking up in tutorials

Disadvantages
- out of practice in learning, writing, etc.
- limitations on time
- extra responsibilities - family?, job?
- lack of peer group support
- " " confidence in academic ability
- memory??
- economic difficulty - finance

Conclusion   Sum up main ideas by comparing:
(a) maturity vs rusty academic skills
(b) strong motivation vs limited time/money
(c) confidence with others vs lack of confidence in SELF

?∴: Adv. & disadv. are equally balanced? OR
One outweighs the other?

The introduction

Follow these guidelines as you prepare the introductory portion of your essay:

- *State your aims or purpose clearly.* What problem or issue are you discussing? Do not simply repeat or rephrase the question. That is one certain way of putting any reader off your work.
- *Make your conceptual framework clear.* This makes it easier for readers to understand the rest of your essay.
- *Set your study in context.* What is the significance of the topic?
- *Outline the scope of your discussion.* Give the reader some idea of the spatial, temporal, and intellectual boundaries of your presentation. What case will you argue?
- *Give readers some idea of the plan of your discussion*—a sketch diagram of the intellectual journey they are about to undertake.
- *Capture the reader's attention from the outset.* Is there some unexpected or surprising angle to the essay? Alternatively, you might capture attention with relevant and interesting quotations, amazing facts, and anecdotes.

TIP

Make your introduction clear and lively. First impressions are very important.

tapers in to cover the detail of the specific issue(s) you are exploring. The conclusion sets your findings back into the context from which the subject is derived and may point to directions for future enquiry.

The best introductions are those that get to the point quickly and that capture the reader's attention (Bate & Sharpe, 1990, p. 12). Like a good travel guide, an effective introduction allows readers to distinguish and understand the main pointers of your essay as they read past them (Greetham, p. 184).

Avoid clichéd, phony, mawkish conclusions (Northey & Knight, 1992, p. 73). For example, "The tremendous amount of soil erosion in the valley dramatically highlights the awful plight of the poor farmers, who for generations to come will suffer dreadfully from the loss of the very basis for their livelihood"; or "Without further action on the

TIP

Good essays get off to a good start.

The discussion

Follow these guidelines as you prepare the discussion portion of your essay:

- *Make your case:* "Who dunnit?"
- *Provide the reader with reasons and evidence to support your views.* Imagine your professor is sitting on your shoulder (an unpleasant thought!) saying "prove that" or "I don't believe you." Disarm his/her skepticism.
- *Present your material logically, precisely, and in an orderly fashion.*
- *Accompany your key points with carefully chosen, colourful, and correct examples and analogies.*

The conclusion

Follow these guidelines as you prepare the conclusion portion of your essay:

- *State your resolution of the problem or question set out in the introduction.* The conclusion ought to be the best possible answer to your essay question on the basis of the evidence you have discussed in the main section of the paper (Friedman & Steinberg, p. 57). It must match the strengths and balance of material you have presented throughout the essay (Greetham, p. 197). Do not introduce new material.
- *Discuss the broad implications of the work*, if appropriate (Moxley, 1992, p. 68).
- *Tie the conclusion neatly together with the introduction.* When you have finished writing your essay, read just the introduction and the conclusion. Do they make sense together?
- Finally, *ask yourself: "Have I answered the question?"*

TIP

Convince your reader with logic, example, and careful structure.

TIP

Make sure the conclusion matches up with the introduction.

problem of spouse abuse, sad stories such as those recounted here will be repeated over and over again." Instead, and, if you can, leave your reader with something interesting to think about (Najar & Riley, 2004, p. 56), such as the wider implications or your informed perspective on future trends.

Some writers like to use **headings** throughout their essay. You are not compelled to use headings in essays—indeed, some professors and some disciplines actively discourage this. (Check with your professor, teaching assistant, or writing centre.) But headings allow readers of your essay to see at a glance its overall structure and, at any stage, to know where they are in the essay's structure. Headings also make it easier to review particular sections and to check a passage or point. These two purposes give a clue to the number and nature of headings that you might include. Provide enough to offer a person quickly scanning the essay a sense of the work's structure or intellectual "trajectory." To check this, write out the headings you propose to use. Is the list logical or confusing, sparse or detailed? Referring back to the essay itself, revise your list of headings until it provides a clear, succinct overview of your work.

TIP

Headings show structure.

If you are writing a particularly long essay, you may need a hierarchy of headings. Three levels should be sufficient for most purposes, although up to five are illustrated in the examples below. Too many headings can add confusion rather than clarity.

Take care to ensure that equivalent heading types are used for equivalent sections in the essay.

Examples of heading styles

BOLD CAPITALS
MEDIUM CAPITALS
MEDIUM ITALIC CAPITALS
CAPITALS AND SMALL CAPITALS
or
BOLD CAPITALS
Bold lower case
Bold italic lower case
Italic lower case
Italic lower case. With text running on . . .
or
BOLD CAPITALS
Bold Upper and Lower Case
Bold italic lower case
Italic lower case

Ensure the material is relevant to the topic

The material you present in your essay should be clearly and explicitly linked to the topic being discussed. When you have finished writing a draft of your essay, read each paragraph asking yourself two questions:

1. Does *all* of the information in this paragraph help answer the question?
2. *How* does this information help answer the question?

On the basis of your answers, edit. This should help you to eliminate the dross.

Ensure the topic is dealt with in depth

Have you simply slapped on a quick coat of paint, or does your essay reflect preparation, undercoat, and good final coats? Have you explored all the issues emerging from the topic? This does not mean that you should employ the "shotgun" technique of essay writing. Do not, in other words, put all the indiscriminate information you can collect on a subject into the pages of your essay.

Instead, be diligent and thoughtful in going about your research, taking care to check your institution's library, statistical holdings, other libraries, and online and information sources. Take notes and, where appropriate, download original text or make photocopies. Read. Read. Read. There is not really any simple way of working out whether you have dealt with a topic in sufficient depth. Perhaps all that can be said is that broad reading, discussions with your professor or teaching assistant, and keeping to the length requested will provide some guidelines.

Quality of evidence

Ensure that your essay is well supported by evidence and examples

You need relevant examples, statistics, quotations from books, articles, and interviews, and other forms of **evidence** to support your case and to substantiate claims. In addition, most readers seek examples that will bring to life or emphasize the importance of the points you are trying to make. You can draw information from good research (for example, wide reading or interviews with appropriate people). Careful use of examples is also an indicator of diligence in research and the desirable ability to link concepts or theory with "reality."

When looking for evidence to include in your essay, do not confine your search to material available on the Web. Your essay marker will most likely be very disapproving of this. Although the Internet is a remarkable and increasingly valuable source of information (see, for example, useful resources like Google Scholar and JSTOR, which provide free access to scholarly works), use online sources wisely, checking to be sure that they are reliable and appropriately academic authorities. The Internet also has the distinct advantage of providing the most current research in a number of areas, but using online sources exclusively sometimes indicates lazy scholarship and neglects vast amounts of high-quality material available from other sources—notably academic journals, reputable newspapers, magazines, and books that are not yet available online.

> **TIP**
> Be sure that research includes more than just Internet sources.

Be critical of *all* your sources and particularly those on the Web. Whose evidence and argument do you accept? Why? How do you know that your source is in any way credible or authoritative? Whose interests does it represent? By way of caution, consider anwr.org, a site promoting oil drilling in the Arctic National Wildlife Refuge. It takes some investigation to find that the site is supported by Arctic Power, a coalition of Alaskan industry groups pressing to open parts of the Refuge to oil and gas development. Arctic Power is underwritten by the state of Alaska with funding from the oil industry.

> **TIP**
> Make sure all of your sources are credible.

Table 8.1 provides some suggestions for scrutinizing the credibility of Internet sources. Simply because something is published, or is on the Internet, does not mean it is true. Indeed, as a 1993 Peter Steiner cartoon published in the *New Yorker* magazine observed, "On the Internet, nobody knows you're a dog."

Table 8.1   Evaluating webpages

Question	How do you answer it?	What does it imply?
Did you find the page or site through a sponsored link?	Some search engines will direct you to sponsored links first. These are usually identified as such.	Information distributed with commercial intent is not always 'balanced'.
From what domain does the page come?	Look at the URL (Uniform Resource Locator). Is the domain, for example: ■ commercial (.com), ■ educational (.edu), ■ government (.gov), ■ non-profit (.org), or ■ miscellaneous (.net)? What country is it from? (e.g., .au for Australia; .nz for New Zealand; .ca for Canada [note: USA-based sites typically have no country identifier]). A Web search for country domain names will yield full lists. Consider whether the domain and country seem appropriate for the site.	Consider the appropri- ateness of the domain to the material. Is this kind of agency a fitting one for the material being presented? Is the mate- rial from the right place?
Who or what agency wrote the page and why? Is the agency reputable?	Good places to start are the ban- ner at the top of the page or any statement of copyright, which is typically located at the bottom of the page. Alternatively, look for informa- tion under links associated with the page and characteristically entitled 'About us', 'Who we are' or 'Background'. Authoring agency details are sometimes located in the URL between the http:// statement and the first / (forward slash), or immediately after a www state- ment (e.g. www.abs refers to the Australian Bureau of Statistics) and www.maf refers to the NZ Ministry of Agriculture and Fisheries). Try truncating back through the URL to find out about the authoring agency. That is, start- ing from the end of the URL, delete one by one each phrase	Web pages are written with intent or purpose— and it is not always the best intent!

Question	How do you answer it?	What does it imply?
	ending with a / (forward slash), pressing enter after each deletion. This may generate new webpages that provide insights to the origins of the page you planned to use. It may also be useful to query the authoring institution's name through a search engine. This may reveal other information that points to funding sources and underlying agendas.	
Is this someone's personal webpage or part of a weblog ('blog')?	Look for a personal name in the URL. This is typically shown in the URL after a ~ (tilde), % (percentage) or /people/, /users/ statement (for example /~jtrout/). Blogs are often identified as such through their title (e.g., Wired Campus Blog); their URL that may contain the word 'blog'; or in webpage text introducing the blog.	The fact that information is presented on a personal page or 'blog' is not necessarily a bad thing. Indeed, some of great value are being written, for example, by people with media connections but without the oversight of an editor. However, you will need to find out whether the author is an expert, credible source. This information may be set out on the site you are looking through. If not, use a good search engine (e.g., Alexa, Google, Yahoo) to query the author's name. If you cannot get any insights into the author (e.g., her credentials, professional role), think seriously about whether you should use information from the page.
When was the page created or last updated?	Look at the bottom of the webpage. This is usually where a 'created on' or 'last updated on' statement is located.	Old pages may contain outdated information. In almost every case, undated statistical or factual information should not be used.
Is the content and layout of high quality?	Check to see if the page looks well produced and that the text is free of typographical errors and spelling mistakes (translated	Scruffy, poorly set out webpages do not necessarily contain inaccurate information but they

Question	How do you answer it?	What does it imply?
	foreign sites may be an exception). Where possible, confirm the plausibility and accuracy of data or other information presented by comparing it with other good sources.	should cause you to question the meticulousness of the author in their information-gathering and presentation.

Adapted from: Barker (2005) and Beck (2005). Barker, in particular, offers very useful and detailed advice on assessing webpages.

Personal experience and observations may be incorporated as evidence in written work. For example, if you have spent several years as a police officer, you may have some valuable insights in an assignment on aspects of the sociology of deviance. Women and men who have spent time caring for children in new suburban areas may have valuable comments to make on the issue of social service provision to such areas. It is certainly valid to refer to your own experiences, but be sure to indicate in the text that it is to those that you are referring, and give the reader some indication of the nature and extent of your relevant experience: for example, "In my 19 years as a police officer in downtown Winnipeg . . . " Where possible, support your personal observations with other sources that readers may be able to consult.

Avoid making unsupported generalizations: for example, "Crime is decreasing daily"; "Pollution is the major cause of respiratory illness." Unsupported generalizations are indicators of laziness or sloppy scholarship and will usually draw criticism from essay markers. Provide support for claims by using empirical evidence or by citing recognized sources. For example, "Statistics Canada has recently released a report entitled *Crime in Canada*, which demonstrates that the crime rate in Canada has been in decline since comparable figures were last collected" or "A new paper in the medical journal *Lancet* suggests that air pollution can be linked to 1,054 deaths in Mexico City since 2000."

KEY CONCEPTS

Using examples

When you use examples, make sure they are

- *relevant*;
- *as current as possible* (this may not be relevant in some fields, such as history or literature);
- *drawn from reputable sources*, such as official statistics, *Hansard*, international journals, or experts in the field (all should be identified fully in your work with an appropriate referencing system); and
- *free from factual errors*.

Ensure accurate presentation of evidence and examples
Keep a tight rein on your examples. Use only those details you need to make your case.

Use of supplementary material

Make effective use of figures and tables
You can use illustrations to make points more clearly, effectively, or succinctly than you can make them in words. People usually remember the information in illustrations more easily than that in text. **Histograms**, **pie graphs**, tables, schematic diagrams, and photos can supplement text but should not duplicate it (Mullins, 1977, p. 40).

When evaluating your use of illustrative material, such as figures, tables, and maps, markers will check to see that you have made reference to the illustration in your discussion and that the illustration makes the point intended. Professors also look to see whether you might have added additional illustrative material to support the points you are making or to better organize the information you have presented. Illustrations do not need to come from your reading. You can create your own illustrations where appropriate.

You should incorporate tables and graphics into your essay with care. Make sure they are relevant, and locate them as close as possible to the text where you discuss them. Be sure to discuss each illustration somewhere in your text. Unless you have a particularly good reason for doing so, do not put figures in an appendix at the end of the essay. Most readers find this very frustrating.

> **TIP**
> A picture is worth a thousand words; it's worth two thousand if you briefly explain its importance in supporting your argument!

Ensure the illustrations are presented correctly
Several types of illustrative material are commonly included in written work. These, and the accepted labels for each, are as follows:

Type of material	Label
Graphs, diagrams, and maps	Figure
Tables and word charts	Table
Photographs	Plate

Tables, figures, and plates can contribute substantially to the message you wish to communicate in a piece of work. But you must take care with their presentation. You are strongly advised to consult chapters 16 and 17 of this book for further information about using maps, figures, and tables.

Written expression and presentation

Your writing should be fluent and succinct

Chapters 12 and 13 will give you more detail on writing style, grammar, and punctuation, and you are advised to read them carefully.

Write simply. Short words and sentences are best. Unless you wish deliberately to obfuscate, there is little room for grandiloquence in effective written communication! Ask yourself whether someone whose first language is not English could understand your essay. If you know someone in that position who is willing to read your essay, give him or her a copy to look over. Or put a draft of your work away for several days and then read it afresh. Ideally, read it aloud: poor expression and odd constructions that were not evident before will leap out to greet you.

TIP

Reading your essay aloud can reveal clumsy expression, poor punctuation, and repetition.

NAVIGATING LEARNING CHALLENGES: GET HELP IF YOU NEED IT

If English is not your first language, or if you know that you have a disability that might interfere with your ability to carefully proofread your own work, be sure to leave extra time for editing your assignments and having someone else look them over. Be careful, though: use only those resources (e.g., writing, academic success, or accessibility services) that are permitted by your university!

Make every word count. Padding is easily detected, and it makes assessors suspicious that you have little of substance to say. Prune unnecessary words and phrases from your work. Remember, the objective in an essay is to answer the question or to convey a body of information—not to write a specified number of words.

Effective paragraphing is an important part of good written communication. A paragraph is a subdivision within a text that marks a break in the subject greater than the break between sentences (Bernstein, 1979, pp. 324–5).

KEY CONCEPTS

Parts of a paragraph

Topic sentence: states the main idea. ("The depletion of the rainforest coast of British Columbia is proceeding apace.")

Supporting sentence(s): "why" and "how" examples to support the topic or to prove the point. ("There is little government action to end land clearance in fragile environments, and private incentives to clear the land remain attractive.")

Clincher: lets the reader know the paragraph is over. May summarize the paragraph, echo the topic sentence, or ask a question. ("There seems to be little hope for the coastal temperate rainforests of Canada.")

It gives your reader a visual cue to separations of subject in your writing and makes reading easier. Although there are exceptions, paragraphs typically comprise the following three parts (Barrett, 1982, p. 118).

In general, a paragraph should be a cohesive, self-contained expression of one idea. If your paragraph conveys a number of separate ideas, rethink its construction. Paragraph length can vary depending on the subject, the font size and layout, the purpose of the writing, and the audience (Bernstein, p. 325). For example, scientific papers are likely to have longer paragraphs than children's books. Newspapers, with small type and narrow columns, will have shorter paragraphs than advanced undergraduate textbooks with their larger type and single column of text.

Paragraphs should relate to one another as well as to the overall thrust of the text. Get into the practice of using transitional sentences at the

KEY CONCEPTS

Transitional phrases
Consider phrases such as
- *another problem associated with . . .;*
- *on the one hand . . .;*
- *on the other hand . . .;*
- *from a different perspective . . .;*
- *elsewhere . . .;*
- *other common . . .;* and
- *a number of issues can be identified . . .*

as devices that allow you to lead your reader from one part of your essay to another.

beginning or end of paragraphs to make explicit the connections between material discussed in each.

Use grammatical sentences
One simple way of detecting difficulties with grammar is to ask a friend to read your essay out loud to you. If that person has difficulty and stumbles over sentence constructions, it is likely that the grammar is in need of repair. Another simple way of avoiding problems is to keep sentences *short* and simple. Not only are long, convoluted sentences often difficult to understand, but they are also grammatical minefields. (See chapter 12 for more details.)

TIP
Think of transitional expressions as road signs: they help the reader navigate your text.

Watch for Road Signs
Students who have English as a second language or who sometimes get lost while they are reading should pay particular attention to transitional expressions. They will help you figure out where an argument is leading.

TIPS for EAL LEARNERS

Use correct punctuation

Check the material in chapter 13 for a review of common punctuation problems. Take particular care with the use of apostrophes. If there is anything you do not understand, ask your academic success or writing centre.

Use correct spelling throughout

Keep a dictionary handy when you are writing essays. Poor spelling brings even the best of work into question. Spelling errors repeatedly emerge as a problem in university-level essays. If you write your essay on a computer, be sure to use the spell-check option before you submit the essay for assessment, *but* remember that distinctions between words such as there/ their, too/two/to, affect/effect, course/coarse, its/it's, principle/principal will not show up. Sometimes, too, it will flag words as being incorrect when in fact you are using a correct, but unconventional, spelling (e.g., quoting Shakespearean English). Check, too, that your spell-checker is using the appropriate form of English (e.g., Canadian English, rather than US or UK English). If you are unsure of a word's spelling, and if you do not recognize the alternatives offered by the spell-check, go to a Canadian edition of a dictionary. It will tell you what the different alternatives offered by the spell-check actually mean and which of them is correct. Do not be like the student who wrote "Shakespeare defecates his mistress in this sonnet." She meant "denigrates," of course. A quick check in a dictionary would have saved the student a lot of embarrassment.

Use a Proofreader

Spelling errors and sloppy presentation reflect poorly on your work. Whenever possible, students who do not have English as their first language or who have trouble catching mistakes in their own writing should be sure to consult an outside reader to look over their assignments.

If you write using paper and pen or pencil, go to a writing or academic success centre, or consult a learning strategist (if you have been given access to this service) for assistance. Ask them to look over your paper with an eye to the spelling and grammatical errors. If you know that you are prone to making certain mistakes, such as mistakenly adding or omitting a final "s" on a word or reversing letters, be sure to make them aware of this before they start reading.

Make sure your work is legible and well set out

Poor presentation can prejudice your case by leading the reader to assume sloppiness of thought.

(Bate & Sharpe, p. 38)

Essays that are difficult to read because of poor handwriting can infuriate your marker. It is difficult to maintain a sense of your case, argument, or evidence if reading must be interrupted repeatedly to decipher individual words. Wherever possible, use a computer to produce the final copy of your paper.

To allow room for your professor's comments, double-space all work and leave adequate margins. Usually, your professor requires you to submit essays that are typed in twelve-point, Times New Roman font, double-spaced, with one-inch margins on all sides. (If you have selected "Metric" as the default measurement system in your display options, your margin will be 2.5 centimetres.) Print your assignment on only one side of standard (8.5 in. by 11 in.) paper.

Well-presented work suggests pride of authorship. You are likely to find that presentation does make a difference—to your own view of your work as well as to the view of the assessor.

Your assignment should be a reasonable length

A key to good communication is being able to convey a message with economy (consider the communicative power of some short poems). Take care not to write more words than your professor has asked for. Most people marking essays do not want to read any more words than they have to. Avoid masking a scarcity of ideas with verbose expression. If you find you do not have enough to say in an essay, perhaps you need to do some more research—not more writing.

Sources/referencing

An introductory word of advice on references—when writing an essay, be sure to insert citations as you are writing. It is very difficult to come back to a paper to try to insert the correct references. Make sure, too, when you are collecting information for an essay that you record the bibliographic details of *all* your sources. This makes it easy to prepare the reference list.

Ensure you have an adequate number of appropriate sources

Markers will consider very carefully the quality of evidence you use in your work. You are expected to demonstrate that you have conducted extensive research appropriate to the topic and to the level of the course. Depending on the discipline within which you are writing, first-year essays might draw from secondary sources, such as books and journals, whereas third-year research essays might require library research, interviews, fieldwork, and information derived from other primary information sources.

You will be expected to draw your evidence from, and substantiate claims with, *up-to-date*, *relevant*, and *reputable* sources. Reputable sources might include scholarly journals, textbooks, high-quality websites (see Table 8.1),

> **TIP**
>
> Keep a full record of all your sources. It will save you a lot of time and work when you prepare your final reference list.

major newspapers (for example, the *New York Times*, the *International Herald Tribune*, the *Globe and Mail*, the *National Post*, *Christian Science Monitor*, the *Financial Post*) and magazines (such as *National Geographic*, the *Economist*, *Science*, the *New England Journal of Medicine*). But be careful about all your sources. Simply because something is written in a journal, newspaper, or on the Web does not necessarily mean it is "true." Indeed, in some disciplines, certain kinds of reference materials are not considered acceptable evidence for some arguments. For instance, in the health sciences, a newspaper article discussing causal links between cigarette smoking and lung cancer would not be appropriate evidence to substantiate that link. But the article might be a useful indicator of public concern about such a connection. If you are in any doubt, ask your professor or teaching assistant.

In much the same way as there is no answer to the question "How long is a piece of string?" there is no specific number of sources you should consult for any particular kind or length of assignment. For instance, you cannot assume that 20 references is the right number for a first-year, 2,000-word essay or that 30 is the correct number for a third-year 4,000-word research report. However, you should not place heavy reliance on a small number of references. Most markers give some weight to the *number and range of references* you have used for your work. This is to ensure that you have established the soundness of your case by considering evidence from a broad range of possible sources. For example, the person marking your paper might be suspicious of an essay examining the consequences of hospital privatization for Canadian rural health-care delivery if the essay was based heavily on documents produced only by the Liberal Party or by the NDP (New Democratic Party).

You should be careful of any information published on the Internet. Anyone can post his or her opinions without subjecting them to peer review or authentication by recognized research methods. Some sites are useful for what they reveal about public opinion on a topic but cannot be accepted as authoritative (see Table 8.1). Some book reviews, for example, contain promotional material from publishers and errors of fact. Frequently, opinions about medical topics are prepared by those with commercial interests in medications or products said to have therapeutic value. As a basic rule of thumb, websites ending with ".edu" or ".gov" tend to be most reliable for academic research.

Make sure you acknowledge your sources adequately

Ideas, facts, paraphrases, and quotations must be attributed to the source from which you derived them. Failure to acknowledge sources remains a common and potentially dangerous error in student essays (see Burkill & Abbey, 2004). Serious omissions may constitute plagiarism. (See the discussion of plagiarism in chapter 14.) You must make acknowledgements by using an appropriate system of referencing. (See chapter 14 for details.)

Quite often, people new to writing essays save the acknowledgement of all the references contained in a paragraph until the end of that paragraph. There they place a string of note identifiers or names, dates, and page numbers. This is incorrect and annoying. The reader has no way of establishing which ideas, concepts, or facts are being attributed to whom. You should place references as close as possible to ideas or illustrations to which they are connected.

If you are *quoting* someone *directly*, there are four golden rules to follow:

> **TIP**
>
> Citing sources fully and correctly is an important academic skill. Take the time to learn how it is done.

- *Reproduce the text exactly*. Spelling, capitalization, and paragraphing must mirror that of the original source. If there is a misspelling or error of fact, put the word "*sic*" in square brackets immediately after the error. This lets your reader know that the mistake was in the original source and that you have not misquoted. Your main text and the quotation should be grammatically consistent. This sometimes requires that you add or remove words. If you find that you must omit unnecessary words, use three periods (. . .), known as an **ellipsis**, to show that you have deleted words from the original text. If you need to add words, put those you have added within square brackets. Make sure you do not change the original meaning of the text through your omissions or additions.

- When making a direct quotation of less than about 40 words, you should incorporate the quote into your own text, indicating the beginning and end of the quote with double quotation marks. The in-text reference or numerical reference (see chapter 14) is usually placed after the closing quotation marks. For example,

    He described Hispaniola and Tortuga as densely populated and "completely cultivated like the countryside around Cordoba" (Colon, p. 165).
    He described Hispaniola and Tortuga as densely populated and "completely cultivated like the countryside around Cordoba."[5]

- If you are making a direct quotation of more than 40 or 50 words, you should not use quotation marks, but rather indent and use single-spacing as shown in the example here:

    Ursula Franklin, a metallurgist, research physicist, author, and educator, provided this insight:
    I want to know as much as possible about the house that technology has built, about its secret passages and about its trapdoors. And I would also like to look at

technology in the way C.B. Macpherson looked at democracy—in terms of the real world. Technology, like democracy, includes ideas and practices; it includes myths and various models of reality. And like democracy, technology changes the social and individual relationships between us. It has forced us to examine and redefine our notions of power and of accountability.

(Franklin, 1999)

- A blank line immediately precedes and follows the quotation.
- *Use quotations sparingly.* Only use a quotation when it outlines an idea or example so well that you cannot improve on it, when it contains a major statement you must document, or when the quotation itself *is* the evidence or example that supports your point.
- *Integrate the quotation into your text.* Justify its inclusion. Let the reader know what it means for your work.

See chapter 14 for more detail on quoting and acknowledging the works of others.

Make sure your in-text referencing style is correct and consistent

Full and correct acknowledgement of the sources from which you have derived quotations, ideas, and evidence is a fundamental part of the academic enterprise. Acknowledging the contribution of others to the essay you have written should not be difficult if you follow the instructions on referencing provided in chapter 14.

Make sure your reference list is correctly presented

The most common—and most easily rectified—problems in essay writing emerge from incorrect acknowledgement of sources. Repeatedly in students' essays, referencing is done incorrectly, and reference lists are formatted incorrectly. Many people who mark essays consider that problems with the relatively simple matter of referencing reflect more serious shortcomings in the work they are reading. It is advisable, then, to follow the instructions on referencing very carefully. If you do not understand how to refer to texts in an essay, ask for help from your teaching assistant, reference librarian, writing tutor, or learning skills counsellor.

Before you submit an essay for assessment, be sure that all in-text references have a corresponding entry in the list of *Works Cited* or *References*. Further, in most cases, this list should include *only* those references you have actually cited in the paper.

TIP

In some other cultures, students are encouraged to use direct quotations from authorities as a sign of respect; moreover, acknowledging the source is viewed as "patronizing" since the reader is assumed to know the origins of the quotation. This is *not* the case in Canadian universities. If you are uncertain about how best to acknowledge sources, it is important to get guidance from a reliable university service on this matter.

(Felicity Fallon, 7)

THE MATTER OF SCHOLARSHIP

There is one intangible factor that has been omitted from the assessment schedule in Figure 8.1 earlier in the chapter: scholarship. High-quality scholarship is one of the most important qualities of a good essay. Your essay should clearly be a product of *your* mind, of *your* logical thought. Your professor will react less than favourably to an essay that is merely a compilation of the work of other writers. In considering matters of scholarship, essay markers are searching for judicious use of reference material combined with *your individual insights*.

While scholarship requires that you draw from the work of other writers, you must do so with discretion. Use direct quotations from secondary sources sparingly (and, if you do use quotations, be sure to integrate them into the rest of your text). Keep paraphrasing to a minimum.

You might argue that novice status in the discipline means that you must rely heavily on other people's work. Obviously, you might encounter problems if you are asked to write an essay on a subject that, until a few weeks ago, might have been quite foreign to you. But do not be misled into believing that in writing an essay, you must produce some earth-shattering exposition on the topic you have been assigned. Instead, your professor is looking for evidence that you have read on the subject, *interpreted* that reading, and set out appropriate evidence based on the interpretation that satisfactorily addresses the essay topic. Remember the advice from the beginning of this chapter. Your professor wants you to explain clearly what you think and what you have learned about a specific topic.

> **TIP**
>
> Essay markers want to know what you think and have learned about a specific topic.

GLOSSARY

analyze Explore component parts in order to understand how the whole thing works. It can also mean to examine closely.

clincher May summarize the paragraph, echo the topic sentence, or ask a question. It lets the reader know the paragraph is over.

compare Look at similarities and differences between ideas, places, events, etc. (often used in conjunction with contrast).

contrast Give a detailed account of differences between selected phenomena (often used in conjunction with compare).

describe Outline the characteristics of some phenomenon without necessarily interpreting them.

discuss Examine critically, using argument.

ellipsis Three periods (. . .) used to show that you have deleted words from the original text.

essay Brief literary composition that states clearly what you think and have learned.

essay plan A series of broad headings that will form the framework on which your essay will be constructed.

evaluate Appraise the worth of something and make a judgment.

evidence Information used to support or refute a statement or conclusion.

freewriting Method of planning an assignment that involves (a) "stream of consciousness" writing without concern for overall structure and direction, followed by (b) careful revision.

heading A word or phrase at the beginning of each section that allows a reader to quickly scan the essay in order to gain a sense of the work's structure or intellectual "trajectory."

histogram Graphs in which observed values are depicted by horizontal or, more commonly, vertical, bars whose area is proportional to the value(s) portrayed. Thus, if class intervals depicted in the histogram are of different sizes, the column areas will reflect this.

paragraph A cohesive, self-contained expression of an idea usually constituting part of a longer written document. Typically comprises three parts: topic sentence, supporting sentence(s), and clincher.

pie graph Also known as circle graph. Circular graph in which percentages of some whole are depicted as "slices" of a round pie.

sketch diagram A sketch of the ways in which key words associated with the material you will discuss are connected to one another.

supporting sentence(s) Provide the "why" and "how" examples to support the topic or to prove the point in a paragraph.

topic sentence States the main idea of a paragraph.

SUGGESTED FURTHER READING

Anderson, J., & Poole, M. (2001). *Assignment and thesis writing* (4th ed.). Milton, ON: John Wiley.

Barry, Lynda. (2008). *What it is*. Montreal: Drawn & Quarterly.

Buckley, Joanne. (1998). *Fit to print: The Canadian student's guide to essay writing*. Toronto: Harcourt Brace & Company.

Dietsch, Betty Mattix, Sauer, Lara, & Lovering, Andrea. (2003). *Reasoning and writing well* (Canadian ed.). Toronto: McGraw-Hill Ryerson.

Elbow, Peter. (1981). *Writing with power: Techniques for mastering the writing process*. New York: Oxford University Press.

Elbow, Peter. (1973). *Writing without teachers*. New York: Oxford University Press.

Harvey, Michael. (2003). *The nuts and bolts of college writing*. Indianapolis: Hackett Publishing.

Kjortshoj, Keith. (2009). *The transition to college writing*. New York: St. Martin's Press.

Taylor, Karen, Avery, Heather, & Strath, Lucille. (1991). *Clear, correct, creative: A handbook for writers of academic prose*. Peterborough, ON: Academic Skills Centre, Trent University.

RELATED WEBSITES

www.writing.utoronto.ca/images/stories/Documents/intros-and-conclusions.pdf
Freedman, Leora, & Plotnick, Jerry. University of Toronto. "Introductions and conclusions."

www.writing.utoronto.ca/images/stories/Documents/organizing.pdf
Plotnick, Jerry. University of Toronto. "Organizing an essay."

www.writing.utoronto.ca/images/stories/Documents/quotations.pdf
———. University of Toronto. "Using quotations."

www.writing.utoronto.ca/images/stories/Documents/paragraphs.pdf
Procter, Margaret. University of Toronto. "Developing coherent paragraphs."

www.writing.utoronto.ca/images/stories/Documents/wordiness.pdf
———. University of Toronto. "Wordiness: Danger signals and ways to react."

http://owl.english.purdue.edu/owl/section/1/1/
Purdue Online Writing Lab. "The writing process."

Arguing Through: Preparing and Presenting Written Argument

It is a capital mistake to theorize before you have all the evidence. It biases the judgment.

Sir Arthur Conan Doyle, 1888

The previous chapter has given advice on writing academic essays. This chapter will look more closely at a particular kind of essay: one where you are asked to argue a point of view on a controversial topic, or to prove or disprove a specific hypothesis. Essays of this kind are set very often, to give students experience in thinking critically about a particular topic and in expressing their opinions logically and persuasively. Typical examples of this kind of essay topic are: "Greenhouse gases are said by many to be causing global warming and unusual weather patterns. Do you agree?"; "Heredity or environment: which is more important in determining an individual's personality?"; "What is the purpose of anti-feminist satire in any two of Chaucer's *Canterbury Tales*?" In answering any of these questions, you need to form an opinion about a controversial topic and to justify that opinion in a convincing way by arguing in support of the opinion you have chosen.

This chapter will define what is meant by "argument" in academic and professional contexts, set out the essential components of an extended argument, discuss different kinds of evidence, describe some pitfalls in reasoning, and suggest some methods of structuring an argumentative essay.

HOW DO WE DEFINE AN ARGUMENT?

There are many different kinds of arguments, ranging from the "Yes, you did," "No, I didn't" of the schoolyard through the "My team is better than your team" pub-style debate or the slightly more sophisticated "You should do the dishes because I cooked the dinner," "But I did all the shopping and cleaned the bathroom" of the domestic arena. In academic and professional settings, a different kind of argument is expected: one that is based on logic and evidence rather than emotion or faith. When you are asked to present an argument for or against a claim, your professors expect something like, "A connected series of statements or reasons intended to establish a position; a process of reasoning" (*The New Shorter Oxford English Dictionary*, 1993).

Another definition that sums up the kind of argument required is "an argument is a set of claims, some of which are understood or intended to support the other(s)" (Rudinow and Barry, 2004, p. 80).

In academic contexts, one statement is not an argument. One statement may be a claim or a generalization: for example, "The government should pay for university students' education." To develop that claim into an argument, you need at least one other statement that supports it: for example, "because an educated workforce benefits the whole community." The second statement supports the first one and provides the basis for making your case:

> *Claim:* The government should pay for university students' education.
>
> *Supporting statement:* Because students' education benefits the whole community.

Someone who did not agree with you might reply with an opposing claim: "University students should pay for their own education," supported by the statement that "students benefit financially from having a degree, and the community should not have to contribute to an individual's prosperity."

> *Claim:* University students should pay for their own education.
>
> *Supporting statement:* The community should not have to pay to ensure an individual's future prosperity.

In each case, it is the supporting statement that displays the strength or weakness of a claim.

Because the supporting statements carry the weight of your argument, you must be able to demonstrate their legitimacy by providing convincing evidence for them. You must also establish clearly their logical connections to your claim.

To go a little further, then, we can see that an argument has three essential components:

- **A hypothesis or claim set out in a clear and simple statement**
  For example, "The violence shown on television is causing damage to our society."
- **One or more supporting statements (often referred to as premises)**
  For example,

  Most people watch television and witness violence in the programs they see. [You must establish this premise before you can move on to the next ones.]
  Violence on television encourages susceptible adult viewers to imitate it.
  Violence on television also causes emotional damage to children who see it.
  Violence on television makes violent actions in society as a whole seem normal and acceptable.

- **Evidence for, or proof of, your supporting statements**
  For example, to support the premises in the argument above, you might use the following:
- *Recently researched, relevant statistics* outlining the extent of television viewing in the population in general and children in particular. You would also need recent and relevant figures on the percentage of programs where violent acts are shown and recent figures that link violent acts by viewers to their television viewing.
- *Recent descriptions of individual cases* where a link has been shown between viewing of violent programs and violent acts by viewers or disturbed behaviour in children.
- *Expert opinion* that there is a link between violent behaviour or emotional disturbance in children and adults and their viewing of violent acts on television.

If you can provide all this, or produce some other kind of convincing evidence, you can now confidently state your conclusion, that "the violence shown on television is causing damage to our society."

This is an **inductive argument**, that is, an argument that builds a case for the probability of its claim being true. An inductive argument can only ever establish that a claim is *likely* to be true, not that it *is* true. The argument above would establish your initial claim as a strong one, but an opponent, using the same methods, could also build up a strong case for the claim that "the violence shown on television is not causing damage to our society."

Inductive and deductive arguments

The term "inductive" is used to describe the form of argument where you reason from **premises** (supporting statements) that are known to be true, or where you can provide evidence for their being true, to come to a conclusion that is probably, but not certainly, true. The truth of an inductive argument cannot be conclusively established. This is one reason why some topics remain controversial: their truth or falsity cannot be finally proved.

The term "**deductive**" is used to describe the form of argument where no evidence is needed because you argue from premises that are known to be true to a conclusion that necessarily follows from those premises. Deductive arguments can always be proved true or false. If the premises of a deductive argument are true, and the argument's reasoning is valid, then the conclusion will always be true. If one or more of the premises is untrue and/or the reasoning is false, then the conclusion will always be false. Following are examples of typical deductive arguments: "All dogs have a good sense of smell. Rover is a dog. Therefore, Rover must have a good sense of smell."; "If you study hard for your exam, you are sure to pass. You have studied hard. Therefore, you are sure to pass."

Because deductive arguments are so clear-cut, you will seldom be asked to write an essay that depends solely on deductive reasoning. Deductive reasoning, however, can be an invaluable tool in arguments that also require inductive reasoning. More information about deductive reasoning is set out later in this chapter.

WHAT MAKES A STRONG INDUCTIVE ARGUMENT?

Because the conclusions you reach in an inductive argument are only likely rather than certain, it is necessary for you to build a strong case and to use persuasion as well as logic and evidence to convince your audience that your claim is more likely to be correct than not. To make a

> **TIP**
>
> Be aware that most inductive arguments can be countered by equally valid opposing ones, so that you must make sure your reasoning and evidence are strong.

> **TIP**
>
> Remember that deductive arguments are complete in themselves and need no outside information.

EXERCISE

INDUCTIVE VS. DEDUCTIVE ARGUMENTS

Identify which of the following is an inductive and which is a deductive argument:

1. Beavers build dams. This lake is full of dams. There must be beavers here.
2. Hockey's the best! Only a crazy person would pass up a chance to go to the Stanley Cup.

convincing inductive argument, you need more than the basic framework set out so far.

The strength of an inductive argument depends on the following as a base:

<table><tr><td>

TIP

If you are not choosing your own essay topic, but have been assigned a claim to argue for or against, look at it carefully. If it seems extreme or vague, then you know you will have trouble, and your first step should be to limit the claim, providing a logical justification for doing so.

</td></tr></table>

1. **You must have an understandable and clearly defined thesis or claim.**
   If your claim is too extreme or too vague, no one will take any notice of your argument. If, for example, you claimed that "violence on television is a plot by the government to cause civil unrest in the modern world," you would have a difficult time supporting this and an even more difficult time persuading your audience to stay with you while you tried. If you argued that "violence on television marks the apotheosis of metrosexual hegemony in a decadent Western culture," you would be in even more trouble. And if you argued that "violence on television is a very bad thing," you would leave yourself open to a long argument about the definition of "a bad thing" and you would never be able to get to your real case. Think about your claim and define clearly what you believe, so that you are arguing about that specific claim. The claim that "the violence shown on television is damaging our society," for example, is *specific*, *clear*, and *not too extreme*. You would be able to find reasons and evidence to support or oppose it.

2. **Your supporting statements, or premises, must be sensible, relevant, and significant.**
   You must use a clear, logical chain in putting your argument together. Use the tools of rational argument (some of the most important of these are set out below), and ensure that you are not depending on any false reasoning (some common kinds of false reasoning are discussed below). In addition, you must ensure that you can find and provide evidence and examples to support each of the premises you put forward.

   You may have many reasons for making a particular claim. In an argumentative essay, concentrate on the ones that your audience is most likely to understand and accept. For example, you might claim that students should not be required to attend tutorials. Your main reason might be that you find tutorials boring. This is a personal reason, however, and it would be better to concentrate on supporting statements that are more generally applicable, and for which you may be able to find supporting evidence. For example, tutorials stifle individual initiative and creativity; tutorials are not as beneficial as time spent in the library; and attendance at classes would be a matter of individual choice, allowing students to take responsibility for their own learning. Do not forget that you would need to find evidence to support those premises.

3. **You must supply thorough and accurate evidence to demonstrate the truth of each supporting statement.**

   Once you rely on a supporting statement, you must be able to justify it. If one premise is discredited, it undermines the credibility of your argument as a whole. For example, in the argument about television violence, you must be able to cite specific instances where adults have imitated violent acts they saw on television and, as a result, committed harmful violence in the community. If you cannot provide such evidence, one of your supporting statements will be useless as part of the argument. (Acceptable kinds of evidence are described below, along with unacceptable kinds.)

4. **You must acknowledge, and explain your rejection of, the opposing position to your own.**

   You need to show that you are aware that there is another point of view and to explain briefly what you see as the major objection(s) to it. For example, "Some people would argue that people are well able to distinguish real life from what is depicted on television and that only those already prone to violence are influenced by what they see. The evidence, however, suggests otherwise . . . ."

5. **You must anticipate the major objections to your own case and answer them.**

   By answering possible objections to your own case, you undermine the opposition's case and, at the same time, show that you have thought about weaknesses in your own argument and have dealt with them on logical grounds. For example,

   It is true that there are many reasons for the violence and crime we see in today's society and that violence on television is only one factor. It is one factor, however, that we could control if we wanted to, and one factor that we could remove from the complex chain of cause and effect undermining a civil society.

6. **You must choose the most effective way of organizing your argument.**

   You should not necessarily deal with these points in the order set out above. Your statement of claim, often called a **thesis statement**, must come first, but you may wish to deal with the opposing case before you begin to present your own reasons and evidence, or you may wish to present your own case before dismissing the opposing one. Choose the order that you think will have the strongest impact for your chosen subject and your particular audience. An effective organization of your material will make your argument more persuasive.

TIP

Usually a mixture of different kinds of reasoning and evidence is more convincing than an argument based on only one kind.

WHAT IS ACCEPTABLE REASONING AND EVIDENCE IN DEVELOPING AN ARGUMENT?

There are many kinds of reasoning and evidence, depending on the nature of your argument. For most arguments, some combination of the following is necessary to convince an audience of the truth of your claim.

Deductive reasoning

Deductive argument is a valuable tool, but its use has many dangers. If you can argue deductively and do it correctly, your argument will always be valid, and if the premises are true as well, the conclusion must be true. A deductive argument is a form in which you reason from premises that are known or assumed to be true, to a conclusion that necessarily follows from those premises. In the standard example of this form, you work out the truth of a statement about one specific instance by proving that it is one example of an already proven general principle. Following is the classic example:

> *Premise:* All persons are mortal.
> *Premise:* Socrates is a person.
> *Conclusion:* Therefore, Socrates is mortal.

We argue this way all the time without thinking about it. In the following argument, if you accept that the first supporting statement, or premise, is true, then the conclusion must be true:

> *Premise:* All people should know how to communicate clearly.
> *Premise:* Students are people.
> *Conclusion:* Students should know how to communicate clearly.

We present this kind of reasoning in an abbreviated form whenever we apply a general rule, but it can be used at other times as well. You could use deductive argument as part of your case in the argument about violence on television, for example:

> *Premise:* All forms of violence cause damage to society.
> *Premise:* Violence shown on television is a form of violence.
> *Conclusion:* Violence shown on television causes damage to our society.

Theoretically, this argument by itself is enough to prove your claim, as long as the first premise is accepted as true. In "real life," however, you would need more than this to convince an audience of skeptics.

You need to be wary of deductive arguments. They are often used wrongly, either because one or other of the premises is untrue or because the reasoning is invalid. For example,

Premise: All boys love cars.
Premise: Aubrey is a boy.
Conclusion: Aubrey loves cars.

In this case, the reasoning is valid but the first premise is not necessarily true, so the conclusion is not necessarily true. The first premise in this case is what is known as a false generalization. Many people rely on false generalizations in their arguments. Such generalizations are tempting, but easy to disprove. You need only one example of a boy who is not interested in cars to demonstrate that not "all" boys love cars, and so the preceding argument is faulty.

Another misuse of deductive argument goes like this:

Premise: All people have hair on their bodies.
Premise: This dog has hair on its body.
Conclusion: This dog is a person.

In this case the premises, or supporting statements, are true, but the reasoning is not valid. The problem is obvious in the preceding example but less obvious in the following one:

Premise: All terrorists oppose the government.
Premise: Joe Bloggs opposes the government.
Conclusion: Joe Bloggs is a terrorist.

The argument above is invalid and has the same form as the one before it. There could be many reasons for Joe Bloggs's opposing the government that have nothing to do with terrorists. Nevertheless, this is a fairly common misuse of deductive argument and one you should look out for.

Yet another common misuse of deductive argument has the following pattern:

Premise: All boys love cars.
Premise: Jane is a girl.
Conclusion: Jane does not love cars.

In this case, the first premise is not necessarily true, and the reasoning is also faulty.

Many people misuse deductive arguments in different ways. Watch out for this kind of mistake in your own work. It is not always as easy to spot as in the above examples.

Valid cause-and-effect reasoning

Cause-and-effect reasoning is a very strong form of inductive argument, but often it is very difficult to establish a clear chain of sufficient and necessary cause and effect for any phenomenon in a complex world. Smoking causes cancer, but not always; speed causes accidents, but not always, and so do other things; dropped matches cause brush fires but only under certain conditions; certain medications cure disease, but other factors may increase or inhibit their efficacy. Cause-and-effect reasoning must be supported by strong and detailed evidence.

Argument by analogy

Analogy means comparison, and argument by analogy seeks to show that because two or more things are alike in some ways, they will be alike in other ways as well. This is a valid form of reasoning as long as you can establish that the things you are comparing really are alike. For example, scientists use analogy as part of the experimental process of determining whether a new medication will be safe and effective in humans: if it works on rats, it may work the same way on humans. Meteorologists use analogy in deciding whether a particular storm threatens to cause damage: if a storm of similar type in a similar position has caused damage in the past, it may do so again. The validity of this kind of argument depends on there being close and detailed similarity between the things compared. Like other forms of reasoning, argument by analogy is open to abuse. Some problems with arguing from analogy are set out below.

Argument based on empirical generalization

Argument based on empirical generalization is very commonly used and abused. If you can show that a particular claim is true of a limited sample, you can make a general conclusion based on that sample. In the argument about violence on television, for example, if your audience accepts that violence on television has been shown to have a bad effect on a representative sample of the general population, then it is reasonable to conclude that it has a bad effect on society in general. If you can show that many smokers suffer more illness and die earlier than non-smokers, then you can argue that smoking should be banned. Of course, your sample size must be large enough, and representative enough of the population as a whole, for you to be able to make this kind of claim.

Valid research

Research is essential as the underlying basis for all of the forms of reasoning described above. There are many different kinds of research. Scientists, economists, historians, mathematicians, and linguists, for example, all use different research methods and different kinds of evidence that are appropriate for their disciplines. There is no substitute for original research, but for students the next best thing is using reliable secondary sources.

The opinions of those who are acknowledged experts in their own fields

When we seek evidence in textbooks or articles in professional journals, we are using secondary sources or expert opinions because we do not have the expertise or the time to conduct our own research. These are valid sources of evidence, but you must be sure that your expert really is one, that he or she has appropriate qualifications in the field of your argument, that he or she has no bias that might affect the way the research was conducted, and that he or she has done the appropriate research to support his or her opinions. Your own research, or consulting expert opinion, will provide you with the valid statistics, sound consistent examples, valid analogies, and/or proof of cause-and-effect relationships that you need to support your argument.

> **TIP**
>
> Always check the qualifications of any expert whose research or opinions you cite in support of your case.

WHAT IS UNACCEPTABLE REASONING OR EVIDENCE?

There are many well-recognized fallacies in presenting arguments. Some of the most frequently used but unacceptable kinds of so-called reasoning and evidence are set out below.

Unsubstantiated generalizations

Unsubstantiated generalizations are the most common examples of poor reasoning and lack of evidence. If you make a generalization, be sure that you can provide evidence of its accuracy. Often the generalizations used, for example, in advertising, politics, and friendly disagreements at a local bar are based on nothing more than the personal interests or prejudices of the company, party, or person who uses them:

> "All Canadians think that this is the best policy"; "All over the country, family values are the major talking point of the day"; "Cats prefer Yummos to any other food"; "Champions wear Bart's Body Braces"; "Everyone knows that you can't trust people

with small ears"; "All teenagers are irresponsible"; "All politicians are corrupt"; "The weather is always perfect in August"; "Dogs never bite their owners."

Isolated individual examples

Isolated individual examples are known as anecdotal evidence. Examples are crucial in building a strong argument, but they must be consistent and numerous enough to provide a reliable sample of the population or the group involved in your statement. Your personal feelings, or those of your friends and relatives, must be consistent with those of the majority if they are to carry any weight. Following are typical examples of anecdotal evidence:

> "My next-door neighbour has smoked 50 cigarettes a day for 40 years and she doesn't have cancer"; "My friend once drank a bottle of vodka in 20 minutes and it didn't hurt him"; "I love rug-hooking; it will be the next big thing in the youth holiday market."

False analogy

The use of analogy is a strong tool of rational argument, but the use of false analogy is very common in superficial argument, where things are compared on the basis of superficial or insignificant similarities and then those similarities are used to make a point. This kind of argument can be misleading when similarities are highlighted and major differences are ignored:

> "Tigers have four legs, big teeth, and a tail and are very dangerous; cows also have four legs, big teeth, and a tail. Obviously, they are also very dangerous"; "The terrorist was wearing jeans and sandals. He also had dark hair, and a beard. That man has jeans, sandals, dark hair, and a beard. He is obviously a terrorist."; "The crime was committed by someone who went to Saint Martha's School. Joe went to Saint Martha's School. He must be a criminal."

TIP

Remember that statistics can be manipulated very easily.

Irrelevant or insignificant statistics, examples, or other information

Statistics and examples can be very misleading, as in the following examples:

> "Forty per cent of adults watch the news daily on television; therefore, more than half the population is not interested in current affairs"; "Seventy per cent of all criminals eat breakfast regularly, so eating breakfast regularly obviously causes people to commit crimes"; "Eighty per cent of doctors surveyed recommend broccoli as a remedy for headache" (when only five doctors were in the survey).

Hearsay

Never rely on **hearsay**, something that you heard from someone else but have never observed yourself and that has no supporting evidence:

"Her sister's next-door neighbour knows a woman who . . . "; "My boss's niece saw that happen and she told the secretary that . . . "

Unqualified opinion

The opinion of actors or sports champions may be very valuable in arguing about their own fields of expertise, but there is no reason to take their word on electrical appliances, medicines, or human nutrition:

> "The champion swimmer knows that Paddlers Pool Rice Pop is the most nutritious breakfast food on the market"; "'Cross-ways audio systems are the best on the market,' says film star Overly Drest."

TIP

A celebrity is not necessarily an expert.

Personal attack

Attacking the person rather than the argument is a common but invalid form of argument:

> "How could someone who has no children and does not like sport have any opinions worth hearing?"; "That actor is rude and aggressive, so all his films must be lousy."

Quoting out of context

Quoting out of context can give a false meaning to something heard or read to suit the argument of the person quoting. For example, "Critics say this movie was 'an unforgettable experience,'" when the full statement by the critic was, "This movie was so bad, sitting through it was, unfortunately, an unforgettable experience."

TIP

Check quotations carefully before relying on them as evidence. Are they complete? What is their context? Is the author reliable?

Omission of inconvenient information

This is very similar to the fallacy immediately above:

> "This amazing remedy significantly helped a majority of patients in the trial" (omitting to mention that the minority, 40 out of 100, died).

Arguing from ignorance

You cannot use the absence of evidence about something to prove that the opposite is true. For example, "There is no evidence that no one has ever come back after death to talk to their relatives; therefore, they must have done so"; "Can you prove that fairies do not exist? OK, so they do."

False dilemma

Setting a false dilemma is a way of stating a case dramatically. It attempts to convince the reader or listener that the only alternative to a stated position

EXERCISE

IDENTIFYING UNACCEPTABLE REASONING OR EVIDENCE

For each of the following, identify the type of unacceptable reasoning or evidence represented.

1. My friends and I all prefer wine to beer. I think that within the next five years, the beer brewing industry in Canada will shut down.
2. The teaching assistant said that 80 per cent of the students had answered at least 15 out of 20 of the multiple-choice questions correctly (omitting to mention that only 5 per cent of the students had passed the short-answer part of the exam).
3. My friend said that no one who gets an undergraduate degree at our university is accepted into graduate school here.
4. Torontonians are snobs.
5. I bought these new running shoes because I read that a lot of the top models say they're good for your feet.
6. My friend, Gail, who is from Nova Scotia, spends a lot of time reading. People from the East Coast are well read.
7. In his teaching portfolio, the professor wrote that his student had said that she would "want to take a course with him again" when what she actually wrote was "I would have to be crazy to want to take a course with him again."
8. 100 per cent of the students who responded to the survey said that they found the workshop "very helpful." (Only two students filled in the survey.)
9. There's no evidence that the teaching assistant doesn't hate me, so I think that I actually deserved an "A" on the essay instead of the "D" that she gave me.
10. If the Canucks don't get into the playoffs this year, they'll never have another chance.
11. Well, since you're an American, I don't see how you could possibly know anything about hockey.

is the exact opposite of it, when, in fact, there may be another, or many other, positions available between the two extremes. The best-known example of this fallacy is, "If you are not with me, you are against me."

Other examples are, "If you do not love dogs, you must hate them"; "Everyone who does not vote for my party is voting for chaos"; "Either the storm will hit and we will all die or it will pass by and we will all live happily ever after."

A WORD OF WARNING

You must remember that underlying many arguments are unspoken premises or beliefs that are held by particular groups or individuals that cannot be shaken by logical argument. This is particularly true for arguments

TIP

In arguments about ethical, moral, or emotional issues, look for hidden premises underlying your own case and any opposing one. Take those premises into account in arguing your case.

about moral or ethical issues. It is very difficult to change someone's mind about, say, euthanasia or abortion, because you and your opponents or your audience may have different belief systems, which override any other consideration. Someone who believes that life begins at conception and that human life is sacred may never agree that any abortion is justified, whereas someone who believes that life for a fetus begins when he or she can live independently of his/her mother's blood circulation may have a completely different view. It is for this reason that the controversy about these issues is ongoing.

In less extreme cases, you still need to think about the underlying assumptions of your own arguments and those of others. At the beginning of this chapter, in the example about violence on television, the argument assumes agreement with the underlying premise that violence is inherently bad, and so there is no need to prove that. This would seem to be a safe assumption, but it could be challenged. In other cases, a variety of underlying assumptions may be firmly held by different people, but the assumptions may be less obvious.

This is true in the debate on how to deal with taking illicit drugs in our society, for example. Some people find drug taking so abhorrent that they follow a hard line on total bans and advocate severe punishment for those who transgress. Other people assume that drug taking is a disease and not a crime and that a medical model should be followed in dealing with addicts. A third group believes that people should be free to make their own choices about how to live, including the choice to take drugs. Proponents of each viewpoint may feel that their belief is so obviously right that it does not need to be demonstrated, and each group can end up with a weak argument by failing to state and support a major premise.

A SUMMARY OF THE REQUIREMENTS FOR A STRONG ARGUMENTATIVE ESSAY

There are many ways to organize an argumentative essay, but no matter what organizational approach you choose, you always need the following:

1. **An introduction, usually about 20 per cent of the essay's total length, that**
   - puts the topic into context;
   - explains why it is worth discussing;
   - sets out your claim or thesis statement; and
   - signals the areas you intend to cover.

2. **The body of the argument, approximately 60 per cent of its total length, in separate paragraphs, that**
    - lists your supporting propositions or premises and the evidence for each of them;
    - describes (briefly) and negates the opposing argument; and
    - answers the major objections to your own case.
3. **A conclusion that is approximately 20 per cent of your essay and that**
    - states or restates your major claim or thesis;
    - summarizes your main points;
    - goes further than your introduction to make a final overall judgment, summary, or comment on what you have said. It emphasizes your claim's implications or significance; where appropriate, it
        » suggests a solution to a problem;
        » recommends a course of action to be followed; and
        » suggests an area of research to be undertaken as a result of your conclusion.

TIP
A summary of your major points is not enough to provide a conclusion for your essay. A conclusion must go further than mere summary.

SOME HINTS FOR PLANNING AN ARGUMENTATIVE ESSAY

1. Before you begin your research, formulate your thesis or claim and your supporting statements for it. Once you have done this, you can target your research areas more precisely, and you can consider the strengths and weaknesses of your case.
2. You should also set out what you think are the major supporting statements for the opposing case to your own. This will help you to find evidence that will refute those statements.
3. Begin your research by ensuring that you can find evidence for each of your supporting statements. Check the evidence for the other side. You may need to change some of your argument, depending on the information you find.
4. Make sure that you have listed all the necessary bibliographic information about your sources, especially page numbers. You will need that information for your references and reference list.
5. When your research is complete, begin on the body of your essay, perhaps leaving the introduction until last. It is usually easier to start with your most important point. You can reorganize things later.

6. Once you have a rough draft, think about how to organize your argument in the most effective way. Logical, well-thought-out organization, along with clear, concise English, is one of the main persuasive tools in argumentative essays.

GLOSSARY

analogy   A comparison.

deductive argument   An argument where no evidence is needed because you argue from premises that are known to be true to a conclusion that necessarily follows from those premises.

hearsay   Something that you heard from someone else but have never observed yourself.

inductive argument   An argument that builds a case for the probability of its claim being true.

premise   A supporting claim.

thesis statement   Statement of claim.

SUGGESTED FURTHER READING

Booth, Wayne C. (2003). *The craft of research*. (2nd ed.). Chicago: University of Chicago Press.

Gage, John T. (1991). *The shape of reason: Argumentative writing in college*. New York: Macmillan Publishing Company, 1991.

Lunsford, Andrea, & Ruszkiewicz, John. (1999). *Everything's an argument*. Boston/New York: Bedford/St. Martin's.

Skwire, David. (1985). *Writing with a thesis: A rhetoric and reader*. New York: Holt, Rinehart and Winston.

RELATED WEBSITES

www.writing.utoronto.ca/images/stories/Documents/critical-reading.pdf
Knott, Deborah. "Critical reading toward critical writing." University of Toronto.

http://owl.english.purdue.edu/owl/resource/659/01/
OWL, Purdue Online Writing Lab. "Logic in argumentative writing."

www.unc.edu/depts/wcweb/handouts/argument.html
Writing Center, University of North Carolina at Chapel Hill. "Argument."

ANSWER KEY TO EXERCISE

Inductive vs. Deductive Arguments
1. Deductive argument
2. Inductive argument

Identifying Unacceptable Reasoning or Evidence

1. Isolated individual examples
2. Omission of inconvenient evidence
3. Hearsay
4. Unsubstantiated generalization
5. Unqualified opinion
6. False analogy
7. Quoting out of context
8. Irrelevant or insignificant statistics, examples, or other information
9. Arguing from ignorance
10. False dilemma
11. Personal attack

Stating Facts:
Writing Research Reports
and Laboratory Reports

The great tragedy of science—the slaying of a beautiful hypothesis by an ugly fact.

T.H. Huxley, 1893–4

This chapter provides a short overview of writing research reports and laboratory reports. By providing guidance on how to write these kinds of reports, the following pages may also help you to undertake the research and laboratory work successfully.

WHAT ARE REPORT READERS LOOKING FOR?

Research and laboratory reports typically answer five classic investigative questions (Eisenberg, 1992, p. 276).

Eisenberg's 5 investigative questions
- What did you do?
- Why did you do it?
- How did you do it?
- What did you find out?
- What do the findings mean?

KEY CONCEPTS

The person reading or marking your report seeks clear and accurate answers to these questions. Because reports are sometimes long and complex, the reader will also appreciate some help in navigating his or her way through the document (Windschuttle & Elliott, 1994, p. 261).

Make the report clear and easy to follow

A well-written report uses

- easily understood language;
- a well-written introduction;
- suitable headings and subheadings; and
- a comprehensive table of contents (if appropriate).

Some forms of reports—especially laboratory reports—will answer the five investigative questions through a formal, highly structured progression (such as introduction, methods, results, discussion) that is written in a way that would allow another researcher to repeat the work. For example, a pharmacologist conducting an experiment on the human physiological implications of a new drug will conduct the study as impartially as possible and record his or her research procedures in sufficient detail to allow someone else to reproduce the study exactly. For some forms of enquiry, *replication* is an important means of verifying results.

In other forms of research, such as those involving qualitative research methods (for example, interviews, participant observation, textual analysis), results are confirmed in different ways. As a consequence, the research report may be written differently. It will usually answer the five questions identified above, but less emphasis will be given to ensuring replicability. It is more important that qualitative research reports be written in a way that would allow other people to confirm the *reliability* of your sources and to check your work against other related sources about the same or similar topics. Consider, for example, the way a murder trial is conducted. The murder cannot be repeated to allow us to work out who the murderer was (replication). Instead, lawyers and police assemble evidence to reconstruct the crime as fairly and accurately as possible. This process is known as *corroboration*. Your report should be a *fair* and *reasonable* representation of events.

GENERAL LAYOUT OF A REPORT

As the preceding paragraphs may have suggested to you, there is no single correct research report style even though most reports will usually answer Eisenberg's five investigative questions. The best way to organize a research report is determined by the type of research being carried out, the character and aims of the author, and the audience for whom the report is written. Accordingly, the following guidelines for report writing cannot provide the recipe for a perfect research report. Keys to a good report include well-executed research and the will to communicate the results of your work effectively.

TIP

Find "model" reports to help guide you through your first report-writing efforts.

Having acknowledged that there is no single correct report-writing style, it is fair to say that over time a common pattern of report presentation has emerged. That pattern reflects a strategy for answering the five investigative questions identified above. Because it has been used so often, it is also a structure of presentation that many report readers will expect to see. If you are new to report writing, and unless you have been advised otherwise, it may be useful to follow the general pattern outlined below. If you are more experienced and believe there is a more effective way of communicating the results of your work, try out your own strategy. Remember, however, that you are guiding the reader through the work; you will have to let your audience know if you are doing anything they might not expect.

Short research reports and laboratory reports generally comprise a minimum of seven sections. Long reports may add some or all of the extra materials outlined below. It is likely that most reports you are asked to write early in your university career will be short ones. By third or fourth year, longer reports might be expected.

Although these headings point to an order of report presentation, there is no need to write the sections in any particular sequence. Indeed, you may find it useful to follow Woodford's advice to label several sheets of paper with the headings Title, Introduction, Methods, Results, and so forth, and use these to jot down notes as you work through the project (in Booth, 1993, p. 2). Then begin your report by writing the easiest section (the Methods section in many cases).

Table 10.1   Contents of a report

Short report	Long report
Title page	Title page
	Letter of transmittal
Abstract/executive summary	Abstract/executive summary
	Acknowledgements (sometimes placed after Discussion or immediately before References)
	Table of contents
Introduction (what you did and why)	Introduction
Materials and methods (how you did it)	Materials and methods
Results (what you found out)	Results
Discussion (what the results mean)	Discussion
	Recommendations
References	References
	Appendices

TIP

There is no need to write your report in the same order as it will be presented.

The following pages outline the form and function of the common components of research reports. Discussion also elaborates on some of the matters that contribute most significantly to effective research presentations in an academic setting. Those same matters form the basis of the research report assessment schedule in Figure 10.1.

Figure 10.1   Research report assessment schedule

Student name: **Grade:**

Assessed by:

The following is an itemized rating scale for various aspects of research report perform-ance. Sections left blank are not relevant to the attached assignment. Some aspects are more important than others, so there is no formula connecting the scatter of ticks with the final lage for the report. A tick in either of the two boxes left of centre means that the statement is true to a greater (outer left) or lesser (inner left) extent. The same principle applies to the right-hand boxes.

If you have any questions about the individual scales, final comments, final grade, or other aspects of this assignment, please see the assessor.

Purpose and significance

Statement of problem or purpose is clear and unambiguous					Statement of problem or purpose is unclear or ambiguous
Research objectives outlined precisely					Research objectives unclear
Disciplinary, social, or personal significance of research problem made clear					Problem not set in context
Documentation fully outlines evolution of research problem from previous research findings					No reference to earlier works or references incorrect

Description of method

Most appropriate research method selected					Research method selected is inappropriate
'Sample', case(s), or study area appropriate to purpose of enquiry					'Sample', case(s), or study area is unsuitable
Complete description of study method					Inadequate description of study method

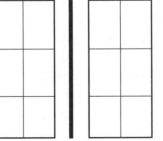
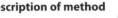

Quality of results

Evidence of extensive
primary research

Limitations of sources
made clear

Relevant results
presented in appropriate
level of detail

Little or no evidence of
primary research

Inappropriate sources
accepted without
question

Relevant results
omitted or suppressed

Discussion and interpretation

No errors of
interpretation
(for example, logic,
calculation) detected

Limitations of
findings made clear

Discussion connects
findings with relevant
literature

Many errors of
interpretation

Limitations of findings
not identified

No connection between
findings and other
works

Conclusions

Significance of
findings made clear

Conclusions based on
evidence presented

Stated purpose of
research achieved

No significance
identified

Little or no connection
between evidence and
conclusions

Little or no
contribution to
solution of problem
or achievement of
purpose

Use of supplementary material

Effective use of
figures and tables

Illustrations presented
correctly

Detailed statistical
analyses and tables
placed in appendices

Illustrative material not
used when needed or
not discussed in text

Illustrations presented
incorrectly

Excessively detailed
findings in text

Written expression and presentation

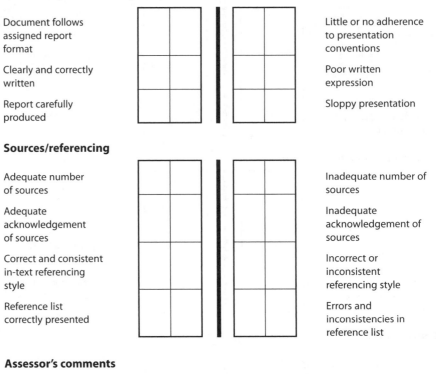

| Document follows assigned report format | | Little or no adherence to presentation conventions |

| Clearly and correctly written | | Poor written expression |

| Report carefully produced | | Sloppy presentation |

Sources/referencing

| Adequate number of sources | | Inadequate number of sources |

| Adequate acknowledgement of sources | | Inadequate acknowledgement of sources |

| Correct and consistent in-text referencing style | | Incorrect or inconsistent referencing style |

| Reference list correctly presented | | Errors and inconsistencies in reference list |

Assessor's comments

Preliminary material

Title page

The best titles are usually short, accurate, and attractive to potential readers. A title should indicate exactly what you have studied. Use a subtitle if you need a fuller description. When you have finished writing your report, check that the title matches the results and discussion. An example of a functional and informative title is "Transport policy and land use planning in Singapore, 1985–2005." This title lets the reader know the topic, place, and time. An example of a bad title on the same subject matter is "Transport and land use." If a large number of variables were part of the study, the title might say "Several factors of . . . " or "Various influences on . . . " There is no need to add redundant phrases like "A study of . . . " or "A report on . . . "

You can modify these recommendations to suit the academic setting in which

THE TITLE PAGE

The title page of a report should also include the following:

- your name, position, and organizational affiliation
- name of the person and/or organization to whom the report is being submitted
- date the report was issued

you find yourself. For example, date of issue might be the due date or the date you submit the assignment for assessment. The person to whom the report is submitted may be your professor.

Letter of transmittal

A letter of transmittal is sometimes included. This letter personalizes the report for the reader who commissioned (or asked for) the report and typically

- explains the purpose of the letter ("Enclosed is the final report on wetland management issues in the Saint Margaret's Bay region that was commissioned by your organization.");
- sets out the main finding of the report and any other vital issues likely to be relevant;
- acknowledges any significant assistance received ("We are indebted to the Saint Margaret's Bay Stewardship Association for allowing us access to their extensive photographic records of post-1985 change in the salt marsh."); and
- offers thanks for the opportunity to conduct the research ("We would like to thank the Nova Scotia Environmental Network for engaging us to conduct this research.") (Mohan, McGregor & Strano, 1992, p. 227).

Abstract/executive summary

Of all sections of the report other than the title, this is the most likely to be read. It is important, therefore, to make it easy to understand. An abstract is a coherent and concise statement, intelligible on its own, which typically provides succinct answers to each of the five investigative questions outlined at the beginning of this chapter: What did you do? Why did you do it? How did you do it? What did you find out? What do the findings mean?

Abstracts are limited in length (usually 100–250 words) and are designed to be read by people who may not have the time to read the whole report. They are *not* written in the form of notes. All information contained in the abstract must be discussed within the main report. Do not write an abstract as if it is the alluring back-cover blurb of a mystery novel. Let your readers know what your research is about—do not leave them in suspense. Put the abstract at the beginning of your report, although it will usually be the last section you write.

Abstracts may be subdivided into two main types, *informative* and *indicative*, although they may be written in a style that combines features of each.

> **TIP**
>
> Many readers decide whether or not to read a report on the basis of its title and abstract; make sure these are clear and accurate.

An **informative abstract** typically summarizes primary research, and offers a concise statement of details of the paper's content including, for example, aims, methods, results, and conclusions.

Example of an informative abstract

Asera, R., Bagarukayo, H., Shuey, D., & Barton, T. Searching for solutions: Health concerns expressed in letters to an East African newspaper column. *Health Transition Review*, 6(2), 169–78.

Abstract

This study examines health-care questions from an unusual data set: 1252 unsolicited letters written over a three-year period to an advice column in an East African newspaper. Analysis of the letters was a non-intrusive method of ascertaining prevalent health questions and opinions. People wrote seeking information, advice, solutions, and reassurance about health problems. Emotions expressed in the letters ranged from hope to fear and frustration. The written format allowed questions that are generally too embarrassing or stigmatized to present in other public or interpersonal settings. More than half the total letters raised questions about sexual behaviour, sexually transmitted diseases, and HIV/AIDS. The letters present not only personal health concerns but also expectations of health-care quality and reflections on the medical options presently available in Uganda. As a whole, the letters express dissatisfaction not only with the outcomes of health-care encounters but also with the process. Of the letter writers with specific physical complaints, more than one-third had already sought medical care and were dissatisfied with the results. The letters were seeking solutions, especially for alleviation of symptoms and discomfort. Almost equally prevalent was a plea for accurate and relevant health information; people not only want to feel better, but they also want to understand their own health.

An **indicative abstract** outlines the contents of a paper, report, or book, but does not recount specific details. It is commonly used to summarize particularly long reports and book chapters.

Example of an indicative abstract

Committee on Space Debris, Aeronautics and Space Engineering Board, Commission on Engineering and Technical Systems, National Research Council. (1995). *Orbital debris: A technical assessment*. Washington, DC: National Academy Press.

Abstract

Since the beginning of space flight, the hazard of space collision has grown along with the increasing number of objects orbiting the earth. This book offers recommendations for targeted research on the debris population and the specific risks to spacecraft, effective international exchange of information, requirements for reducing debris from future launches, and improved spacecraft protection measures. The book explores methods of tracking and cataloguing the debris population in orbit. It also discusses the tools and techniques used to assess the specific risks to spacecraft and to develop protective measures such as shielding. Finally, the book evaluates approaches to reducing the growth rate in the debris population, including changing disposal practices during space flights and forcing large rocket bodies out of orbit.

Abstracts usually comprise a single paragraph, although long abstracts may require paragraphing. They do not usually contain tables, figures, or formulae, and they should not discuss anything not covered in the paper or report. All unfamiliar terms should be defined, as should **acronyms** (for example, NATO, NAFTA) and non-standard abbreviations (for example, dBA, pJ). Avoid referring to other work in an abstract. If you do refer to specific works or individuals, they must, of course, be included in the list of references associated with the full paper.

It is a matter of common style that issues included or discussed in the main paper are presented in the present tense, whereas what the author did and thought is written in the past tense (for example, "This report describes the nature of chemical weathering on . . . "; "It was discovered that . . . "; "Moreover, weathering had the effect of . . . "; "The report concludes that . . . ").

Acknowledgements

If you have received valuable assistance and support from some people or organizations in the preparation of the report, you should acknowledge them. As a general rule, thank those people who genuinely helped with aspects of the work, such as proofreading, preparing figures and tables, solving statistical or computing problems, taking photos, or typing.

Table of contents

This should accurately and fully list all headings and subheadings used in the report, with their associated page numbers. The table of contents occupies its own page and must be organized carefully with appropriate spacing. Make sure that the numbering system used in the table of contents is the same as that used in the body of the report.

Included after the table of contents, and on separate pages, are a list of figures and a list of tables. Each of these lists contains, for each figure or table, its number, title, and the page on which it is located. If your report uses many abbreviations and acronyms, provide a list of these too, but make sure that you also define each one fully when it first appears in the text.

Introduction: Why did you do this study?

The introduction of a report answers the following questions:

- What question is being asked? (If appropriate, state your hypothesis.)
- What do you hope to learn from this research?
- Why is this research important? (What is the social, personal, and disciplinary significance of the work? This usually requires a **literature review**.)

> **TIP**
>
> Use the introduction to convince your audience to read the rest of your report.

When you write your introduction, imagine that readers are unfamiliar with your work and that they really do not care about it. Let your audience know why this report is important and exactly what it is about, but do not include data or conclusions from your study. When readers know what you are going to discuss, they are better able to grasp the significance of the material you present in the remainder of your report.

When your readers have finished reading your introduction, they should know exactly what the study is about, what you hope to achieve from it, and why it is significant. If they have also been inspired to read the remainder of the report, so much the better!

Literature review

> **TIP**
>
> A good literature review makes clear the relationships between your work and what has previously been done in the area.

As part of, or soon after, your introduction, you may need to write a literature review to provide the background to and justification for your research. The literature review is sometimes presented as a separate part of the report, after the introduction and before the discussion of materials and methods. A literature review is a comprehensive, but pithy and critical, summary of publications and reports related to your research. It should discuss significant other works written in the area and make clear your assessment of those works.

As Macauley suggests, the literature review serves a number of functions. It may help to

- prevent you from "reinventing the wheel" (that is, replicating the earlier work of others);
- identify gaps in the literature and potential research areas;
- increase your breadth of knowledge in the field and highlight information, ideas, and methods that might be relevant to your project;
- identify other people working in the same area; and
- put your work into intellectual and practical perspective by identifying ways in which it may contribute to, fit in with, or differ from available work on the subject.

Starting a literature review can be difficult. It is probably useful to identify the parent discipline(s) with which your research is associated (for example, geography, hydrology) and go to recent issues of their leading journals to gather information on the topic area as broadly as it might be defined. Draw from the references in those articles to get some sense of the history of your research topic area and to identify key authors, texts, and articles. Gather those texts and read them. You may also find it helpful to consult the Social Sciences Citation Index (SSCI) or the Sciences Citation Index (SCI) to trace the intellectual genealogy of key references forward through time (speak to your college or university's research librarian about this helpful technique).

Once you have gathered and read relevant resources, you can set out writing the literature review. As a rule of thumb, a good literature review might normally discuss the truly significant books written in the field, notable books and articles produced on the broad subject in the past four or five years, and all available material on your narrow, specific research area. As noted above, the review should provide the reader with an understanding of the conceptual and disciplinary origins and significance of your study. It requires careful writing. As Reaburn (in Central Queensland University Library, 2000) observes,

> Students will get a pile of articles and will regurgitate what article one said, what article two said. I can't emphasize enough, a well written literature review must evaluate all the literature, must speak generally, with general concepts they have been able to lift from all the articles, and they must be able to evaluate and critically analyze each one, then link and make a flow of ideas. Rather than separate little boxes, each box representing an article, make a flow of ideas, generalize and use specifics from one or two articles to back up a statement.

Your literature review should not be a string of quotations or a review of findings of other authors' work simply strung together. Do not make

the mistake of trying to list and summarize all material published in
your area of work. Rather, organize the review into sections that present
themes and trends related to your research. Integrate all those little pieces
of knowledge you have found in your reading into a coherent whole. Your
completed literature review should be a critical analysis of earlier work set
out in such a way that the reader is led to a point where it becomes evident
why your research work is being conducted (Behrendorff, 1995, p. 4).

You will probably find it helpful to look at examples of good literature
reviews in your area of interest to gain a sense of how they are written.
Short reviews are included as part of research papers in virtually every
good academic journal.

Materials and methods: How did you do this study?

You should provide a precise and concise account of the materials and
methods used to conduct the study and why you chose them. Let your
reader know exactly how you did the study and where you got your data.
A good description of materials and methods should enable readers to
duplicate the investigative procedure even if they had no source of information about your study other than your report. In qualitative studies,
however, duplication of procedure is unlikely to lead to identical results.
Instead, the outcome may be results that corroborate, substantiate, or,
indeed, refute those achieved in the initial study.

Depending on the specific character of the research, the methods section of a report comprises up to three parts (Dane, 1990, p. 219–21),
which may be written and presented as a single section or under separate
subheadings: **sampling**, **apparatus**, and **procedure**.

Sampling/subjects

In the sampling or **subjects** section of your report, your reader will appreciate answers to the following questions:

- *Who/what* specific group, plant, animal, place, or object have you chosen to study?
- *Why* did you make that choice?
- *How* did you select the unit(s) of study? What specific sampling technique did you employ (for example, snowball, simple random, typical
case, cluster area, random traverse)? There is no need to go into great
detail about the technique, such as describing any computer programs
used in your sampling, unless the procedure was unusual.

- *What* are the limitations and shortcomings of the data or sources? In
some cases, it may be more appropriate to consider these matters in the
discussion.

If you are reporting a field study, a general description of the study site is needed. Do not forget to include figures, photographs, and maps if they are appropriate.

Apparatus or materials

Provide a concise description of any special equipment or **materials** used in your study. For example, briefly describe any experimental equipment or questionnaires used in your work. In some more advanced studies, you may also be expected to put the name and address of equipment manufacturers in parentheses. Do not hesitate to use figures and plates in your description of apparatus.

> **TIP**
> Don't hesitate to illustrate.

Procedure

This section contains specific *details* about how the data were collected, response levels, and the methods used to interpret the findings. For example, if your study was based on a questionnaire survey or experimental procedure, tell your readers about the process of questionnaire administration or about the experiment in enough detail to allow them to replicate your procedures. What statistical tests did you decide to use? It is important to *justify* your selection of data collection and statistical procedures in this section. Why did you choose one method over others? Give references to support your selection.

What are the advantages and disadvantages of the procedure you selected, and how did you overcome any problems you encountered? You might consider it more appropriate to confine discussion of this last question to the discussion section of your report.

Where appropriate (for example, research involving human or animal subjects), in discussing procedure, you should also indicate how the work satisfied relevant ethical guidelines.

Results: What did you find out?

The **results** section of a research report is typically a dispassionate, factual account of findings. It outlines what occurred or what you observed. State clearly whether any hypotheses you made can be accepted or rejected, but, in general, you should not discuss the significance of those results here. That is saved for the next section of the report. For example, you may have conducted a study that suggests that all seals on a small offshore island will starve to death unless something is done to control their population. You would save your discussion of ways to resolve that problem for a later section of the report.

Although it is not customary to present conclusions and interpretations in the results section, in some qualitative and laboratory reports

> **TIP**
> The results section is important, but save time, space, and energy to write your interpretation of the results.

it is considered appropriate to combine the results with an interpretive discussion. If you have any doubt about what is appropriate, ask your professor or teaching assistant.

A key to effective presentation of results is making them as comprehensible to your readers as possible. Towards this end, it may be appropriate to begin your discussion of results with a brief overview of the material to follow; then elaborate. You might also consider presenting your results in the chronological order in which you discovered them.

Use maps, tables, figures, and written statements creatively to summarize and convey key information emerging from the study. If you have provided results in figures and tables, do not repeat all the data in the text; emphasize only the most important observations. You should place tables and figures within the text of your report as soon as possible after you mention them but without interrupting the text. However, if you have particularly detailed and lengthy data lists or figures that supplement the report's content, these may be better placed in an appendix.

If you have not already done so, the results section is an appropriate place to identify the limitations of your data.

Discussion and conclusion: What do the findings mean?

> I am appalled by . . . papers that describe most minutely what experiments were done, and how, but with no hint of why, or what they mean. Cast thy data upon the waters, the authors seem to think, and they will come back interpreted.
>
> (Woodford, 1967, p. 744)

TIP

Use the discussion to explain results and explore significance.

The **discussion** is the heart of the report. It is also the part that is most difficult to write and, after the title, abstract, and introduction, is the section most likely to be read thoroughly by your audience. Readers and assessors will be looking to see if your work has achieved its stated objectives.

KEY CONCEPTS

What the discussion does

The discussion has two fundamental aims:

- To *explain* the results of your study. Why do you think the patterns—or lack of patterns—emerged? Interpretations should be supported with references to appropriate literature.
- To *explore* the significance of the study's findings. What do the findings mean? What new and important matters have been raised?

Compare your results with trends described in the literature and with theoretical behaviour. Embed your findings in their larger academic, social, and environmental contexts. Make explicit the ways in which your work fits in with that conducted by other people and the degree to which it might have broader importance. David Hodge makes the point: "Remember that research should never stand alone. It has its foundations in the work of others and, similarly, it should be part of what others do in future. Help the reader make those connections" (Hodge, 1994, p. 3).

The concluding sections of the report might also offer suggestions about improvements or variations to the investigative procedure that might be useful for further work in the field. Where do we go from here? Are there other methods or data sets that should be explored? Has the study raised new sets of questions? (Hodge, p. 3). Any thoughts you have must be *justified*. Many students find it easy to offer suggestions for change, but few are able to support their views.

Recommendations

You may wish to add a **recommendations** section that suggests courses of action or solutions to problems. In some reports, recommendations are included within the conclusion, but more commonly they are accorded a free-standing place. On occasion, recommendations are placed at the front, following the abstract/executive summary.

References

As with essays and other forms of written communication, you must acknowledge all references. For guidance on citing references, see chapter 14.

Appendices

You should place material that is not essential to the report's main argument and that is too long or too detailed to be included in the main body of the report in an **appendix** at the end of the report. However, your appendix is *not* a place to put everything you collected in carrying out your research but for which there is no other place in your report. Each appendix contains different material and each should be numbered clearly.

> **TIP**
> Don't use appendices as a dumping ground for data.

WRITTEN EXPRESSION AND PRESENTATION

Language of the report

Some audiences reading research and laboratory reports still expect the report to be written in "objective," dispassionate, third-person language (for example, "it was considered" rather than "I considered"). You should consider that expectation when writing your report. If you choose to write in a more personal style, which reflects the social creation of knowledge, some audiences may be distracted and unconvinced by your "personal bias." Whatever choice you make, remember that simply because a report is written in an "objective" manner does not mean that it is any more accurate than a report written in more personal language. If you have any questions or concerns about the style of language you should use in your report, ask your professor, or, for a lengthy discussion on issues around this point, see Berg and Mansvelt, 2000.

Another matter of language that warrants attention is the use of **jargon**. The word "jargon" has two popular applications. Most commonly, it refers to technical terms used inappropriately or when clearer terms would suffice. More accurately, it means words or a mode of language intelligible only to a group of experts in a particular field of study (Friedman & Steinberg, 1989, p. 30). There will be occasions in report writing when you will find it necessary to use jargon in the second sense of the word. You should try to resist the temptation to use jargon in the more common, first sense of the term. Remember, you are writing to communicate ideas to the intended audience as clearly as possible. Use the language that allows you to do that. KISS (that is, Keep It Simple, Stupid) your audience. For a more detailed discussion of jargon, see chapter 12.

Two final points include checking that your report's text and figures "move from the general to the specific . . . for individual sections and for the report as a whole" (Montgomery, 2001, p. 143–4) and ensuring that your report, despite its many sections, reads as a single, integrated document. This is especially important if your report is the output of a group project and sections have been written by different people or teams. It may involve the sometimes lengthy tasks of rewriting some sections, reordering elements of the report, and ensuring that all references, figures, and tables are formatted uniformly.

> **TIP**
>
> Make sure your report is coherent and formatted consistently.

Presentation

Be sure that your report is set out in an attractive and easily understood style. Care in presentation suggests care in preparation. *Care* in presentation is to be emphasized here, not gaudiness and decoration. People tend to be suspicious of overly "decorated" reports, and in a professional environment, such as consulting, they may also question the costs of production.

Get the fundamentals straight

- Use the same-sized paper throughout, though there may be some occasions when the use of same-sized sheets is impractical (for example, when you are using maps).
- Number all pages.
- Be sure the different parts of your report stand out clearly.
- Use lots of white space—but do be judicious about your use of paper.
- Use SI (*Système International*) units (that is, metric) in describing measures; use a clear and consistent hierarchy of headings. An example is set out below.

Example of heading hierarchies in a report

1. INTRODUCTION
   1.1. Background
   1.2 Aims
   1.3 Objectives

2. METHODS
   2.1 The questionnaire
   2.2 Sample group

3. RESULTS
   3.1. Response rate
   3.2. Findings
      3.2.1. Who is fearful in urban space?
      3.2.2. Precautionary strategies taken to avoid perceived threats
      3.2.3. Residents' views on means to reduce levels of fear

4. CONCLUSIONS

5. RECOMMENDATIONS
   5.1. Public solutions to fear of violence in urban space
   5.2. Individuals' solutions

6. REFERENCES

7. APPENDICES
   (i)   The questionnaire
   (ii) Tabulated responses

WRITING A LABORATORY REPORT

A laboratory report is a particular form of research report. Hence, the preceding advice on report writing applies. Laboratory reports dispassionately and accurately recount experimental research procedures and results.

You should write your report so that another student-researcher could repeat the experiment in exactly the same way as you did (assuming, of course, that you employed correct procedures) and could compare their results with yours. You must be both meticulous in discussing methods and accurate in your presentation of results. Meticulous does not mean tedious. Try not to overdo the detail. Be as concise as possible while maintaining accuracy and comprehensibility. Record those things that are important. What did *you* need to know to do the experiment? Put that in your report.

Setting out a laboratory report

By convention, laboratory reports follow the order of research report presentation outlined earlier in this chapter, that is:

- title page;
- abstract;
- introduction;
- materials and methods;
- results;
- discussion;
- references; and
- appendices.

Depending on the specific nature of your experiment, your laboratory supervisor may not require all of these sections to be included. For example, if your report is simply an account of work you undertook during a single class laboratory time, it is possible that there will be no need for you to include an abstract, references, and appendices. But your professor or teaching assistant may be impressed if you take the care and attention to note how your day's laboratory work is related to your lecture material. Clearly, though, if your laboratory work is conducted over a longer period than a single class, you will have the opportunity to consult relevant reference materials.

GLOSSARY

acronym A word formed from the first initials of words (e.g., ROM, NATO, KISS, LOL).

apparatus A concise description of any special equipment or materials used in your study.

appendix The section of your report containing material that is not essential to the report's main argument and that is too long or too detailed to be included in the main body of the report.

discussion The part of the report in which you explain results and explore significance.

indicative abstract An abstract that outlines the contents of a paper, report, or book, but does not recount specific details.

informative abstract An abstract that summarizes primary research, and offers a concise statement of details of the paper's content, including, for example, aims, methods, results, and conclusions.

jargon Words or a mode of language intelligible only to a group of experts in a particular field of study.

literature review A comprehensive, but pithy and critical, summary of publications and reports related to your research.

materials See **apparatus**.

procedure The section of your report containing specific details about how the data were collected, response levels, and the methods used to interpret the findings.

recommendations The section of your report in which you suggests courses of action or solutions to problems.

results A dispassionate, factual account of findings.

sampling The part of a report that answers such questions as who or what you have chosen to write about, why you made that choice, how you selected the units—or subjects—of your study, and so on.

subjects See **sampling**.

SUGGESTED FURTHER READING

Day, R.A. (1998). *How to write and publish a scientific paper*. Oryx: Phoenix & New York.

Gulston, Lawrence. (2004). *Nelson guide to report writing*. Toronto, ON: Thomson Nelson.

Hay, I. (1999). Writing research reports in geography and the environmental sciences. *Journal of Geography in Higher Education, 23*(2), 125–35.

Lewis, Roger, & Inglis, John. (1982). *Report writing*. Cambridge: National Extension College.

McMillan, V. (2001). *Writing papers in the biological sciences*. Boston: Bedford Books.

RELATED WEBSITES

http://158.132.164.193/cill/reports.htm
Centre for Independent Language Learning. "Academic report writing template."

**www.engineering.utoronto.ca/Directory/Student_Resources/
Engineering_Communication_Program/Online_Handbook/Types_of_Docu-
ments/Lab_Reports.htm**
Engineering Communication Centre, University of Toronto. "Laboratory reports."

**www.umanitoba.ca/student/u1/lac/media/Writing_a_Science_Lab_
report_07.pdf**
Learning Assistance Centre, University of Manitoba. "Writing a science lab report."

http://owl.english.purdue.edu/owl/resource/726/01/
OWL, Purdue Online Writing Lab. "Handbook of report formats."

http://owl.english.purdue.edu/owl/resource/656/1/
OWL, Purdue Online Writing Lab. "Writing report abstracts."

www.writing.utoronto.ca/advice/specific-types-of-writing/abstract
Procter, Margaret. University of Toronto. "The abstract."

www.writing.utoronto.ca/advice/specific-types-of-writing/literature-review
Taylor, Dena. University of Toronto. "The literature review: A few tips on conducting it."

Making Sense: Writing Annotated Bibliographies, Summaries, and Reviews

There is no such thing as a moral or an immoral book. Books are well written or badly written.

Oscar Wilde, 1891

Your academic endeavours will often require you to summarize and make sense of the works of other people. This chapter provides some advice on writing **annotated bibliographies**, **summaries** or **précis**, and book and article **reviews**—exercises that specifically require you to interpret and abridge longer pieces of work comprehensibly. Where appropriate, the discussion sets out the criteria that readers and assessors usually consider in evaluating these kinds of work. You will find assessment criteria for different types of summary assignment in Figures 11.1 and 11.2.

PREPARING AN ANNOTATED BIBLIOGRAPHY

An annotated bibliography is a list of reference materials, such as books and articles, in which you provide author, title, and publication details for each item (as in a bibliography) and a short review of that item. The review might typically be up to 150 words long. Annotated bibliographies are customarily set out with the items in alphabetical order (by authors' surnames). Some annotated bibliographies are, however, written in the form of a short essay that quickly and concisely offers the same bibliographic material and critique, but in a more literary style than an annotated list.

The following are examples of annotated bibliographies. The first two provide a short synopsis and critique.

Example: Annotated bibliography 1

Yelloly, M., & Henkel, M. (Eds.). (1995). *Learning and teaching in social work: Towards reflective practice*. London: Jessica Kingsley Publications.

A major contribution to the literature on professional education and training, *Learning and Teaching in Social Work* addresses significant contemporary themes in the post-professional education of social workers and related professionals, and examines the nature of professional education, its changing epistemological environment, and processes of teaching and learning. Essential reading for those engaged in education and training for social work, counselling, and psychotherapy, the book will also be of value to other professions, notably teaching and nursing.

Example: Annotated bibliography 2

Craig, R.B. Illicit drug traffic and US–Latin American relations. *Washington Quarterly*, 8, 105–204.

Argues that the US government and general population are primarily interested in Latin America because it is the major source of hard and soft drugs. The control of drugs cultivation, processing, and shipping now ranks in importance in US eyes with illegal immigration, the debt crisis, and fighting communism. Also looks at US relations with Bolivia, Peru, and Colombia.

This is an example of an annotated bibliography written in essay form.

Example: Annotated bibliography 3

I know of no geographical research on the condom, and virtually nothing on the geography of sexual relations, although the fine and pioneering work by a geographer—Symanski, R. (1981), *The immoral landscape: Female prostitution in western societies*, Toronto: Butterworths—is increasingly referenced by other human scientists. Numerous short reports on condom use and propagation are given in almost all issues of *World AIDS*, while many articles and reports in the "AIDS Monitor" of *New Scientist* deal with condom use (Gould, 1993, p. 215).

A good place to see examples of annotated bibliographies is the Internet. Simply search for annotated bibliographies in your area of specialization.

What is the purpose of an annotated bibliography?

Annotated bibliographies provide people in a particular field of enquiry with some commentary on books and articles available in that field.

They discuss the *content*, *relevance*, and *quality* of the material reviewed (Engle, Blumenthal, & Cosgrave, 2004). Annotated bibliographies may also give a newcomer to a body of work a perceptive review of material available. Your professor might ask you to write an annotated bibliography to make you familiar with a particular body of literature in your discipline area.

What is the reader of an annotated bibliography looking for?

Although the content may vary depending on the purpose of the list, readers of annotated bibliographies typically expect to see the following three sets of information, although many annotated bibliographies exclude the element of critique.

Information provided by an annotated bibliography

Details: full bibliographic details (author, date of publication, title, volume or edition number, pages, publisher, place of publication).
Summary: a clear indication of the content (and argument) of the piece. Consider including, for example, material on the authors' aim in writing the piece, their intended audience, their claim to authority, and key arguments they use to support points.
Critique: critical comment on the merits and weaknesses of the publication or on its contribution to the field of study. Some of the things you might also consider evaluating are appropriateness of the article to its intended audience, whether it is current, and, importantly, its engagement with other significant literature in the field.

WRITING SUMMARIES OR PRÉCIS

Summaries (sometimes called précis) restate the essential contents of a piece of writing in a much more limited number (usually specified) of words than the original text. Abbreviation of the text is accomplished by presenting the main ideas in alternative wording, leaving out most examples and minor points.

Your précis must accurately *represent* the text in condensed form. It should be a scaled-down version of the original text. Unlike a review, a précis does *not* contain interpretation of the issues raised. It is *not* evaluative. There is no need for you to provide your reaction to the author's ideas.

Brevity and *clarity* are crucial ingredients of a summary or précis. Let your reader or assessor know, in as few words as possible, what the summarized text is about. Do not prepare a précis that is as long as the article itself. Imagine your audience sitting opposite you with a bored glaze about to appear across their eyes. Spare them the details. Give them

TIP
A good précis spares the details and focuses on key matters.

enough information to understand what the text is about but not so much that they might just as well have read the original.

This leads us to one of the most common shortcomings of summaries or précis: failure to say what the original author's *main argument* is. Imagine someone has asked you to tell her about a movie you have recently seen. One of the most important things she will want to know, and in relatively few words, will be *essential details of the plot*. For example, readers probably do not want to know the names of Cinderella's evil sisters, the colour of her ball gown, or the temperament of the horses. Instead, they want to know the essence of the story that brought Cinderella together with her Prince Charming.

Once you have written your summary, reread it with the following question in mind: "Could I read this précis aloud to the author in the honest belief that it accurately summarizes his or her work?" If the answer is "no," modify your work. You might also ask yourself, "Would someone who has not read the original text have a good sense of what it is about after reading this précis?" Again, if the answer is "no," you have some changes to make.

What is the reader of a summary or précis looking for?

The criteria in the précis assessment schedule in Figure 11.1 can be used as guidelines for successfully completing your assignment.

Provide full bibliographic details of the text
At the start of your précis, you should provide the reader with a full reference to the work you are summarizing.

KEY CONCEPTS

The summary or précis

The précis should include the following details of the work being summarized:

- authors' names
- date of publication
- title
- edition
- publisher
- place of publication

For example,

Flyvbjerg, B. (2001). *Making social science matter*. Cambridge: Cambridge University Press.

Clearly identify the text's subject matter

After you have written the reference, you should provide a short statement that lets your readers know what the reviewed text is about. For instance, you may be reviewing a book on "advances in biological warfare techniques" or another on "recent developments in chaos theory."

Clearly identify the purpose of the text

Having stated what the text is about, you need to let the reader of your review know precisely what the *aim* of the text is. The distinction between a text's subject matter and its purpose is illustrated by the following introductory sentences of Bourne and Ley's edited collection on the social geography of Canadian cities:

> This is a book *about* the places, the people and the practices that together comprise the social geography of Canadian cities. Its *purpose* is both to describe and to interpret something of the increasingly complex social characteristics of these cities and the diversity of living environments and lived experiences that they provide.
>
> (Bourne & Ley, 1993, p. 3, emphasis added)

In his preface to *Recent America*, Dewey Grantham also distinguishes between the aim and the purpose of the text:

> *Recent America* seeks to provide a relatively brief but comprehensive survey of the American experience since 1945. The emphasis is on national politics and national affairs, including international issues and diplomacy, but some attention is given to economic, social, and cultural trends. I hope that this volume will serve as a useful introduction to a fascinating historical epoch.
>
> (Grantham, 1987, p. x)

> **TIP**
>
> Be sure to distinguish between the subject matter and the purpose of the text you are summarizing.

FIGURE 11.1   Précis assessment schedule

Student name: **Grade:**

Assessed by:

The following is an itemized rating scale for various aspects of a précis. Sections left blank are not relevant to the attached assignment. Some aspects are more important than others, so there is no formula connecting the scatter of ticks with the final percentage for the assignment. A tick in either of the two boxes left of centre means that the statement is true to a greater (outer left) or lesser (inner left) extent. The same principle applies to the right-hand boxes.

If you have any questions about the individual scales, final comments, final grade, or any other aspects of this assessment, please see the assessor.

Description

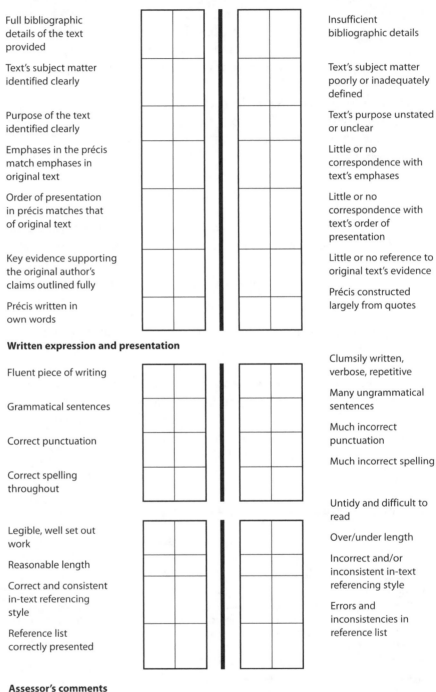

| Full bibliographic details of the text provided | | | | Insufficient bibliographic details |

Text's subject matter identified clearly — Text's subject matter poorly or inadequately defined

Purpose of the text identified clearly — Text's purpose unstated or unclear

Emphases in the précis match emphases in original text — Little or no correspondence with text's emphases

Order of presentation in précis matches that of original text — Little or no correspondence with text's order of presentation

Key evidence supporting the original author's claims outlined fully — Little or no reference to original text's evidence

Précis written in own words — Précis constructed largely from quotes

Written expression and presentation

Fluent piece of writing — Clumsily written, verbose, repetitive

Grammatical sentences — Many ungrammatical sentences

Correct punctuation — Much incorrect punctuation

Correct spelling throughout — Much incorrect spelling

Legible, well set out work — Untidy and difficult to read

Reasonable length — Over/under length

Correct and consistent in-text referencing style — Incorrect and/or inconsistent in-text referencing style

Reference list correctly presented — Errors and inconsistencies in reference list

Assessor's comments

You must think carefully about the distinction between a text's subject matter and its purpose. Usually a book or article will discuss some topic or example in order to make or illustrate a particular point. For example, a volume exploring the financing of a First Nations and Inuit integrated health service may actually be attempting to contribute to broader discussions of Canada's health-care system.

Ensure emphases in the précis match emphases in the original text

In the summary, you should give the same relative emphasis to each area as do the original text's authors (Northey & Knight, 1992, p. 59). If, for example, two-thirds of a paper on monitoring water pollution from the Lake Louise ski area is devoted to a discussion of the legalities of obtaining the water samples, your précis should devote two-thirds of its attention to that issue. This helps to provide your reader with an accurate view of the original text.

Ensure that the order of presentation in the précis matches that of the original text

Just as you should give the same emphasis to each section as the original text's author, you should also follow the article/book's order of presentation and its chain of argument (Northey & Knight, p. 59). Make sure you have presented enough material for a reader to be able to follow the logic of each important argument. You will not be able to give every detail. Present only the critical connections. If you are reviewing a website, this advice on following the order of presentation may be redundant given the non-linear structure of some Internet resources. Consider, instead, trying to follow the order of the site indicated by the layout of inline links on the site's home page.

> **TIP**
>
> Summarizing a website presents unique challenges.

Outline fully the key evidence supporting the original author's claims

You should briefly mention the crucial evidence provided by the authors to support their arguments (Northey & Knight, p. 59). There is no need to recount all the data or evidence offered by the authors. Instead, refer to the material that was the most compelling and convincing.

Ensure that the précis is written in your own words

Write the précis in your own words, although you may, of course, elucidate some points with quotations from the original source. Do not construct a précis from a collection of direct quotations (or text that is, with minor alteration, loosely quoting without attribution) from the text you are summarizing.

WRITING A REVIEW

TIP

Reviews are vital, critical guides to new resources.

A review is an honest, concise, and thoughtful description, analysis, and evaluation of some text, such as a book, journal article, or research report. Reviews serve an important role in the professional and academic world. They let people know of the existence of a particular text as well as pointing out its significance. They also warn prospective users about errors and deficiencies (Calef, 1964). So many new publications are appearing that we need to be selective about what we read.

KEY CONCEPTS

Why write reviews?

Professors usually ask you to write reviews for one or several of the following reasons:

- to familiarize you with a significant piece of work in the field
- to allow you to evaluate the importance of a text to the discipline you are studying
- to allow you to practise your capacity for critical thought

What are your review markers looking for?

People who read reviews, including those marking your review, typically want *honest* and *fair* comments on

- what the reviewed item is about (*description*);
- details of its strengths and weaknesses (*analysis*); and
- its contribution to the discipline (*evaluation*).

Figure 11.2 shows the criteria for assessment of a book or article review. The next few pages of guidelines and advice will help you to deal with these matters.

A review should be interesting as well as informative. So, while your assessor will probably expect you to deal with the following matters in the course of your review, there are no rules concerning the order in which you should present them. Instead, you should set out the material in a way that is both comprehensive and interesting. You should read a few reviews in professional journals in your discipline area to see how they have been laid out and ordered before you write your own. Your review should be composed of the following sections: description, analysis, and evaluation.

FIGURE 11.2   Book/article review assessment schedule

Student name: **Grade:**

Assessed by:

The following is an itemized rating scale for various aspects of a review. Sections left blank are not relevant to, or are beyond the scope of, the attached assignment. Some aspects are more important than others, so there is no formula connecting the scatter of ticks with the final percentage for the assignment. A tick in either of the two boxes left of centre means that the statement is true to a greater (outer left) or lesser (inner left) extent. The same principle applies to the right-hand boxes.

If you have any questions about the individual scales, final comments, final grade, or any other aspects of this assessment, please see the assessor.

Description

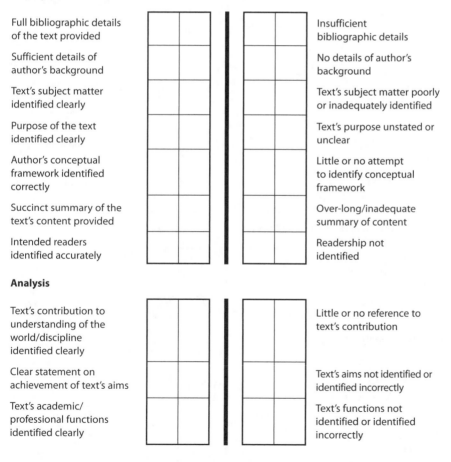

Full bibliographic details of the text provided		Insufficient bibliographic details
Sufficient details of author's background		No details of author's background
Text's subject matter identified clearly		Text's subject matter poorly or inadequately identified
Purpose of the text identified clearly		Text's purpose unstated or unclear
Author's conceptual framework identified correctly		Little or no attempt to identify conceptual framework
Succinct summary of the text's content provided		Over-long/inadequate summary of content
Intended readers identified accurately		Readership not identified

Analysis

Text's contribution to understanding of the world/discipline identified clearly		Little or no reference to text's contribution
Clear statement on achievement of text's aims		Text's aims not identified or identified incorrectly
Text's academic/ professional functions identified clearly		Text's functions not identified or identified incorrectly

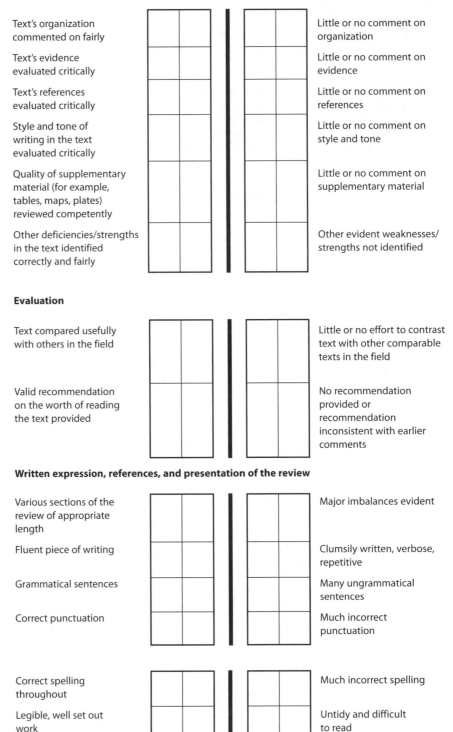

Analysis

Text's organization commented on fairly | | | | | Little or no comment on organization

Text's evidence evaluated critically | | | | | Little or no comment on evidence

Text's references evaluated critically | | | | | Little or no comment on references

Style and tone of writing in the text evaluated critically | | | | | Little or no comment on style and tone

Quality of supplementary material (for example, tables, maps, plates) reviewed competently | | | | | Little or no comment on supplementary material

Other deficiencies/strengths in the text identified correctly and fairly | | | | | Other evident weaknesses/ strengths not identified

Evaluation

Text compared usefully with others in the field | | | | | Little or no effort to contrast text with other comparable texts in the field

Valid recommendation on the worth of reading the text provided | | | | | No recommendation provided or recommendation inconsistent with earlier comments

Written expression, references, and presentation of the review

Various sections of the review of appropriate length | | | | | Major imbalances evident

Fluent piece of writing | | | | | Clumsily written, verbose, repetitive

Grammatical sentences | | | | | Many ungrammatical sentences

Correct punctuation | | | | | Much incorrect punctuation

Correct spelling throughout | | | | | Much incorrect spelling

Legible, well set out work | | | | | Untidy and difficult to read

Reasonable length	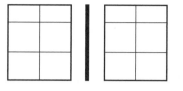	Over/under length
Correct and consistent in-text referencing style		Incorrect and/or inconsistent referencing style
Reference list correctly presented		Errors and inconsistencies in reference list

Assessor's comments

Description: What is the reviewed item about?

Description or summary is an important part of a review. You should imagine that your audience has not read the text you are discussing and that their only knowledge of it will come from your review. Give them a comprehensive but concise outline of the text's content and character. But do not make the mistake of devoting almost all of the review to description—if you do that, your reader might as well go to the original text! As a rule of thumb, try to keep the summary to less than half the total length of your review.

Provide full bibliographic details of the text

You should provide a full and correctly set out reference to the work under review so that others may consult or purchase it (and so the person grading your paper knows that you have reviewed the correct text). Readers of your review will be interested to know

- who the work's authors/editors are;
- the name of the book's publisher; and
- where the volume was published.

It is sometimes helpful also to state how many pages are in the text (and, if a book, its purchase cost, although this is rarely required for classroom reviews). Here is an example of a complete book review reference:

Moulaert, F., Rodriguez, A., & Swyngedouw, E. (Eds.). (2002). *The globalized city: Economic restructuring and social polarization in European cities*. New York: Oxford University Press, xxii and 279, plates, tables, figs, and index. US$85.00 cloth (ISBN 0-19-926040-0).

This text has 279 pages plus twelve pages of introductory material (acknowledgements, title page, contents pages, notes on contributors). The hardback edition costs US$85.00. If a paperback existed, its price would also be recorded here. This book also includes photos, tables, diagrams, and an index. It does not appear to have a bibliography, maps, or a glossary, but these would be listed if present.

Bibliographic details are normally placed at the top of the review. The book review section of almost any academic journal will provide an example for you to follow.

Give sufficient details of the authors' background

If you consider it appropriate, and know of the authors' expertise in the area they are writing about, give a brief overview of their background and reputation (Marius & Page, 2002, p. 213; Northey & Knight, 60). It may also be helpful to consult the Internet or a *Who's Who* publication to find out a little more about any specific author's affiliation and credentials. You might consider whether the authors have written many other books and articles in this area and whether they have an abundance of practical experience. Readers unfamiliar with the subject area will often appreciate some information on the authors' apparent credibility or area of expertise (see discussion in chapter 4 on the importance of evaluating expertise).

Clearly identify the text's subject matter

See the previous section, "Writing a Summary or Précis," for details.

Clearly identify the purpose of the text

This was also discussed in the section above. See the notes for "Writing a Summary or Précis" for details.

Correctly identify the author's conceptual framework

Texts are written from a particular perspective. Authors have a way of viewing the world and of arranging their observations into some specific and supposedly comprehensible whole. That way of thinking about the world is known as a **conceptual framework**. You might imagine a conceptual framework to be rather like the text's skeleton on which the flesh of words and evidence is supported. As a reviewer, one of your tasks is to expose that skeleton, letting your reader know how the authors have interpreted the issues they discuss. How have the authors made sense of that part of the world they are discussing?

In your review, you might combine identification of the conceptual framework with a **critique** of it. Does the author make inappropriate assumptions, and are there inconsistencies, flaws, and weaknesses in the intellectual skeleton? For example, an author might argue that a particular feature of capitalism in Canada has been massive job losses, associated with the adoption of new labour-saving technologies in industry. A reviewer might suggest that this reflects a simplistic view of human–technology relations under capitalism and go on to point out that service

TIP

Try to uncover the intellectual scaffolding that gives the book you are reviewing coherence.

sector employment has risen at the same time as industrial job losses have occurred. Moreover, the reviewer might suggest that while some industries have atrophied, others have emerged and grown.

Provide a succinct summary of the text's content

Readers want some idea of what is in the book or article. Describe the contents in sufficient detail for them to understand what the text is about. This might require stating what is in various parts of the text and how much space is devoted to each section. You might want to integrate the summary of content with your evaluation of the text or prefer to keep it separate (Northey & Knight, p. 61). If you are new to review-writing, it is usually safer to keep the two separate. Write the summary first, then the analysis.

Accurately identify the intended readers of the text under review

The reader of a review is usually interested to know what sort of audience the author of the original text was addressing. In many cases, the author will include a statement on the intended readership somewhere early in the volume. For example, in his preface to *The Slow Plague*, Peter Gould says that his book is "one of a series labeled *liber geographicus pro bono publico*—a geographical book for the public good, which sounds just a bit pretentious until we translate it more loosely as 'a book for the busy but still curious public'" (Gould, p. xiii–xiv).

Similarly, in the preface of his book *Recent America*, Dewey Grantham explicitly recognizes his readers: "I hope that the volume [*Recent America*] . . . will interest students and general readers alike" (Grantham, p. x).

KEY CONCEPTS

Why identify the intended audience?

Identifying the intended audience of the reviewed text serves at least two important purposes:

- You will be helping your readers decide whether the original text will be of any relevance to them.
- You will be providing yourself with an important foundation for writing your critique of the text.

From both Gould and Grantham's statements above, it is reasonable to conclude that their books ought to be easy to read, stimulating, and written for a lay audience. If they are not, there is an important flaw in their books. A book or article intended for experts in the field may legitimately use technical terms and express complex ideas. A version of the same

TIP

Be sure to identify a text's intended audience and review it with that audience in mind.

information for children, though, would be simplified with a completely different vocabulary. You should write your review with the relationship between intended audience and content/style in mind.

Analysis: Details of strengths and weaknesses

So far you have let your reader-assessor know a few basic descriptive details about the text you are reviewing. Now you need to let everyone know what you consider to be the weaknesses *and* strengths of the text. Being negative about a volume under review does not necessarily suggest that you are smarter than the author; indeed, it can be more difficult and challenging to demonstrate how good a text is. If you believe that the material you are reviewing has no significant weaknesses, you should say so. But you should also point out its specific strengths.

As Calef observes, analysis is usually the weakest feature of book reviews: "All authors deserve sympathetic, appreciative analyses of their books; too few authors get them. Many reviewers concentrate on the authors' mistakes and discuss the books as they should have been written" (Calef, p. 1).

It is essential that when you write your review you consider the aims of the original text's authors. *Analyze the book on the authors' terms.* Have the authors achieved their aims?

In your analysis, you should above all *"be fair, be explicit, be honest"* (Calef, emphasis added). To these ends, you should explain why you agree or disagree with the authors' methods, analysis, or conclusions.

In organizing their analysis of a text, many reviewers point out the utility and successes of the book or article first and then move on to point out the deficiencies. You may find that pattern a useful one to follow.

TIP

Be fair, be explicit, and be honest when you write a review.

Clearly identify the text's contribution to your understanding of the world or of your discipline

In evaluating the text's contribution to the discipline, you should begin with the assumption that the author has something useful to say, rather than trying to explain whether you agree or disagree with that contribution. What is that contribution? Has the author helped *you* to make sense of things? What has been illuminated?

State clearly whether or not the text achieved its aims

Think carefully about the author's objectives and compare those with the content of the text. Do they match one another? You would be derelict in your duty as a reviewer if you had stated what the reviewed text's aims were but failed to say whether or not they had been met. (Imagine how frustrated you would feel if someone told you there was an article in a magazine about how to make a lifetime fortune in twenty-one days and when you read those pages you found that the article failed to deliver what it promised.)

Clearly identify the text's academic or professional functions

Ask what educational, research, or professional functions the text might fulfill. For example, is the book or article likely to be a useful resource for people in the same class as you, for other undergraduate students, or for leaders in the field?

Accentuate the positive. For example, an author may think that the book's audience ought to be final-year undergraduate students, but you—as an undergraduate student reviewer—believe the book would better serve a first-year audience. Rather than simply stating that the text is inappropriate for its intended audience, let your reader know which audience the text might best serve.

Comment fairly on the text's organization

Say whether you believe the reviewed text is well organized or not. Within this, think about the ways in which the book/paper is subdivided into chapters/sections. Do the subdivisions advance the book's purpose or are they obstructive? Do they break up and upset an intellectual trajectory? Support your standpoint with examples.

Critically evaluate the text's evidence

An author's evidence should be reliable, current, drawn from reputable sources (such as official statistics, Hansard, international journals, or experts in the field), and should support claims made in the text. Would the results of the original text stand up to replication (if the study was done again, is it likely that the results would be the same?) or corroboration (are the results of the study substantiated by other related evidence?)?

Make clear your assessment of evidence used in the text. Is it compelling or not? If, for example, you are skeptical about the repeated use of quotations drawn from *National Enquirer* to support a discussion of bribery in Ottawa, you should let the reader know. Back up your assessment of the evidence with reasons for your conclusion. If you are able, and if it is necessary, suggest alternative and better sources of evidence.

Critically evaluate the text's references

Readers and assessors of your review will wish to know if the reviewed work has covered the available and relevant literature reasonably well. If there are major shortcomings in the references, it is possible that the text's authors may not be fully aware of material that might have informed their work. If you are new to your discipline, you might protest, sometimes quite justifiably, that you cannot offer a meaningful judgment about the strength of the reference material. Nevertheless, you ought to be thinking about this question and answering it where possible.

Critically evaluate the style and tone of writing in the text

Among other things, readers of a review may be trying to work out whether to buy or read the reviewed text. Therefore, questions foremost in the mind of some will be whether the text is written clearly and if it is interesting to read. Is the text's writing repetitious? Detailed? Not detailed enough? Boring? Is the style clear? Is it tedious, unnecessarily abstract, jargon-laden, offhand? Particularly if you think there are problems with the style of writing, it is appropriate to support your criticisms with a few examples.

You should also comment on the tone of the book. Let your reader or assessor know if the text is accessible only to experts in the field or if it is a coffee-table publication, or something in between. Of course, criticisms about the tone of the text should be written with reference to the intended audience. It would probably be unfair, for instance, to condemn a book on the grounds that it used technical language if it was written for an audience of experts.

Ensure that the quality of supplementary material (for example, figures, plates) is reviewed competently

Many books and articles make extensive use of supplementary material such as tables, plates, and figures. In reviewing the text, you should comment on the quality of these materials and their contribution to the text's message. Graphic and tabular material in the text being reviewed should be relevant, concise, large enough to read, comprehensible, and should provide the details of sources.

TIP

Support criticisms in your review with evidence.

Correctly and fairly identify any other deficiencies/strengths in the text

After a close reading of the text, you should be able to identify any weaknesses and strengths you have not already discussed. Remember, you do not have to find things wrong with the text you are reviewing. Being critical does not require you to be negative. Similarly, you should not pick out minor problems within the text and suggest that they destroy the entire book. However, if there are genuine problems, be explicit about what they are, giving examples where possible.

Evaluation: Contribution to the discipline

In the first section of the review, you described the text being reviewed. You then went on to outline the text's strengths and flaws. Now you have to make a judgment. Is the text any good? You may find it useful to be guided by the central question: "Would you advise people to read (or buy) the text you have reviewed?"

Compare the text's usefulness with others in the field
If you have the expertise in the field, appraise the text being reviewed in terms of its use as an alternative to work already available. It may be helpful to consult library reference material to see, for example, how many other volumes on the same or a similar topic have been produced recently. If you are reviewing a website, search for competitors and compare them. Compare the book/article factually with its predecessors. What subjects does it treat that earlier volumes did not? What does it leave out? (Northey & Knight, p. 60). Remember to cite correctly any additional sources you use.

> **TIP**
> Think about how the text you are reviewing stacks up against its competitors.

Make a valid recommendation on the worth of reading the text
A fundamental reason for writing reviews is to let readers know whether a particular book or article is worth consulting. Your recommendation should be consistent with the preceding analysis of its strengths and weaknesses. For example, it would be inappropriate to criticize a book or article mercilessly and then conclude by saying that it is an important contribution to the discipline and should be read by everyone interested in the area. It is worth restating a point made earlier. In your review *be fair, be explicit, be honest.*

Written expression, references, and presentation of the review

Make sure the various sections of the review are of appropriate length
Assessors will consider the balance between description, analysis, and evaluation when marking a review. A description of the text is important, but it should not dominate your review. As noted earlier, unless there are special reasons, the description should usually be less than half of the total length of the review.

Your own writing should be clear, concise, and appropriate for your audience. Detailed advice on the written expression assessment criteria shown in the assessment schedule for reviews in Figure 11.2 can be found in chapter 8.

Some examples of reviews

Before you start writing a review, you will find it helpful to look to high-quality academic journals in your field for good examples. Reviews are typically printed towards the end of the journal. Below, and as a preliminary guide, are some slightly revised versions of reviews published in the *Library Journal*. You will see that despite their brevity, the reviews address many of the issues discussed in this chapter.

Example review 1

Angell, M. (1996). *Science on trial: The clash of medical evidence and the law in the breast implant case*. New York: Nostalgia, 288.

Angell, executive editor of the *New England Journal of Medicine*, addresses the controversy over silicone breast implants, which were banned and the subject of huge lawsuits despite dubious scientific evidence of harm. She suggests that lawyers and journalists have misinterpreted scientific results and ignored evidence, leading to the public's growing mistrust of science and the scientific method. Replacing cynicism with a more balanced ability to view scientific results critically is crucial for our health, notes Angell. But her case for scientific objectivity is disappointingly murky. She sweepingly dismisses the validity of controversial ideas only now being thoroughly researched (for example, alternatives to technological medicine, criticisms of male biases in science), which undermines her credibility. Still, this remains a compelling book recommended for lay and academic audiences.

(Adapted from: *Library Journal* 1996, p. 121 (12))

Example review 2

Meredith, M. (2005). *The fate of Africa: A history of fifty years of independence, public affairs*. New York: Perseus Publishing, 800.

A scholar of Africa necessarily becomes an expert on death. In Meredith's tome, death comes in huge numbers and in many ways: through famine, ethnic strife, racial injustice, and at the hands of ruthless dictators. It came in the days of European colonialism, but in post-colonial Africa, death pervades the continent. Meredith (*Our Votes, Our Guns: Robert Mugabe and the Tragedy of Zimbabwe*) writes with sobriety, intelligence, and a deep knowledge of Africa as he describes individuals responsible for deaths unimaginable to much of the rest of the world. A well-known example is the carnage among Hutus and Tutsis in Rwanda, claiming 800,000 lives in 100 days in 1994—more people were killed more quickly than in any other mass killing in recorded history. Much of this tragic history has been told in part elsewhere, but Meredith has compiled the text covering the entire continent. Only in the last few pages does Meredith answer the question of Africa's fate—and he thinks it's bleak. This is a valuable work for those who wish to understand Africa and its besieged peoples, and for audiences interested in environmental and life sciences.

(Adapted from: *Library Journal* 2005, p. 130 (12))

Example review 3

Mommsen, H. (1996). *The rise and fall of Weimar democracy*, trans. E. Forster and L.E. Jones. Chapel Hill: University of North Carolina, 608.

This translation makes available to the English-speaking world an important historical work published in 1989 by a prominent German historian. The period from 1919 to 1933 was a time of great political, social, economic, and artistic upheaval in Germany. In this magisterial work, the author looks at the Weimar period from the viewpoint of social and economic history, providing a lucid yet detailed account of the complexities of this era without attempting to pull the strands out of their context in order to find the "roots" of the Nazi period that followed. By doing so, he both sheds light on this interesting period and provides a convincing overall picture of Germany's road from parliamentary democracy to dictatorship during the interwar years. Because of its depth and detail, this book is not for casual readers, but it covers a complex subject with admirable clarity and is certain to become a classic. Everyone interested in European history should read this book.

(Adapted from: *Library Journal* 1996, 121 (12))

GLOSSARY

annotated bibliography A list of reference materials, such as books and articles, in which the author, title, and publication details for each item and a short review of that item are provided.

conceptual framework A specific and supposedly comprehensible whole.

critique Critical comment on the merits and weaknesses of the publication or on its contribution to the field of study.

précis See **summary**.

review An honest, concise, and thoughtful description, analysis, and evaluation of some text, such as a book, journal article, or research report.

summary A clear indication of the content (and argument) of the piece.

SUGGESTED FURTHER READING

Finnbrogason, Jack, & Valieau, Al. (2006). *A Canadian writer's guide*. Toronto, ON: Thomson Nelson.

Swales, John, & Feak, Christine B. (2004). *Commentary for academic writing for graduate students: Essential tasks and skills* (2nd ed.). (*Michigan Series in English for Academic & Professional Purposes*). Ann Arbor: University of Michigan Press.

RELATED WEBSITES

**www.writing.utoronto.ca/advice/specific-types-of-writing/
annotated-bibliography**
Knott, Deborah. University of Toronto. "Writing an annotated bibliography."

www.library.cornell.edu/olinuris/ref/research/skill28.htm
Olin and Uris Library, Cornell University. "How to prepare an annotated bibliography."

http://owl.english.purdue.edu/owl/resource/614/01/
OWL, Purdue Online Writing Lab. "Annotated bibliographies."

www.writing.utoronto.ca/advice/specific-types-of-writing/book-review
Procter, Margaret. University of Toronto. "The book review or article critique."

http://library.ucsc.edu/ref/howto/literaturereview.html
University of California–Santa Cruz University Library. (2005). "How to . . . write a literature review."

Writing Well: Language and Sentence Structure

Read over your compositions, and wherever you meet with a passage which you think is particularly fine, strike it out.

Samuel Johnson, 1773

Many different elements are involved in writing well, and many of them have been dealt with in other sections of this book. You must

- know your subject;
- have a clear idea of your purpose for writing;
- organize your material logically; and
- divide your text into clear and appropriate paragraphs.

This chapter deals with the words you use and the way you arrange those words to improve the effectiveness of your academic writing. It covers aspects of vocabulary, non-discriminatory language, and sentence structure.

WHAT IS GOOD WRITING?

Good writing is an essential element of clear and effective written communication, but what constitutes "good writing"? There are probably as many answers to that question as there are writers and readers. A style of writing that is effective in one situation might be quite ineffective in another. What is suitable for one audience might be totally inappropriate for a different one. The art of writing well is the art of matching your style of writing to your purpose and to the specific audience you are addressing.

In creative writing, for example, the writer's purpose might be to convey a feeling or atmosphere or to express a distinct personality. J.K. Rowling is a good writer. She entertains millions of people and makes a great deal of money by doing so. Her style, however, would be completely inappropriate for your sociology essay. William Shakespeare is a great writer but he would never get on the *FictionDB* authors' list. If you can write like Dr. Seuss, then do it! But not in your chemistry lab report.

Writing for academic purposes is usually **functional writing**. Although the writer's personality should come through, the main purpose of functional writing is to focus not on the writer, or the emotions of the writer or reader, but on the information or ideas being explained, with as little interference as possible. Good writing in this context achieves its purpose by conveying the ideas in the mind of the writer to the mind of the reader with a minimum of confusion, distortion, and delay. The audience for academic writing is fairly easy to identify. Academic writers should assume an audience of people much like themselves and direct their writing to

KEY CONCEPTS

The "six Cs" of good writing

Clear: Your writing should be straightforward, logical, unambiguous: academic readers are not looking for suspense or mystery. They want to know "what's what" and "that's that."

Complete: Your writing should contain all necessary details: your readers will expect your writing to form a complete whole. They will not want to have to consult other sources to make your reasoning or descriptions comprehensible.

Concise: Your writing should contain no unnecessary details or ornaments: readers want to get straight to the point without spending time on irrelevant detail or padding.

Considerate: Your writing should show that you are aware of your readers: always think about your audience as you write. What do they want to know? How can you make your writing easier to understand? How can you make your writing lively and interesting?

Concrete: Your writing should not be vague or abstract. Always be specific to make your writing accurate, credible, and vivid: for example, "there were 1,500 people at the concert," not "there were lots of people at the concert"; "These events happened 55 years ago," not "these events happened many years ago."

Correct: Your writing should be correct in word usage, grammar, punctuation, and spelling: poor expression will make your writing hard to understand and will also make it seem unprofessional and careless. Many people do know how to structure sentences, punctuate, and spell, and, rightly or wrongly, they will judge the quality of your work by your ability to do the same.

that audience. For this purpose and this audience, it is easier to define the characteristics of good writing.

Good functional writing uses the "six Cs." It is *clear, complete, concise, considerate, concrete*, and *correct* (adapted from Dwyer, 1993, p. 202).

ACHIEVING THE GOALS OF GOOD FUNCTIONAL WRITING

In order to write well for academic purposes, you must make your writing as accessible as possible without sacrificing depth of content or shades of meaning. This involves, above all, a wide vocabulary. The more words you have at your command, the wider the choice you have in selecting the right word for the right occasion. It also involves knowing accepted forms of sentence structure and punctuation. A feeling for these matters comes partly through practice in writing and partly through wide reading.

Good writers are necessarily good readers. Chapter 3 of this book advised you to read widely to increase your reading speed and to improve your comprehension. If you know how other writers use words in functional writing, you will be well on the way to knowing how to use them yourself. Go to professional journals in your field, not only for information about essay topics, or topics set for examinations, but also for general knowledge about how writers in your field use words.

It is no use, of course, reading widely and discovering new words if you do not know what they mean. A good dictionary is an invaluable tool for a writer. When you see a new word, look it up. Keep a dictionary handy whenever you have a writing task to do. There are many dictionaries on the market; one of the most useful ones for students to have on their desk at home or in residence is the *Canadian Oxford Dictionary*. A more compact version of this—for example, the *Paperback Oxford Canadian Dictionary*—might be useful to have in your backpack or university locker, if you have one. Students who use laptops, netbooks, smartphones, or tablets connected to wireless networks can take advantage of online dictionaries, many of which may be available to you through arrangements made by your university's library. Dictionary.com is a useful site for quickly checking the basic meaning or spelling of a word, but be careful about words that might have specifically Canadian spellings ("pyjamas," "labour," "analyze," "cheque," and so on). Remember, too, that even familiar words can have unexpected nuances, and looking them up in a comprehensive dictionary can often give you some new way of thinking, to say nothing of the correct spelling.

TIP

Reading widely is the best way to increase your vocabulary and to develop a feeling for what is the right word in a particular context.

CHOOSING THE RIGHT WORD

Often the right word is the shortest and simplest word that will convey the meaning you want concisely and unambiguously. Academic writing is not, however, texting: it is sometimes necessary and appropriate to use long words. Never reject a word that means exactly what you want just because it is long, but do not choose a word *just* because it is longer or sounds more "academic" than a simple word. Where the two have the same meaning, it is often wise to choose the simpler and better-known one. Your audience will thank you. For example,

KEY CONCEPTS

Using simple words

Use	Do not use
need	require
use	utilize
try	endeavour
find out	ascertain
go	proceed
before	prior to
begin/start	commence
harmful	deleterious
buy	purchase

NAVIGATING LEARNING CHALLENGES
Using Plain Language

Students who feel insecure about their English because it is not their first language or they have been diagnosed with a learning disability often turn to a thesaurus to make their writing sound more scholarly. This is not a good practice: generally, the word that first comes to mind is the best word to use!

Be concise

Use the minimum number of words that will convey *exactly* the meaning you want. For example,

Using concise language

Use	Do not use
because	as a consequence of/on account of/due to the fact that
about	in relation to/with reference to
if	in the event that
since	in view of the fact that
now	at this point in time
has	is provided with

Be precise

Always use concrete and specific words and phrases rather than abstract general ones.

Using precise language

Use	Do not use
Next month/On 24 August . . .	In the foreseeable future . . .
We are planting 1,000 new trees each month.	A process of reforestation is under way.

Avoid slang or colloquial language

We use informal language, called **slang** or **colloquial language**, in speech, and sometimes in literature, but it is not appropriate in formal writing. There are several reasons for avoiding spoken forms in written work. Most slang is particular to certain age, social, or cultural groups and so might not be understood in the same way by everyone: for example, "wicked" and "sick" might be terms of approval for you but not for your parents or even your older siblings. Some people find certain kinds of slang offensive. Slang goes in and out of fashion, and outdated slang looks and sounds silly, whereas writing is fixed once it is published. Slang tends to distract the reader from the subject of the writing to the personality of the writer, and so a neutral style is more effective for functional writing.

> **TIP**
>
> In professional writing, use straightforward, simple language, choosing vocabulary that expresses your meaning clearly and precisely.

Avoid jargon

Jargon, like slang, has its place in specific kinds of writing where you know your reader will understand it. "Jargon" is the technical language of a particular vocational or professional group. Those who belong to the same group understand their own jargon and might find it convenient. Those who do not belong to that same group might find it incomprehensible. It is quite inappropriate to use jargon in writing for a general audience or in places where a word in general use will do as well. Within any professional or vocational group, the members might use jargon for convenience, but far too often they use it to baffle or impress outsiders or, worse, because they are too inconsiderate to realize the needs of their audience.

Computer experts and academics compete with doctors and lawyers to win first prize for impenetrable language. One doctor might write the following to another doctor:

> **Example**
>
> This patient has been suffering from increasing orthopnoea which culminated last night in an attack of severe paroxysmal nocturnal dyspnoea . . .

In writing the same thing to someone who is not a doctor, he or she should write the following:

> **Example**
>
> This patient cannot lie flat without becoming breathless. The problem has been getting worse and last night she had a severe choking attack . . .

No doubt you can think of examples from other fields. Although the first example above would be quite appropriate within the context of medical communication, it is probably meaningless for most of the rest of us. Inappropriate use of jargon wastes time, leads to confusion, and annoys readers.

Beware of easily confused words

It is easy to make spelling errors that will not be picked up by your computer's spell-check. You should always proofread carefully to check your own spelling and use a dictionary if you are unsure of meanings or correct spelling. Many writers are tricked by words that that sound alike but have different meanings and different spellings. For example, there is a big difference between *piece* and *peace; here* and *hear; there, their*, and *they're*; and *meet* and *meat.* Using the wrong word can be embarrassing. At best, it makes your writing seem careless, and, at worst, it alters your meaning or makes it hard to understand. Some other commonly confused words of this kind are *weather/whether, course/coarse, past/passed, site/sight/cite, two/too/to, principle/principal, break/brake, complement/compliment, discrete/discreet*, and *it's/its.*

Other words can cause trouble because they have similar spellings even though they do not sound exactly alike and their meanings are different. *Quite* and *quiet*, for example, are often confused, as are *loose* and *lose*. Once again, only a dictionary and wide reading experience will help you avoid this kind of error. Some other frequently confused words of this kind are *desert/dessert, accept/except, moral/morale, allude/elude, formerly/ formally, affect/effect, personal/personnel, illusion/allusion, access/excess, aural/oral*, and *sever/severe*.

NAVIGATING LEARNING CHALLENGES
Seek Proofreading Help

Some students, particularly those who do not have English as their first language or who have learning disabilities that make it difficult for them to detect these kinds of errors, should leave time to have their written assignments looked over by staff in university writing, academic success, or accessibility services.

EXERCISE

EASILY CONFUSED WORDS

Choose the correct words in each of the following sentences:
1. My high school principal/principle made it a principal/principle never to drink coffee in the afternoon.
2. Her moral/morale was low because she didn't understand the question on the sociology test about the difference between moral/morale and ethical behaviour.
3. Her parents were happy that, because she was just 16, she didn't have access/excess to pubs and other places where people were drinking to access/ excess.
4. He thought he'd better get the pockets of his pants fixed; otherwise, he was going to loose/lose all of his loose/lose change.

USING NON-DISCRIMINATORY LANGUAGE

An important aspect of good writing is choosing a suitable tone to match the subject you are writing about, the purpose for which you are writing, and the audience you are writing for. Much of that tone comes through the vocabulary you employ to communicate your thoughts and ideas. To be considerate to your readers, you should use language or forms of expression that will not offend them or denigrate them on the basis of their gender, race, country of origin, religion, sexual orientation, or age. As you prepare an essay, report, or talk, try to use non-discriminatory terminology. Universities, government departments, and many private businesses in Canada have policies that require employees to use non-discriminatory language; by getting into the habit of using this language now, you will be preparing yourself for writing in the workplace.

The *Language Portal of Canada*, a Government of Canada publication, observes the following:

> The diversity of Canada's population in terms of origin, descent, ethnicity, race, language, culture and other characteristics is reflected in language. Because language plays a leading role in group relations and conflicts, it is important for writers to reflect diversity in a positive light by using non-discriminatory language and avoiding stereotypes.
>
> (Language Portal, 2010)

You can avoid using discriminatory language very easily without resorting to the kinds of linguistic contortions that people sometimes joke about. Using non-discriminatory language does not mean that you have to use phrases like "vertically challenged" or "police persons." Set out below are some of the common forms of discriminatory language and how you can avoid them. The information is adapted from *Editing Canadian English* (Editors' Association of Canada, 2000).

Using language and descriptions that refer to both genders

The most common form of discrimination in language occurs when all human beings are referred to as "men." This excludes women from the

KEY CONCEPTS

Using inclusive language

Write	Do not write
Our parents/ancestors lived a different life	Our fathers/grandfathers lived a different life
In the stone age, humans were hunters and gatherers	In the stone age, men were hunters and gatherers
The best person/applicant for the job	The best man for the job
Dress will be formal/informal	Dress will be black tie/sports jacket
Housekeeper	Cleaning lady
Flight attendant	Stewardess
Sales associate/salesperson	Salesman
Humanity/people/the human race	Mankind
Sewer/maintenance hole	Manhole
Staff/staffing/workforce	Manpower
Police officer	Policeman
Letter carrier/postal worker	Mailman

activity, role, or occupation under discussion and makes women's roles invisible. Although it is less common, it is equally discriminatory to exclude men by referring to some general human activity, characteristic, or occupation as exclusively female.

You will notice that using the gender-neutral terms listed above, and others like them, will often improve your writing by making it more specific.

One problem that arises with using gender-neutral language in English is that English does not have a singular pronoun that refers to both men and women. The third person pronouns in English are "he," "she," and "it." The masculine forms of the pronoun, "he," "his," and "him," are often used to refer to both men and women. There are several ways of writing the third person singular pronoun in English sentences to overcome this problem.

If you do not have to repeat the words too many times, use "he or she," "his or her," or "him or her."

> **Example**
> The lecturer should communicate clearly with his or her students. He or she has a responsibility to make sure that the students understand him or her.

If you find this too clumsy, you can often rewrite a sentence so that it uses only plural forms.

> **Example**
> Lecturers should communicate clearly with their students. They have a responsibility to make sure that the students understand them.

If the sentence does not lend itself to this kind of rewriting, you can write the sentence a different way, so that you get rid of the difficult pronouns altogether.

> **Example**
> Students must be able to understand their lecturer, and it is the lecturer's responsibility to make sure that students do understand by communicating clearly with them.

Sometimes it is possible to rewrite a sentence in several different ways to avoid gender-specific pronouns. The method you use to do this will depend on the structure and meaning of the sentence.

Using language that avoids stereotyping and discrimination

There are some other kinds of discriminatory language that you should try to avoid in your writing:

- *Trivialization:* usually sees women's activities denigrated and often implies that women behave more irrationally and emotionally than men. For example, women "bicker" whereas men "disagree"; a woman is called "office girl" whereas a man is called "filing clerk"; men are "assertive" where women are "aggressive"; men are "cautious" where women are "timid."
- *Stereotyping:* characterizes men or women in ways that empha-size characteristics supposedly typical of the whole group of men or women. For example, men might be depicted as "unemotional," "uncaring," "clumsy," or "strong." Women might be depicted as "emotional," "passive," "fragile," or "neat."
- *Parallel treatment in non-parallel situations and vice versa:* sometimes takes the form of women having their role defined through their rela-tionship with a man. For example, "man and wife"; "Mrs. Smith, wife of famous Formula One driver George Smith . . ." Less commonly, the reverse applies, as Denis Thatcher discovered in the 1980s as "Mar-garet Thatcher's husband." Another form of this non-parallelism in language occurs in phrases like "men and girls" or "men and ladies."

Avoiding racist language

Racism is the discriminatory treatment of people on the basis of their race, ethnicity, or nationality. It has its basis in a clear distinction between an "in-group" and an "out-group." Language might be racist in a number of different ways. You should try to avoid the kinds of writing listed below:

- *Describing an in-group as the norm and an out-group as a deviation from the norm:* The ethnic status of the in-group is rarely mentioned, whereas that of out-group members is given. This often happens in news head-lines. For example, "Francophones take Ontario political position"; "Korean gang threat."
- *Using euphemisms to describe the actions of an in-group towards out-groups:* For example, "detainment of Tamil refugees in Canada" might mean that the refugees have been imprisoned.
- *Using stereotypical terms to describe out-groups:* For example, Vietnamese immigrants might be depicted as "nimble-fingered" and, therefore, suited to working as sewing machine operators; Chinese immigrants might be described as always having "business acumen."

- *Using ethnic and racial slurs that set the out-group apart from the in-group:* For example, derogatory names and adjectives such as "Newfie," "blochead," or "Bluenoser."

STRUCTURING CLEAR SENTENCES

The way you structure your sentences has an important influence on your writing style. Written communication involves words arranged in recognizable patterns. The most important pattern is the sentence, and to write clearly and concisely, you must be able to structure clear and grammatically correct sentences. Although the sentence patterns of imaginative and informal writing can be varied and free, sentences in functional writing should be structured to achieve clarity and to avoid ambiguity.

Writing complete sentences

A **sentence** is a group of words that

- begins with a capital letter;
- ends with a period, exclamation mark, or question mark;
- contains a subject (who or what the sentence is about), except for imperatives, discussed at the end of this section;
- contains a finite verb (a "doing" word that tells what the subject does, has, or is; a finite verb is a "finished" or main verb that makes sense on its own); and
- expresses a complete thought (is a main or principal clause).

> **Example**
> After consulting her advisers, *the queen* (subject) *decided* (finite verb) to dismiss parliament.

Sentences are often much more complex than this, but the basic framework of any sentence in functional writing must always be a subject and a finite verb. Sometimes a sentence might have more than one subject, it might have more than one word in the subject, and it might have more than one verb.

> **Example**
> *The queen* (subject) and *her group of experienced advisers* (subject) *have decided* (finite verb) to dismiss parliament and *will act* (finite verb) swiftly on that decision.

It might have a number of additional phrases or clauses:

> **Example**
> *The queen* (subject), who was concerned about the danger of revolution, *decided* (finite verb) to dismiss parliament from that very day and *acted* (finite verb) swiftly on the decision before the end of the day's session.

A sentence can also be very simple:

> **Example**
> *The queen* (subject) *acted* (finite verb).
> *She* (subject) *dismissed* (finite verb) parliament.

No matter how simple or how complicated a sentence is, the principle remains the same. If you do not have a subject and a finite verb, you do not have a sentence.

> **Example**
> After consulting her advisers, the queen deciding to dismiss parliament.

This group of words is not a sentence. It has a subject (the queen) but it does not have a finite or complete verb ("deciding" is a participle that needs another part of the verb to make it complete). Because the verb is not complete, the sentence is not a complete thought. It makes no sense on its own.

In the same way,

> **Example**
> The queen decided to dismiss parliament. After consulting her advisers.

"After consulting her advisers" is not a sentence because it is a prepositional phrase; it has no subject and no finite verb. It cannot, therefore, make sense on its own.

Even though a group of words has a subject and a finite (or complete) verb, it might not be a complete thought. It might not make sense on its own. Neither of the examples below is a complete sentence. Each one needs another statement to complete it.

> **Example**
> After consulting her advisers, if *the queen* (subject) *decided* (finite verb) to dismiss parliament.
> After consulting her advisers, when *the queen* (subject) *decided* (finite verb) to dismiss parliament.

These **sentence fragments** are made up of dependent clauses and phrases, and they need a principal or independent clause to complete their meaning:

> **Example**
> After consulting her advisers, if *the queen* (subject) *decided* (finite verb) to dismiss parliament, *she* (subject) *would have to act* (finite verb) quickly.
> After consulting her advisers, when *the queen* (subject) *decided* (finite verb) to dismiss parliament, *she* (subject) *acted* (finite verb) quickly.

Groups of words that are incomplete, like the examples above, are called sentence fragments. Many people write sentence fragments instead of complete sentences. We see and hear them all the time in advertising and other popular media: "Like our new lobster and fish duo"; "Have never taken 'no' for an answer"; "Civil unrest!" As you can see from the examples, fragments are clumsy and often confusing.

There are many different sentence patterns that are not demonstrated here, but they all have the same basic rules. There is one exception. Orders or **imperatives** might not have their subject explicitly stated:

> **Example**
> Go away!
> Leave the room!
> Be quiet!

These are all sentences. They all make sense on their own. The subject, so clearly implied that it does not need to be stated, is "you" in each one.

Keeping sentences short

In general, in functional writing, sentences should be short. Short sentences are easier to follow than long ones, and you are less likely to get their structure muddled. Many people advise that a sentence conveying information should be no more than 20 words. It is a good idea to vary the length of your sentences so that your writing does not become monotonous, but try not to go above the 20 word limit. Long sentences need more punctuation than short ones, and this provides more possibilities for error or confusion.

> **TIP**
> Every sentence must have a subject (either stated or clearly implied) and a complete or finite verb.

Sentences are clearer if they deal with only one idea at a time. If you want to make a comparison, or to qualify what you are saying, begin a new sentence.

> **Example**
>
> Although it is a good idea to read as much as possible because it will help to improve your writing style, it is not a good idea to spend so much time reading that you never have time for writing assignments or talking to your colleagues, and so the advice usually given is that students should spend one hour of each day in general reading. [65 words]

The sentence above is grammatically correct, but it is so long that by the time you get to the end, you have forgotten the beginning. It might be written in the following more straightforward way:

Remember, however, that each sentence must have a subject and a finite verb, and it must be a complete unit of meaning.

TIP

If you find that you are using words like "and," "while," "where," "although," "when," and "if" many times, your sentences are probably too long and might need to be broken into smaller units.

> **Example**
>
> It is a good idea to read as much as possible because it will improve your writing style. However, too much time spent in reading will leave you with no time for writing assignments or talking to colleagues. Therefore, we usually advise students to spend one hour each day in general reading.

The run-on sentence or the comma splice

A very common error in sentence structure is for writers to run two sentences together with no **conjunction** and no punctuation (or merely a comma) between them. This seems to happen when writers get so tied up in what they are saying that they forget they have to put out signposts for their readers to show the relationships between the different sections of their writing.

> **Example**
>
> The book was very useful, it showed me how to cook.
> I read a lot, my friend doesn't read at all.
> The book was interesting, therefore I had to finish it.

Each of the examples above has two separate units of meaning and so must be divided in a way that makes that clear. This type of **run-on sentence** can be corrected in three different ways.

Make the two statements into two separate sentences.

> **Example**
>
> The book was very useful. It showed me how to cook.
> I read a lot. My friend doesn't read at all.
> The book was interesting. Therefore, I had to finish it.

Join the two statements with a joining word (conjunction) that shows how they are connected.

> **Example**
> The book was very useful *because* it showed me how to cook.
> I read a lot *but* my friend doesn't read at all.
> The book was interesting *and therefore* I had to finish it.

Separate the two statements with a semicolon.

> **Example**
> The book was very useful; it showed me how to cook.
> I read a lot; my friend doesn't read at all.
> The book was interesting; therefore, I had to finish it.

Use the semicolon to connect the two sentences only if they are closely related in meaning and if you feel confident that you know how to use semicolons. The first two methods of punctuation are easier and safer for most student writers.

Using active and passive verbs

A verb expresses action of some kind, and it always has a subject. When a verb is in the active voice, the subject of the verb is clearly identified as the one who performs the action.

> **Example**
> *Scientists* (subject) *perform* (active verb) many experiments.
> *Most patients* (subject) *feel* (active verb) anxious before surgery.
> *Books* (subject) *provide* (active verb) most information for students.

When a verb is in the passive "voice," as it is called, the subject of the verb is acted upon rather than acting. This is why the verb in this kind of construction is called passive. For example, the sentences above written with the verbs in the passive voice would look like this:

> **Example**
> *Many experiments* (subject) *are performed* (passive verb) by scientists.
> *Anxiety* (subject) *is felt* (passive verb) by most patients before surgery.
> *Most information* (subject) for students *is provided* (passive verb) by books.

Although both sets of examples say the same thing, you can see that the examples using passive voice use more words, are less direct, sound impersonal, can sound pompous, and are weaker in their impact on the reader than the examples using the active construction. The reader has to think longer to work out the meaning of the passive constructions. This effect is more noticeable in a more complex sentence that uses passive constructions:

> **Example**
> The work in this area is being assessed and a decision will be reached next week about whether the surveys will be done by students as part of their project. [30 words]

The same sentence using active voice would be as follows:

> **Example**
> We are assessing the work in this area and will decide next week whether students will do the surveys as part of their project. [24 words]

In general, use active voice unless you have a particular reason for choosing a passive construction.

There are situations in which passives are preferable. For example, you might deliberately want to remove the emphasis from the "doer" of an action because what is done is more important.

> **Example**
> The information has been collected and will be collated as soon as possible.
> Smoking is prohibited.

In the sentences above, the reader's interest might lie with the information rather than with who has done the collecting or collating and with whether he or she can smoke rather than with knowing who has done the prohibiting.

The passive voice is also very useful when you do not know the "doer" of an action:

> **Example**
> The books were taken from the library.
> The DVD was ruined because it was left in the sun.

The passive voice is frequently used by bureaucracies to conceal who did what, and by pompous writers in the mistaken belief that by avoiding first person pronouns they can make their opinions more authoritative.

You should not use the passive to avoid responsibility for your actions or opinions.

> **Example**
>
> The data were examined and it was concluded that the rates were too high.
> Your manuscript has not been accepted and it will be returned to you.

Both of these sentences would be much better in the active voice:

> **Example**
>
> I/we examined the data and concluded that the rates were too high.
> I/we have not accepted your manuscript and will return it to you.

EXERCISE

ACTIVE AND PASSIVE VOICES

Change the following sentences, written in the passive voice, into active sentences.
1. The latte was put on the counter by the barista.
2. The sentences were turned from passive to active voice by the student.

Using parallel structure

Your sentences will be easier to understand if they are consistent in their structure. In any sentence that presents two or more ideas or pieces of information, the different ideas or items you list must be presented in the same form. This is called using **parallel structure**.

> **Example**
>
> The causes of the typhoid outbreak were that there was no clean water, poor housing conditions, and eating contaminated food.

The three causes listed here are not explained in the same way, and so it is hard for the reader to make connections between them. The sentence reads much better like this:

> **Example**
>
> The causes of the typhoid outbreak were that the water was not clean, the housing conditions were poor, and people were eating contaminated food.

In the second version of the sentence, each factor has been listed using the same structural elements (the verb "was" or "were") and so it is easy to compare the items with each other. The sentence could also be written like this:

> **Example**
> The causes of the typhoid outbreak were the lack of clean water, the poor housing conditions, and the contamination of the food supply.

In this case, a different structural element has been used: the nouns "lack," "conditions," and "contamination." There are several ways of writing any one sentence. You should choose the one that you think expresses your meaning most clearly and concisely, but you must make sure that the elements within the sentences are expressed in the same way.

Another example of the same problem can be seen in the following sentence that has bullet points:

KEY CONCEPTS

Faulty parallelism
There are three factors that lead to good writing:
- *choosing* the appropriate vocabulary
- clear *organization* of ideas
- to *make* sure sentences are well structured

This example is inconsistent and hard to follow. The sentence can be corrected most easily by beginning each item in the list in the same way:

KEY CONCEPTS

Using parallel structure
There are three factors that lead to good writing:
- *choosing* the appropriate vocabulary
- *organizing* ideas clearly
- *making* sure sentences are well structured

There are other ways of writing this sentence correctly, depending on which structure you choose.

Many different kinds of sentences can be muddled in this way. You need to proofread carefully to check for this kind of error. Remember, the longer the sentence and the more ideas it contains, the more possibility there is for confusion.

EXERCISE

FAULTY PARALLELISM

Correct the faulty parallelism in the following sentence.

The principal causes of my recent excitement with North American popular culture are James Cameron's *Avatar*, that I can easily get frozen yogourt all over town, and I agree that *The King's Speech* was the best picture of 2010.

FINDING OUT ABOUT CORRECT GRAMMAR

This chapter has dealt with some of the most common problems students have with structuring clear sentences. In doing so, it has touched on some grammatical rules but has not done so comprehensively or in any depth. To provide even a basic guide to English grammar is beyond the scope of this book. If you are concerned about some aspects of your writing that are not dealt with here, you can consult one of many excellent books on usage and style. Fowler's *Modern English Usage*, for example, was first published in 1926 and became a standard reference work but is now dated. It has been replaced by *The New Fowler's Modern English Usage*, edited by R.W. Burchfield (Oxford University Press). There is also a handy concise edition called *Pocket Fowler's Modern English Usage* (Oxford University Press), which is probably the most useful edition for students today. The *Oxford Guide to Canadian English Usage* by Margery Fee and Janice McAlpine (Oxford University Press) and *Editing Canadian English* by the Editors' Association of Canada (revised second edition) are also very useful references for Canadian writers.

GLOSSARY

colloquial language See **slang**.

conjunction A joining word (and, or, nor, but, yet, for, so).

functional writing Focuses not on the writer, or the emotions of the writer or reader, but on the information or ideas being explained, with as little interference as possible.

imperatives Sentences that are stated as orders, with the subject ("you") understood.

jargon The technical language of a particular vocational or professional group.

parallel structure Presenting two or more ideas or pieces of information in the same form.

racism Discriminatory treatment of people on the basis of their race, ethnicity, or nationality.

run-on sentence an unwieldy sentence made up of two or more independent clauses joined by conjunctions.

sentence A group of words expressing a complete thought; it begins with a capital letter, ends with a period, question mark, or exclamation point, and typically contains a subject and a complete or finite verb.

sentence fragment Dependent clauses and phrases lacking principal or independent clauses necessary to complete their meaning.

slang Informal language.

stereotype Use an oversimplified, standardized approach to assign characteristics to a group of people.

trivialize Denigrate people by using language that serves to diminish them (e.g., calling men "assertive" and women "aggressive" when they display the same behaviour).

SUGGESTED FURTHER READING

Australian Government. (1994). *Style Manual for Authors, Editors and Printers*. Sydney: Australian Government Publishing Service.

Allen, Robert. (Ed.) (1999). *Pocket Fowler's Modern English Usage*. Oxford: Oxford University Press.

Burchfield, R.W. (Ed.) (1996). *The New Fowler's Modern English Usage*. (3rd ed.). New York: Oxford University Press.

Editor's Association of Canada. (2000). *Editing Canadian English*. (2nd ed.). Toronto: Mcfarlane Walter & Ross.

Fee, Margery, & McAlpine, Janice. (2007). *Oxford Guide to Canadian English Usage*. New York: Oxford University Press.

Glenn, Cheryl, & Gray, Loretta.(2006). *Hodges Harbrace Handbook*. Scarborough, ON: Thompson/Wadsworth Publishing.

Norton, Sarah, & Green, Brian. (1983). *The Bare Essentials: English Writing Skills*. Toronto: Holt, Rinehart and Winston of Canada.

Strunk, William, & White, E.B. (1999). *The Elements of Style*. New York: Longman.

Williams, Joseph M. (2006). *Style: Lessons in Clarity and Grace*. New York: Pearson-Longman.

RELATED WEBSITES

www.ucc.vt.edu/stdysk/vocabula.html
Cook Counseling Center, Virginia Tech. "Vocabulary: An ongoing process."

www.writing.utoronto.ca/images/stories/Documents/passive-voice.pdf
Corson, Tim, & Smollett, Rebecca. University of Toronto. "Passive voice: When to use it and when to avoid it."

www.noslangues-ourlanguages.gc.ca/bien-well/fra-eng/style/ethnicracial-eng.html
Language Portal of Canada, Government of Canada. (2010). "Eliminating ethnic and racial stereotypes."

www.writing.utoronto.ca/advice/style-and-editing/unbiased-language
Procter, Margaret. University of Toronto. "Unbiased Language."

www.writing.utoronto.ca/advice/style-and-editing/unbiased-language
Taylor, Dena. University of Toronto. "Hit Parade of Errors in Grammar, Punctuation, and Style."

ANSWER KEY TO EXERCISE

Easily Confused Words
1. My high school principal made it a principle never to drink coffee in the afternoon.
2. Her morale was low because she didn't understand the question on the sociology test about the difference between moral and ethical behaviour.
3. Her parents were happy that, because she was just 16, she didn't have access to pubs and other places where people were drinking to excess.
4. He thought he'd better get the pockets of his pants fixed; otherwise, he was going to lose all of his loose change.

Active and Passive Voices
1. The barista put the latte on the counter.
2. The student turned the sentences from passive to active voice.

Faulty Parallelism
The principal causes of my recent excitement with North American popular culture are James Cameron's *Avatar*, the availability of frozen yogourt all over town, and *The King's Speech*'s well-deserved receipt of the 2010 "Best Picture" award.

13

Dotting "i"s: Using Punctuation Correctly

If the English language made any sense, a catastrophe would be an apostrophe with fur.

Doug Larson

Chapter 8 has already considered some aspects of punctuation, in particular where to use periods. This chapter will cover some other aspects of punctuation that cause problems for many student writers: **abbreviations**, **apostrophes**, capital letters, **colons**, **commas**, **ellipses**, **periods**, numbers, and **semicolons**.

WHY IS PUNCTUATION IMPORTANT?

Using accurate punctuation is essential to writing clearly. Punctuation marks act as signposts to the writer's intentions. Without them, writing would be impossible to decipher (just take a look at Molly Bloom's soliloquy in James Joyce's *Ulysses*!). The good news for modern writers is that over the years, punctuation has become simpler. As technology makes documents easier to read, we need less punctuation to help us separate or combine words, phrases, or clauses. Hyphens, capital letters, and commas, for example, are used less frequently than they were even ten years ago. The bad news is that there are no hard-and-fast rules that apply in every situation. Even experts often disagree about how and when some forms of punctuation should be used. Usage is changing so quickly that something you learned in elementary school could be out of date by the time you start university. What follows is a basic guide to the *essential* rules of using punctuation marks in functional writing. It is by no means complete.

USING ABBREVIATIONS AND OTHER SHORTENED FORMS OF WORDS OR PHRASES

Abbreviations of words and phrases are used in writing to save time and space and to eliminate repetition. It is not appropriate to use abbreviations in formal writing. In a formal essay, for example, you would not use "e.g." instead of "for example," or "i.e." instead of "that is." As a general rule, abbreviate only where not to do so would involve much tedious repetition. In writing notes for your own use, abbreviations are invaluable, but in formal writing they create too informal a tone and suggest that you cannot be bothered spelling things out for your reader. *Abbreviations should be there to help the reader understand, not to save the writer effort.* Abbreviations are commonly used, for example, in scientific, technical, and specialist publications where the same terms appear over and over again and where readers will have a shared knowledge of them.

Some abbreviations, such as e.g., i.e., and symbols for weights and measures, such as kg and km, are so well known that you can use them, *when it is appropriate*, as ordinary words without explanation. RCMP and HTML also come into this category. With most abbreviations, however, you must write out the full word or words the first time you want to abbreviate a word or phrase and put the abbreviation in parentheses immediately afterwards. Once you have made the meaning of the abbreviation clear to your readers, you can use it throughout the rest of your text.

> **TIP**
>
> Abbreviations must be clear, specific, and consistent. Use them to help your reader, not to save time in writing.

> **Example**
> The findings of the International Monetary Fund (IMF) were that . . . with the result that the IMF will now . . .
> The Canadian Union of Public Employees (CUPE) has revised its policy on . . . and academic administrators, according to CUPE, must recognize these new conditions.

The correct form for abbreviations

Abbreviations that consist of the first letter of a word and one or more other letters are usually written with a period at the end.

Abbreviations that have more than one capital letter are written without periods:

> **Example**
> Mon. (Monday), etc. (et cetera), i.e. (id est; that is), e.g. (exempli gratia; for example), Feb. (February), Vic. (Victoria), vol. (volume), dept. (department).

> **Example**
> PEI, NB, SSHRC, CBC, US

Using acronyms

Acronyms are shortened forms of names or titles that are always pronounced as words. They are usually formed from the initial letters of other words or from a number of letters taken from the word or phrase being shortened. Acronyms are always written without periods. Usually, where the full word or title has capital letters, the acronym does as well: for example, WHO, SEATO, CSIS. If the complete word or title does not have capitals, the acronym does not either: for example, sonar (sound navigation and ranging), laser (light amplification by stimulated emission of radiation), scuba (self-contained underwater breathing apparatus), radar (radio detection and ranging). There are some exceptions to this, usually where the acronym is used for the name of a very well-known organization and often accepted as that organization's proper name.

> **Example**
> Unicef (United Nations Children's Fund)
> CUPE (Canadian Union of Public Employees)
> Nato (North Atlantic Treaty Organization)

If the acronym is not very well known or could create confusion for some other reason, it should be written in capital letters:

> **Example**
> POW (prisoner of war)
> MS (manuscript)
> TV (television)
> PS (postscript)

One practice, which used to be widespread, was to place an apostrophe before the "s" in making an abbreviation or acronym into a plural form. This is no longer accepted practice and, as with other words, you should make an abbreviation plural by adding just "s". Following are some examples:

Pluralizing abbreviations	
Write	**Do not write**
All the POWs were sent home.	All the POW's were sent home.
There are three TVs in the house.	There are three TV's in the house.
The MPs are well paid.	The MP's are well paid.

EXERCISE

MAKING ABBREVIATIONS AND ACRONYMS PLURAL

For each of the following, make the singular form plural:
1.   1 MS; 2 MS_   2.   1 TV; 2 TV_

USING APOSTROPHES CORRECTLY

The apostrophe causes more misunderstanding than any other punctuation mark. The rules for its use are simple, but recognizing those rules in practice is very difficult for many people. There are two main uses for the apostrophe: to show possession and to indicate that letters have been left out of a word.

> **Example**
>
> The student's experiment (the experiment of the student)
>
> The committee's decisions (the decisions of the committee)
>
> The animal's characteristics (the characteristics of the animal)

Using the possessive apostrophe

An apostrophe plus "s" following the final letter of a singular noun indicates ownership of the word immediately following.

If a noun is plural and already ends in "s," then, to show possession, you must add an apostrophe alone after the final "s":

> **Example**
>
> The students' experiment (the experiment of the students)
>
> The committees' decisions (the decisions of the committees)
>
> The animals' characteristics (the characteristics of the animals)

Some plural nouns do not end in "s"; for example, "women," "men," "children," "sheep." You should treat these nouns in the same way as the singular forms and add an apostrophe plus "s" to indicate that they are possessive.

Example

The children's toys (the toys of the children)

The women's work (the work of the women)

The men's work (the work of the men)

The sheep's wool (the wool of the sheep)

Remember that the whole point of using an apostrophe to show possession is to distinguish the possessive form of the noun from the simple plural. *You never use an apostrophe to indicate a plural.*

KEY CONCEPTS

Plurals

Write	Do not write
I bought a kilo of tomatoes.	I bought a kilo of tomato's.
The animals slept outside.	The animals' slept outside.
The shoes were a good fit.	The shoe's were a good fit.
There are many books in the library.	There are many books' in the library.

In the preceding examples, the nouns *tomatoes, animals, shoes,* and *books* are the plural forms of *tomato, animal, shoe,* and *book*. None of them possesses anything in these sentences. None of them needs an apostrophe. Using apostrophes in plurals is now very common in ordinary communication, *but it is incorrect.*

Possessive apostrophes are used only with nouns. The pronouns *his, hers, your, my, our, their,* and *its* are already possessive. There is often confusion about *it's* and *its*. The apostrophe shows that *it's* is short for *it is*. Without an apostrophe, *its* means "belonging to it."

Example

The dog is wagging its tail.

It's a happy dog!

EXERCISE

POSSESSIVE APOSTROPHE

Where appropriate, add an apostrophe to make the possessive form:
1. The Trail Smoke Eaters [singular possessive] rule
2. The Trail Smoke Eaters [plural possessive] rule
3. The Trail Smoke Eaters [plural, but not possessive] rule [where "rule" is being used as a verb]!
4. Its (singular possessive) rule

Using the apostrophe to show contractions

When two words are contracted to form one word, an apostrophe is used in place of the missing letters.

Contractions

cannot becomes *can't*

you will becomes *you'll*

do not becomes *don't*

it is becomes *it's*

This use of the apostrophe is straightforward and usually does not cause writers the same problems as the possessive apostrophe.

USING CAPITAL LETTERS

Use capitals in the following positions:

- For the first word in a sentence: The end is nigh.
- For the proper names, or titles, of specific individuals, institutions, official positions, languages, races, countries, and nationalities: This is where Uncle Fred lives (but: This is where my uncle lives); Prime Minister Harper (but: She is a government minister); the University of the Fraser Valley (but: He attends university); French, Canadian, Austria, Hungary, New Zealand.
- For the days of the week, months, and special days of the year: Monday, January, Ramadan, Rosh Hashanah (but: spring, autumn).
- For the title of a relationship if it is taking the place of a specific person's name: I know that Mother will do it (but: I will ask my mother to do it); Did you know that Aunt Lina has gone home? (but: My aunt, who is named Lina, has gone home.)

- For the first word in quoting direct speech: He said, "Once more should do it."
- For the first, last, and every important word in the title of a book, journal, article, painting, musical or dance composition, video, or film: *The Principles of Semantics; The Creature from the Black Lagoon; New World Symphony.* In another style of capitalization, only the first word in a title and subtitle are capitalized.

Capital letters are used less often in modern writing. Some people use capitals to begin any word that is important to them. You should resist this temptation. The importance of one word or name over another is a matter of personal opinion, and your ideas might be very different from those of your readers. Some people, for example, wrongly give capitals to titles such as professor or doctor. A professor or a doctor is no different from a teacher, a nurse, or a firefighter, and none of these occupational titles needs capitalization, except where it is given as the title of a specific individual.

> **TIP**
>
> Capital letters should be used sparingly, and only for specific purposes. Their use is never optional.

> ## EXERCISE
>
> **USING CAPITAL LETTERS**
>
> Add capital letters where necessary.
>
> 1. Do you think that dad will let us go?
> 2. I heard that her mother has wanted a new car since january.
> 3. He asked, "do you suppose that the professor will be away for passover?"

USING COLONS

Colons are expressed by two periods, one above the other. They are often confused with semicolons, which consist of a period above a comma. Colons have very limited applications, but in the three situations in which you can employ them, they serve a very useful purpose. This book is full of colons because it is the kind of book where colons come into their own as a vital piece of punctuation.

Colons mean "as follows" and their main use is to introduce lists, as they have done all through this chapter.

If you look back through this book, you will see the colon used many times. Without colons, many of the examples and lists in the book would have needed much more cumbersome introductions.

USING SEMICOLONS

Semicolons also have very limited functions in modern writing. You could go through your whole life without using a semicolon, and it would not matter since other punctuation will do just as well.

The colon

The colon has three uses:

- to introduce a list of items
- to introduce a quotation
- to separate an example from the statement that introduces it

The semicolon: lists

The place where a semicolon is most useful is in separating the items in a list, where each individual item has subgroups within it that are divided by commas. For example: There were several factors influencing the government's decision: the improved rates of employment, inflation, and foreign debt; the favourable reaction from ethnic groups, new migrants, and social welfare groups; and the good harvests in wheat, barley, and sugar.

In this example, because each item on the list is long and involved, the semicolons clarify the divisions between the different items and make the list easy to follow. Note that the list is introduced by a colon. The separate items on the list should not begin with a capital letter because they are all part of the same sentence. You do not use semicolons to separate single words or short items in a list. For example, "They painted the room in three colours: red, blue, and green." Semicolons are only necessary if each item on the list is long and could confuse the reader. When each item is short, use commas between each one.

You can also use a semicolon to join two independent clauses that you might otherwise join by a conjunction or divide into two separate sentences. The clauses must contain ideas that are quite closely related to one another. This use of the semicolon has been discussed in chapter 8.

Example
The semicolon: Independent clauses

The government will call an early election; it expects to win easily.

EXERCISE

COLONS AND SEMICOLONS

Punctuate where necessary:

We decided to pack a picnic containing our favourite things some poached salmon which is Michelles favourite some cold fiddlehead salad which Kue adores and butter tarts which I love I cant wait it sounds like a great meal!

USING COMMAS

Commas have specific functions in structuring clear sentences. Contrary to popular opinion, you do not just put a comma into a sentence to imitate the way you would break up the sentence if you were speaking. Written expression is different from spoken expression, and by inserting commas as you would in speech, you break up the rhythm of the sentence and often confuse the reader. Many people scatter commas through their sentences in the hope that these magic marks will somehow make everything clear. Too often, they have the opposite effect.

To some extent, you have to use your own judgment about when to use commas, since the rules governing their use are not as hard and fast as those for capital letters, semicolons, or apostrophes. Set out below are guidelines that outline the eight most common uses for commas.

Use a comma before *and, but, for, or, nor, yet*, and *so*, when they separate two independent clauses with different subjects.

> **Example**
> The disease spread very rapidly, and the authorities could not keep it in check.
> *Jane Eyre* is a great novel, but *Wuthering Heights* is more popular with young readers.

Use a comma after an introductory expression, to divide it from the main part of the sentence.

> **Example**
> If you are having trouble with your writing, you should practise by keeping a diary.
> If the test tube is not dry, there might be an explosion.

Use commas around information that is not essential to the sentence's meaning to divide it from the rest of the sentence.

> **Example**
> The documents, which had been completed in a hurry, were delivered to the registrar's office on time.
> Good diet and regular exercise, although not very popular with most people, are the keys to good health.
> The leader, Aamir Khan, will conduct the new surveys.

Use commas between the items in a series if those items could be separated by "and."

TIP

As with capital letters, you should use as few commas as you can, but you must use them in places where they indicate the correct meaning of your sentence.

TIP

The comma inserted before the conjunction joining two independent clauses is sometimes omitted when the clauses are short and to the point.

> **Example**
>
> Vocabulary, grammar, punctuation, and paragraph structure are all important aspects of writing.
>
> Mining involves geologists, surveyors, engineers, mechanics, and workers in many other areas.

In Canada, as in America, writers often place a comma before the "and" in the final pair of a series. This use of the **serial comma**, although not universally accepted, avoids ambiguity.

Most people, though, no longer put commas between the items in a short series of adjectives.

> **Example**
>
> The fragrant green foliage is characteristic of these trees.
>
> They took the old dusty fishing line from its hiding place.

It is not, however, incorrect to do so:

> **Example**
>
> The fragrant, green foliage is characteristic of these trees.
>
> They took the old, dusty fishing line from its hiding place.

Use commas around the name of a person you are addressing.

> **Example**
>
> Your support, Ms.Tran, will be essential to the project.
>
> You said, Ting, that you would be here on time.

Use commas around a word that interrupts the sentence: for example, "however," "moreover," or "therefore."

> **Example**
>
> The causes, however, are more interesting than they appear at first.
>
> We worked hard, moreover, to achieve this score.
>
> The results, therefore, should be interesting.

Use a comma for words in **appostion**:

> **Example**
>
> My best friend, Anil, will be going to the movies with us.
>
> He is going with Dr. Goldman, his English professor, and one of the dons from his residence.

Use a comma to introduce a short direct quotation.

> **Example**
>
> The writer said, "I always think about commas in bed."
>
> John Donne wrote, "No man is an island."

EXERCISE

USING COMMAS

Insert commas where needed:

1. Roz are you going with us?
2. She packed everything into her backpack: her laptop cell phone mp3 player and chemistry textbook.
3. He has one of those dull green canvas coats that everyone is wearing.
4. If I were going though I wouldn't leave until after midnight.

USING ELLIPSES

An ellipsis is three periods in a row. An ellipsis indicates that you have left some words out of a direct quotation. The ellipsis can be very useful in allowing you to leave out parts of a quotation that are not relevant to your purpose, while making clear to the reader that you have done so. It is essential, however, that you do not use the ellipsis to distort or falsify the meaning of the quotation. The part you quote must be true to the intention and spirit of the original. An ellipsis is also used sometimes to indicate that there is more of what you are writing but that you are not putting it all down. This second usage is only appropriate in informal writing.

> **Example**
>
> As the report claims, "There are many factors in determining the state of the economy . . . but the most important is retail sales." (formal usage)
>
> She talked for hours with a list of complaints about the state of the weather, the state of her health, the state of the economy . . . (informal usage, inappropriate for formal writing)

Do not use an ellipsis at the beginning of a sentence.

USING PERIODS

The period signals the ends of sentences and some abbreviations. It is used more often than any other form of punctuation in English. The period has been discussed earlier, in chapter 12 in the section on sentence structure, and in this chapter in the section on abbreviations.

USING NUMBERS

Numbers can be written in figures or words. Whether you use figures or words depends on the context in which you are writing and the position and function of the numbers in your sentences.

In most formal writing, use words rather than figures for numbers of less than 10. Single-digit numbers are easier to understand when they appear in written form.

In narrative or descriptive writing, express numbers of less than 100 in words since figures interrupt the flow of the writing and look inappropriate in a text that uses words exclusively.

In scientific, technical, mathematical, or statistical writing, use figures rather than words because figures and symbols are used often in this context, and precise values are an important requirement of the text.

Do not use figures at the beginning of a sentence in any kind of writing. A sentence must always begin with a word. If you wish to use figures only in your text, you must structure your sentence so that the first word is not a number.

Example

Three hundred new workers are joining the company next week.

Next week, 300 new workers will join the company.

Never write the following:

Example

300 new workers will join the company next week.

Always use figures to express numbers that are accompanied by units of measurement or symbols.

Example

The recommended single dose of this drug is 250 mg twice a day.

The new glasses will cost $5.70 each.

The pipe's diameter is 9 mm and its length is 10 m.

USING QUOTATION MARKS

Quotation marks indicate that you are quoting the exact words of another person. Most publications use double quotation marks for direct quotations, reserving single quotation marks for a quotation within your first quotation.

Example

Alexander Pope wrote, "True Wit is Nature to advantage drest,/ What oft was Thought, but ne'er so well Exprest."

She said, "There are many examples of 'Nature to advantage drest' in the poetry of Pope."

For long quotations, usually those longer than four or five lines and 40 to 50 words, you should not use quotation marks but indent the quotation instead.

Example

According to Jonathan Swift's Gulliver, the Lilliputians had an ideal system of education for their children:

> Their opinion is, that parents are the last of all others to be trusted with the education of their own children: and therefore they have in every town publick nurseries, where all parents, except cottagers and labourers, are obliged to send their infants of both sexes to be reared and educated when they come to the age of twenty moons . . . .

But I doubt that modern readers would agree with his views on the ideal education for children.

As you can see from the examples above, in direct quotations you must keep the spelling and punctuation of the original writer, even if they do not conform to modern usage or are incorrect. If you know that a quotation contains wrong or inappropriate spelling, punctuation, or any other feature that you do not want your readers to hold you responsible for, you should put the word "*sic*" in square brackets immediately after the incorrect word in the quotation: [*sic*]. Sic is a Latin word that literally means "thus" and has been adapted in this context to mean "that is how it was." You should not overdo this device. In the excerpts quoted above, for example, it is unnecessary since it should be obvious that the spelling and punctuation are those of the original writers.

Placing punctuation when quoting

Periods and commas precede closing quotation marks; colons and semicolons follow closing quotation marks; and question marks and exclamation points follow closing quotation marks unless they are part of the material being quoted.

You also use quotation marks to distinguish the titles of short publications and pieces of writing, such as articles from journals or newspapers, chapters of books, short poems, essays, lectures, and songs.

You do not use quotation marks for the titles of books, films, operas, newspapers, journals, or magazines. For these you use italics (for example, *Time Magazine, Gulliver's Travels, The Lion King, British Journal of Educational Psychology*).

FINDING OUT MORE ABOUT PUNCTUATION

This chapter has dealt with some punctuation marks that cause problems for student writers. There are other punctuation conventions that have not been mentioned, either because most people know how to use them or because they are not used very often. If you need more information about English punctuation, you can consult a number of excellent books or websites that deal with punctuation in much more detail (for example, *The Copyeditor's Handbook*, 2006 or the Purdue Online Writing Lab website).

GLOSSARY

abbreviation Shortened form of a word or phrase used in writing to save time and space and to eliminate repetition.

apostrophe A form of punctuation (') used to show possession and to indicate that letters have been left out of a word.

apposition Placing two words (usually nouns) beside one another, with one serving to define the other.

colon A form of punctuation (:) with three uses: introduces a list of items, introduces a quotation, and separates an example from the statement that introduces it.

comma A form of punctuation (,) with a number of uses: it is used between items in a series, to separate two independent clauses joined by a conjunction, to divide an introductory dependent clause from the independent clause that follows it, and to introduce a short quotation.

ellipsis Three periods in a row (. . .), indicating that some words have been left out of a direct quotation.

period A form of punctuation (.) that signals the ends of sentences and some abbreviations.

quotation marks   A form of punctuation (" ") indicating that you are quoting the exact words of another person.

semicolon   A form of punctuation (;) used to separate the items in a list, where each individual item has subgroups within it that are divided by commas, and to join two independent clauses.

serial comma   A comma inserted before the "and" or "or" that precedes the final item in a list.

SUGGESTED FURTHER READING

Baker, Nicholson. (1996). The history of punctuation. In *The size of thoughts*. New York: Random House.

Editors' Association of Canada. (2000). *Editing Canadian English* (2nd ed.). Toronto: McClelland & Stewart.

Einsohn, Amy. (2006). *The copyeditor's handbook*. Berkeley: University of California Press.

Truss, Lynne. (2004). *Eats, shoots & leaves*. New York: Gotham Books.

RELATED WEBSITES

www.sti.nasa.gov/publish/sp7084.pdf
McCaskill, Mary K. Langley Research Center. "Grammar, punctuation, and capitalization: A handbook for technical writers and editors."

www.writing.utoronto.ca/images/stories/Documents/punctuation.pdf
Plotnick, Jerry. University of Toronto. "Punctuation."

http://owl.english.purdue.edu/owl/section/1/6/
Purdue Online Writing Lab. "Punctuation."

www.writing.utoronto.ca/images/stories/Documents/hit-parade-of-errors.pdf
Taylor, Dena, & Procter, Margaret. University of Toronto. "Hit parade of errors in grammar, punctuation, and style."

ANSWER KEY TO EXERCISE

Making Abbreviations and Acronyms Plural

1. MSs

2. TVs

Possessive Apostrophes

1. Trail Smoke Eater's

3. Trail Smoke Eaters

2. Trail Smoke Eaters'

4. Its

Using Capital Letters

1. Do you think that Dad will let us go?

2. I heard that her mother has wanted a new car since January.

3. He asked, "Do you suppose that the professor will be away for Passover?"

Colons and Semicolons

We decided to pack a picnic containing our favourite things: some poached salmon, which is Michelle's favourite; some cold fiddlehead salad, which Kue adores; and butter tarts, which I love. I can't wait; it sounds like a great meal!

Using Commas

1. Roz, are you going with us?
2. She packed everything into her backpack: her laptop, cell phone, mp3 player[,] and chemistry textbook.
3. He has one of those dull[,] green canvas coats that everyone is wearing.
4. If I were going, though, I wouldn't leave until after midnight.

Owning Up: Acknowledging Sources

A man will turn over half a library to make one book.

Samuel Johnson

When you use information that has originally appeared in someone else's work, you must acknowledge clearly where you found it. You must always make the acknowledgement in a consistent and recognizable format. Such acknowledgements are called "references." In your academic work you are expected to draw on evidence from, and substantiate claims with, *up-to-date*, *relevant*, and *reputable* sources. The *number* and *range of references* used for your work are also important.

Citing references

You must cite all references in order to

- acknowledge previous work conducted by other scholars;
- allow the reader to verify your data; and
- provide information so the reader can consult your sources independently.

What must you acknowledge?

You *must* clearly acknowledge your references when you

- *quote* (use the original source's exact words);
- *paraphrase* (express a source's ideas in different words); or
- *summarize* (outline the main points of) information, ideas, text, data, tables, figures, or any other material that originally appeared in someone else's work.

References may be to sources such as books, journals, newspapers, websites, videos, photographs, blog posts, or personal communications (such as letters, emails, or conversations). References must provide enough **bibliographic** information for your reader to be able to find your source easily. "Bibliographic" refers to the key descriptive elements of a publication such as a book, journal article, video, or online resource. These elements include details such as author, date of publication, title, volume number, and page numbers.

Systems of referencing

There are three principal systems of referencing:

- the **APA** (American Psychological Association) **system**, a parenthetical author-date reference system used primarily in the social and behavioural sciences
- the **MLA** (Modern Language Association) **system**, a parenthetical author-page reference system used primarily in the humanities
- the **CMS** (*Chicago Manual of Style*) **system**, which includes a footnoted and endnoted reference system used in the humanities (also called the **Turabian system**) as well as a parenthetical author-date reference system used in the life, physical, and social sciences

All are discussed in the following pages. Of the three systems, the APA system (and variants of it) is the most widely used, although the others sometimes have greater currency in specific disciplines. For example, the APA system is frequently employed in anthropology and sociology, but both disciplines also have reference systems specific to them: the American Anthropological Association system and the American Sociological Association, respectively. The *CMS* author-date system has widespread use in biology and chemistry, although the American Medical Association system is widely used for medicine and public health. You should use the system of referencing that your professor recommends. Whichever system you adopt, though, be sure to consult the most recent edition and to employ the same style throughout any single piece of work.

Despite the frequency with which electronic sources (the Internet, email) are now used, there are few comprehensive, consistent, and definitive guidelines for citing electronic sources (Library of Congress, 2005). The sections below include some efforts to help remedy this by suggesting formats for a wide range of contemporary sources (for example, Facebook, electronic journals, email, or software). Should you have a type of source not included below, adhere to the same fundamental principles that are used in print media referencing. In short, make sure that you give enough details for readers to be able to track down for themselves the source you are citing. Present that information in a sequence that is consistent with the information you provide for your other sources.

THE APA SYSTEM

The APA system comprises two essential components:

- an *in-text author and parenthetical date* or *parenthetical author-date citations* noted throughout your work
- a comprehensive *list of references* cited at the end of the work.[1]

The in-text citation gives the author's (authors') name(s) followed by the parenthetical date of publication. The parenthetical reference gives the surname of the *author(s)* followed by a comma and the *date* of publication; if you are citing a direct quotation, you must follow it with parentheses containing the *page number(s)* where the information or quotation can be found (American Psychological Association, Basics of APA Style Tutorial). The list of references gives the author's full surname and the given name initials, year of publication (in parentheses), the title of the publication, the name of the publisher, and place of publication. Articles in journals should now also include the **DOI** (Digital Object Identifier). Different types of references are discussed more fully below.

In-text references

An in-text reference presents a summary of bibliographic details in the following ways. Take particular note of the ways in which the various references are punctuated.

If the reference is to a direct quotation

> As Bloggs (2006) has so clearly indicated, there is at present a "significant challenge" (p. 50) confronting geography . . .
>
> As has been so clearly indicated, there is at present a "significant challenge" (Bloggs, 2006, p. 50) confronting geography . . .

Either of the citations above is correct; use the form that is least intrusive.

Although the standard APA style does *not* ascribe page numbers to text that is paraphrased or summarized, some professors may want you to do this. It is always wise to consult with your individual professor to determine his or her preference on this matter (Procter, 2010).

---

1   Footnotes may be used within the author-date system to provide, for example, an aside or information supplementary to the main text. Indeed, this is an example of such a footnote. Details on the use of footnotes are provided in the section on "Notes and note identifiers" later in this chapter.

If the reference is to a number of different publications

Several authors (Brown, 2006; Henare, 2004; Biderman, 2005) agree . . .

Note that each reference is separated from the next by a semicolon. If more than one work by the same author is cited, the referenced dates are separated from each other by commas (for example, Hay, 1995, 1996; Hay & Bull, 2002). It is common practice to set out such lists alphabetically by author name, following the form of the "References" section.

If the reference is to a single text written by two people

A recent study (Chan & D'Ettorre, 2002) has shown . . .
Chan and D'Ettorre (2002) have shown that . . .

Note that the names are linked within parentheses by an ampersand (&) but with an "and" if the names are incorporated within the text.

If the reference is to a single text written by three to five authors

- The *first in-text* citation includes all three authors:

  Flurkey, Astle, and Harrison (2010) argue that . . .

- *Subsequent in-text* citations use "**et al.**":

  Flurkey et al. (2010) argue that . . .

- The *first parenthetical* citation includes all three authors:

  Understanding the role of diet in extending the life span of mice (Flurkey, Astle, & Harrison, 2010) . . .

- *Subsequent parenthetical* citations use "et al.":

  Understanding the role of diet in extending the life span of mice (Flurkey et al., 2010) . . .

If the reference is to a single text written by five or more authors

- The *first* and all *subsequent in-text* citations use "et al."

  Bertoni-Freddari et al. (1980) discuss the implications . . .

- The *first* and all *subsequent parenthetical* citations use "et al."

  Demystifying the role of dietary restriction in modulating synaptic structural dynamics in the aging hippocampus (Bertoni-Freddari et al., 1980), they confront . . .

The abbreviation "et al." is short for *et alii* and means "and others."

> **TIP**
> In-text references provide summary bibliographic details only. Full details of each reference should be included in a separate list of references at the end of your work.

If the reference is to an anonymously written work

> This is apparently not the case in Thailand (*Far Eastern Economic Review*, 28 January 2003).
> *Poughkeepsie Yearning* (1963) offers fine testament to this view.

The expressions "Anonymous" and "Anon." should not be used unless this is how the author has been identified in the original work (Williams College Libraries, 2010). Instead, the work's title is given.

If the reference is to work written by a committee or an organization

> OFA (2004) suggests that soil degradation is of major concern to the agricultural community in Ontario.
> Natural disasters have been responsible for significant geological transformation in Newfoundland and Labrador (Natural Resources Canada, 2006).

Occasionally, a publication will have both individual and organizational authors listed. In such cases, it is common practice to treat the individual as author. The organization is mentioned when giving full details in the list of references cited.

If the reference is to one author referred to in the writings of another

> Motor vehicles are a major cause of noise pollution in urban areas (Hassan, in Yeo, 2005).

Avoid such references unless tracing the original source is impossible. You are expected to find the original source yourself to ensure that the information has not been misinterpreted or misquoted by the intermediate author.

Referencing sources other than books and journals

Inevitably, you will find yourself wanting to acknowledge sources such as private correspondence, interviews, television transcripts, and so on. It is best to consult a complete online or print version of the APA system (or whatever other citation system that you are using) to get the most current information about how best to do this.

If the reference is to electronic information

The style of reference provided is the same as that for individual, group, organizational, and committee authors as outlined above. The in-text reference should indicate the author's name (which may be an institution) and provide details of the year in which the reference was created or last amended (for websites this is usually noted towards the end of a page as "Page last updated on . . .").

TIP

Electronic sources present some referencing challenges. Be sure to provide enough information about them to allow someone else to find the source.

The National Aids Information Clearinghouse (2002) guidelines give clear advice on . . .

The full text of David Harvey's (1989) book *The Condition of Postmodernity* is now available online.

The in-text reference for an online resource should *not* include the site or page's URL. This information is included only in the reference list.

KEY CONCEPTS

Citing emails, blog posts, youtube, facebook, and twitter

- *Emails* should be cited as other written communications. They are not included in your reference list.

  > G. Noble (personal communication, 9 August 2010)

  > (G. Noble, personal communication, 9 August 2010)

- *Blog posts* are sometimes written under assumed or screen names. This is the name that you should list as the author of the entry (Williams College Libraries, 2010).

  > In her meditation on "Student success and 'The King's Speech': Imagine a friend listening to you as you work," M.F. (20 September 2010) writes . . . [Web log message]

- *YouTube* sometimes has short videos that you might want to cite. Again, use the screen name for your author reference (Williams College Libraries, 2010).

  > In a bittersweet online video called "Procrastination: Tales of mere existence," AgentXPQ (9 October 2006) bemoans . . . [Video file]

- *Facebook* and *Twitter* do not have clearly defined referencing guidelines created for them in the APA system yet. Scholars wishing to make reference to Facebook or Twitter should consult the Social Media section of the APA Style Blog (American Psychological Association, 2010) for the most current thinking on this matter.

EXERCISE

IN-TEXT REFERENCING USING THE APA SYSTEM

Using the APA in-text system, cite the following:

> The article "Age-Related Macular Degeneration; Research from Ohio State University, Department of Ophthalmology, Yields New Findings on Age-Related Macular Degeneration" appeared as an "anonymous" contribution to *Obesity, Fitness & Wellness Week*. It was published on 12 February 2011. The article, seen on page 2076, looks at recent findings suggesting that the use of PRLs could be beneficial to sufferers of age-related macular degeneration.

List of references

This *alphabetically* ordered (by surname of author) list provides the complete bibliographic details of all sources actually referred to in the text. By convention, it does not include those sources you consulted but have not cited (a full list of *all* references consulted is known as a *bibliography*).

The following examples of correctly formatted references may be useful when you prepare your own reference lists. The examples cover only the most commonly encountered sources. Remember that this is no more than an introduction to the APA style: it is no substitute for the complete print or online version.

KEY CONCEPTS

APA List of references

Note that

- the second and subsequent lines of each reference are indented (this is called a **hanging indent** and a computer command will do it for you);
- only the first letter of book, journal, and article titles is capitalized. The first letter after a colon is capitalized, as well;
- book and journal titles are italicized or underlined; article and chapter titles are *not*; and
- for all journal articles and, whenever possible, for all recent books, a Digital Object Identifier (DOI) must be provided. For example,

Pomerance, M. (2006). Hitchcock quotes: Imagining understanding. *Quarterly Review of Film and Video, 23*, 139–54. doi:10.1080/1050920059049068.

TIP

Bibliographic management software (e.g., EndNote, ProCite, RefWorks, Son of Citation) now makes organizing and setting out references easier than ever before.

Book with a single author
Pomerance, M. (2005). *Johnny Depp starts here*. New Brunswick, NJ: Rutgers University Press.

Multiple entries by same author
If you have cited two or more works written by the same author, they should be listed in alphabetical order by year of publication. If they were written in the same year, add lower-case letters to the year of publication in both the reference list *and* the text to distinguish one publication from another (for example, 1987a, 1987b).

Krugman, P. (1991a). History versus expectations. *Quarterly Journal of Economics. 106* (2), 651–67.

Krugman, P. (1991b). Increasing returns and economic geography. *Journal of Political Economy. 99*, 483–99.

TIP

An incorrectly formatted reference list reflects poorly on your work.

Journal entries
Lack, L.C. (1986). Delayed sleep and sleep loss in university students. *Journal of American College Health. 35*, 105–10.

Meyer, T.D., & Maier, S. (2006). Is there evidence for social rhythm insta-
bility in people at risk for affective disorders? *Psychiatry Research. 14*,
103–14. doi: 10.1016.j.psychres.2005.07.023.

Tempesta, D., Couyoumdjian, A., Curcio, G., Moroni, F., Marzan, L.,
& Ferrara, M. (2010). Lack of sleep affects the evaluation of emotional stimuli. *Brain Research Bulletin. 82*, 104–8. doi: 10.1016/j.
brainresbul.2010.01.014.

Note that although the APA recommends that you include a DOI in your
reference section, in some instances, as in the first entry above, none
might exist.

TIP

Set your reference list
out in alphabetical
order.

EXERCISE

APA REFERENCE LIST

How would the following two journal articles appear in a reference list at the back of
your essay?

1.   A book entitled *Drugs and Society* (10th edition), written by four authors: Glen
     R. Hanson, Peter J. Hanson, Peter J. Venturelli, and Annette E. Fleckenstein. It
     was published in 2009 by Jones and Bartlett in New York.

2.   An article called "Social/Ecological Transformation in Northwest Newfound-
     land" that was written by Lawrence Hamilton, Cynthia Duncan, and Richard
     Haedrich. It appeared on pages 195–215 of the journal *Population and
     Environment*, volume 25, issue 3.

THE MLA SYSTEM

The Modern Language Association (MLA) system is another very frequently used citation method. Most often employed in the humanities,
it has been simplified considerably over the years. In the sciences and
social sciences, it is critical that the information being referenced be as
current as possible, but this is in most cases not an issue in the humanities. That is why the date of the text isn't given as much prominence in
the MLA system as it is in the other (APA, *CMS*, or CSE/AMA) referencing
styles.

Source references are generally placed within parentheses immediately after a direct quotation or paraphrased text. The "signal word" placed
within the parenthetical reference must correspond to the first word on the
left-hand margin of the relevant entry in the reference list or **Works Cited**
section of the paper (Writing Lab, OWL at Purdue, & Purdue University,
2010). Generally, if the author is indicated within the text itself, only a
page number is included within the parentheses; if no specific author is

indicated within the text itself, the author and page number will appear within the parentheses.

> **Example**
> **Parenthetical and in-text citations in the MLA system**
>
> In his meditation on the importance of metaphor, Frye considers the difficulty involved in shaping narrative (14).
>
> "In fiction, the technical problems of shaping a story . . . don't change much in whatever time or culture the story's being told" (Frye, 14).

The MLA system distinguishes between online and hard copy sources by indicating either "online" or "print," respectively, at the end of each entry in the Works Cited section of a research paper. The MLA does not require URLs for online sources, although you may, if you like or if your professor asks for it, include Web addresses in angle brackets (Writing Lab et al., 2010). Notice that all of the significant words in the titles of books and journal articles are capitalized; each author's full given name(s) and surname are included, not simply, as in the APA system, his or her surname and initial(s).

> **Example**
> **Works Cited or Reference List in the MLA System**
>
> Frye, Northrop. *The Educated Imagination*. Toronto: Canadian Broadcast Corporation, 1963. Print.
>
> Kertzer, Jon. "Northrop Frye and the Phenomenology of Print." *University of Toronto Quarterly* 78(1): (Winter 2009): 429–31. Print.
>
> Munk, Linda. "Words with Power: Being a Second Study of 'The Bible and Literature.'" Volume 26 of Collected Works of Northrop Frye (review). *University of Toronto Quarterly* 79.1 (2010): 513–14. Project MUSE. University of Toronto, Toronto, ON. 18 August 2010. http://muse.jhu.edu.myaccess.library.utoronto.ca/ Online.
>
> "Nova Scotia Connection: 'The War Was On.'" *The Elizabeth Bishop Centenary: 1911–2011*. 09 May 2010. Online.
>
> Pomerance, Murray, and John Sakeris, eds. *Popping Culture*. Boston: Pearson/Education, 2009. Print.
>
> Thacker, Robert, ed. *The End of the Story: Critical Essays on Alice Munro*. Toronto: ECW Press, 1999. Print.
>
> Todd, Paula. "Mavis Gallant at 86." *The Globe and Mail*. 10 April 2009. http://www.theglobeandmail.com/books/article978937.ece Online.

THE *CMS* N-B SYSTEM

The *Chicago Manual of Style* (CMS) notes-bibliography system of referencing provides your reader with footnotes or endnotes, rather than in-text, parenthetical citations and a bibliographic reference. It is most frequently used in the humanities (literature, history, and arts).

Footnotes and endnotes

At each point within the text where you have drawn upon someone else's work, or immediately following a direct quotation, place a superscript numeral (for example, [3]); this refers the reader to full reference details provided either as a **footnote** (at the bottom of the page) or as an **endnote** (at the end of the document). If you refer to the same source, say, seven times, there will be seven separate note identifiers within the text that relate to that source, so you must provide seven endnotes or footnotes. This practice is sometimes simplified by providing full bibliographic details in the first endnote/footnote and abbreviated details (author's surname, shortened book title, and page number(s)) in the second note (Writing Lab et al., 2010). The second reference to a source does not need to be as comprehensive as the first, but it should leave your reader in no doubt as to the precise identity of the reference (for example, if there are two books by the same author, you will need to provide enough detail for the reader to work out which text you are noting). In some disciplines, Latin abbreviations such as **ibid**. (from *ibidem*, meaning "in the same place"), **op. cit.** (from *opere citato*, meaning "in the work cited"), and **loc. cit.** (from *loco citato*, meaning "in the place cited") are used for subsequent references as part of that abbreviation process, although this practice is far less common today than it was in the past.

Notes in the *CMS* N-B system are preceded by their corresponding number, followed by a period and a space; notes in the otherwise quite

---

Using the CMS N-B system

Note the following:

- The first endnoted or footnoted reference to a work must give your readers all the bibliographic information they might need to find the work.
- The reference is indented from the note number so that readers can quickly identify the note they are looking for.
- Book and journal titles are italicized or underlined; article and chapter titles are not.
- Article and chapter titles appear in quotation marks.
- The appropriate page number(s) for the material being cited should be included in each note. The bibliography will record the full page range of any article or chapter drawn from a larger work (such as an edited collection or journal). Note that surname and initial are not reversed in notes (but they are in the reference list or bibliography).
- It is not necessary to indicate that a book or article was accessed in a print, rather than an online, format.

KEY CONCEPTS

similar Turabian system are preceded by their corresponding superscript number (Writing Lab et al., 2010).

Example

Footnotes and endnotes in the *CMS* N-B system

1. Mavis Gallant, *The End of the Story: Critical Essays on Alice Munro*, edited by Robert Thacker (Toronto: ECW Press, 1999), 43. [First reference to work]
2. Gallant, *The End*, 43. [Second reference]
3. *Ibid.*, 43. [Subsequent reference *immediately* following previous note]
4. Margaret Atwood, *The Year of the Flood* (Toronto: Vintage Canada, 2010), Kindle edition. [Edition for wireless reading device]
5. Ruth Parkin-Gounelas, "Margaret Atwood: *Feminism and Fiction* (review)," *MFS Modern Fiction Studies* 54.4 (2008): 935–8, accessed 09 October 2010, doi: 10.1353/mfs.0.1557. [Article in online journal: include the DOI if one is available].

Turabian style footnote/endnote

[1] Mavis Gallant, *The End of the Story: Critical Essays on Alice Munro*, edited by Robert Thacker (Toronto: ECW Press, 1999), 43.

Bibliography

The bibliography at the end of a work using the *CMS* N-B system of referencing includes all the works consulted irrespective of whether they are cited within the text. The bibliography is traditionally set out in alphabetical order of authors' surnames to make it easier for the reader to find the full details of sources you have cited in the text. The bibliography contains the same information about the works cited as the footnotes or endnotes, but it is customary to place the author's surname first (rather than his or her initials, which appear first in the notes). Place the work's title first if the author is unknown.

TIP

As you are preparing your work, keep full details of all the references you consult. This will make preparing a reference list easy.

Example

Bibliography in the *CMS* N-B System

Gallant, Mavis. *The End of the Story: Critical Essays on Alice Munro*, edited by Robert Thacker. Toronto: ECW Press, 1999.

THE *CMS* A-D SYSTEM

The *Chicago Manual of Style* (*CMS*) author-date system of referencing provides your reader with short parenthetical citations that usually include the author's surname and the date of publication. More detailed information is available in the References section of the research paper. This system is most often used by the physical, life, and social sciences.

> **Example**
> **References and parenthetical citations in the *CMS* A-D System**
>
> Molles, Manuel, and James Cahil. 2007. *Ecology, Canadian Edition: Concepts and Applications.* Toronto: McGraw-Hill Ryerson.
>
> (Molles and Cahil, 2007, 145)
>
> [Two authors. For four or more, list all authors in the reference list and only the first author and "et al." in the text] (University of Chicago Press, 2010)
>
> Ugalde, Herman, and William A. Morris. 2010. "Deriving geological contact geometry from potential field data." *Exploration Geophysics* 41(1): 40–50. Accessed 12 September 2010. doi: 0.1071/EG09032.
>
> (Ugalde and Morris, 2010, 40–50)
>
> Winnipeg. 2010. "Time to band your trees." Last modified 09 September 2010. http://www.winnipeg.ca/cao/media/news/nr_2010/nr_20100910.stm
>
> (Winnipeg, 2010)

> **Citing email, text messages, and blog posts**
> - *Email* and *text messages* are most commonly cited in-text and not included in the reference list.
>   "On receiving a text message on 12 July 2010 from Chen Shen, the author understood the implications . . ."
> - If you choose to use a parenthetical reference to email or text messages, employ the term "personal communication" (or "pers. comm.") (University of Chicago Press, 2010).
>   (Chen Shen, email message to author, 12 July 2010)
>   (Chen Shen, pers. comm.)
> - *Blog posts* are most commonly cited in-text and not typically included in the references.
>   In his meditation on the evolution of love in his *Your Wise Brain Blog* post on 28 September 2010, Rick Hanson observes . . .
> - If your professor asks you to cite blog posts in the reference list, use the following format:
>   Hanson, Rick. 2010. "The Evolution of Love." *Your Wise Brain Blog*, 28 September.
>   http://yourwisebrain.scienceblog.com/2010/09/28/the-evolution-of-love/?utm_source=feedburner&utm_medium=feed&utm_campaign=Feed%3A+SbBloggers+%28Sciene+Bloggers%29

NOTES AND NOTE IDENTIFIERS

Sometimes you may wish to let your reader know more about a matter discussed in your essay or report but believe that extra information to be peripheral to the central message you are trying to convey. An indication to your reader that this supplementary information exists may be provided within the text through the use of note identifiers such as symbols (for example, *, §, ¶, ‡) or, preferably, superscript numbers (for example, [5]).

THE IMPORTANCE OF ACKNOWLEDGING SOURCES

Correct referencing is an important academic and professional courtesy. Failure to acknowledge fully sources of ideas, phrases, text, data, diagrams, and other materials is widely regarded as a significant transgression of intellectual etiquette. It may even lead to charges of plagiarism and to the imposition of severe penalties (expulsion from a course or from university). Do take the time to become familiar with referencing procedures. If you have any questions not resolved here, consult a good reference style manual, such as *The Gregg Reference Manual* (2004), or ask your professor, teaching assistant, writing tutor, or learning skills counsellor for advice.

GLOSSARY

APA system   American Psychological Association citation system, used primarily for the social and behavioural sciences.

bibliograhy   A listing of the key descriptive elements—author, date of publication, title, volume number, and page numbers—of a publication such as a book, journal article, video, or online resource.

CMS system   *Chicago Manual of Style* citation system, used in the humanities (notes-bibliography system) and the sciences and social sciences (author-date system).

DOI   Digital Object Identifier: a unique string of combined letters and numbers assigned at publication to identify a "persistent" link on the Internet.

endnote   Numbered citation at the end of a research paper, most often associated with the *CMS* (N-B) system.

et al.   Short for *et alii*, meaning "and others."

footnote   Numbered citation at the bottom of page, most often associated with the *CMS* (N-B) system.

hanging indent   The second and subsequent lines of each reference are indented.

ibid.   From *ibidem*, meaning "in the same place."

loc. cit.   From *loco citato*, meaning "in the place cited."

MLA system   Modern Language Association citation system, used primarily in the humanities.

op. cit.   From *opere citato*, meaning "in the work cited."

paraphrase   Express a source's ideas in different words.

summarize   Outline the main points of an argument.

Turabian system   Kate Turabian citation system, similar to the *CMS* N-B system but using superscript numbers for notes.

Works Cited   Reference list of all works cited within the text, used in the MLA system.

SUGGESTED FURTHER READING

American Psychological Association. (2009). *Publication Manual of the American Psychological Assocation*. Washington, DC: American Psychological Association.

Gibaldi. (2009). *MLA Handbook for Writers of Research Papers*. New York: Modern Language Association.

Sabin, William. (2004). *The Gregg Reference Manual: A Manual of Style, Grammar, Usage, and Formatting*. New York: Career Education.

University of Chicago Press. (2010). *The Chicago Manual of Style* (16th ed.). Chicago: University of Chicago Press.

RELATED WEBSITES

www.youtube.com/watch?v=4P785j15Tzk
AgentXPQ. (9 October 2006). "Procrastination: Tales of mere existence."

http://blog.apastyle.org/apastyle/social-media/
American Psychological Association. (2010). "APA style blog."

http://flash1r.apa.org/apastyle/basics/index.htm
American Psychological Association. "Basics of APA style tutorial."

http://bcs.bedfordstmartins.com/resdoc5e/index.htm
Hacker, Diana, & Fister, Barbara. (2009). "Research documentation online" (5th ed.).

http://citationmachine.net/
Landmark Project. (2010). "Son of citation machine."

http://blogs.studentlife.utoronto.ca/academicsuccess
M.F. (2010). "Student success and 'The King's Speech': Imagine a friend listening to you as you work."

www.utoronto.ca/writing/handouts/PDreferencing.pdf
Procter, Margaret. (2010). "Referencing: Why and how across the disciplines."

www.writing.utoronto.ca/images/stories/Documents/documentation.pdf
Procter, Margaret. (2010). "Standard documentation formats."

http://citesource.trincoll.edu/mla/mlablogpost_002.pdf
Trinity College Library. (2009). "Cite source: MLA style—blog post.

www.chicagomanualofstyle.org/home.html
University of Chicago Press. (2010). *The Chicago Manual of Style* (16th ed.).

www.library.unt.edu/govinfo/browse-topics/citation-guides-and-style-manuals/scholarly-and-professional-style-manuals#ama-style
University of North Texas Libraries. (2010). "Scholarly and professional style manuals."

http://library.williams.edu/citing/
Williams College Libraries. (2010). "Citation guide."

http://owl.english.purdue.edu/owl/section/2/
Writing Lab, OWL at Purdue, & Purdue University. (2010). "Purdue online writing lab: Research and citation resources."

ANSWER KEY TO EXERCISE

In-Text Referencing Using the APA System

The article "Age-Related Macular Degeneration; Research from Ohio State University, Department of Ophthalmology, Yields New Findings on Age-Related Macular Degeneration" (12 February 2011) looks at recent findings that suggest that the use of PRLs could be beneficial to sufferers of age-related macular degeneration.

APA Reference List

Hamilton, L., Duncan, C. & Haedrich, R. (2004). Social/ecological transformation in northwest Newfoundland. *Population and Environment, 25*(3), 195–215.

Hanson, G.R., Hanson, P.J., Venturelli, P.J., & Fleckenstein, A.E. (2009). *Drugs and Society* (10th ed.) New York: Jones and Bartlett.

Speaking Out:
Public Speaking

Speech is power: speech is to persuade, to convert, to compel.
Ralph Waldo Emerson, 1880

WHY ARE PUBLIC SPEAKING SKILLS IMPORTANT?

Oral communication skills are recognized by Canadian, American, and overseas business and educational leaders as a central objective of university education. Preparing and delivering a talk may fulfill educational objectives by encouraging you to organize ideas and construct logical arguments. Moreover, public speaking, which often has more impact than writing, is an increasingly important transferable skill.

One of the most challenging speaking skills practised at university is giving an **oral presentation** of, say, 20 to 30 minutes' duration. This chapter is divided into three main parts that attempt to outline some of the "mechanics" of giving such a talk. The first of these parts deals with the vital matter of preparing for the talk, the second with delivering the talk, and the third with coping with post-talk questions.

The discussion that follows is not intended to be a "prescription" for a perfect talk. Instead, it offers guidelines to help you prepare for and deliver your first few oral presentations within a classroom environment. With experience you will develop your own "style"—a form of presentation that may be very effective and yet may transgress some of the guidelines outlined here. Practice will help you to develop your own approach, but you may also want to keep a critical eye on your professors, classmates, and other people giving talks that you attend. Pay attention to the form and manner of their delivery. Try to identify those devices, techniques, and mannerisms that you believe add to, or detract from, a presentation. Apply what you learn in your own talks.

PREPARING TO GIVE A TALK

You cannot expect to talk competently "off the cuff" on any but the most familiar topics. Effective preparation is crucial to any successful presentation. Preparation for a talk should begin some days, or even weeks, before the actual event.

Establishing the context and goals

- *Who is your audience?* Target the presentation to the audience's characteristics, needs, and abilities. The ways in which a topic might be developed will be influenced heavily by the background and expertise of the audience (Eisenberg, 1992, p. 333). Find out how big the audience will be. Audience size may affect the style of presentation. For example, a large crowd will make an interactive presentation somewhat difficult.
- *Where are you speaking?* If possible, visit the venue in which the talk is to be held. Room and layout characteristics can have an effect on the formality of the presentation, the speed of the talk, the attentiveness of the audience, and the types of audiovisual aids that can be employed. Check, for example, to see if the talk is to be given in a large room, from a lectern, with a microphone, to an audience of your classmates and professor seated in rows.
- *How long will you speak?* Confirm how much of the time available is for the talk and how much is intended for audience questions. Avoid the embarrassment of being asked to conclude the talk before it is finished or of ending well short of the deadline. You may be asked to speak as part of a group. It is unfair on other group members if you speak for more or less time than you have been assigned.
- *Why are you speaking?* The style of presentation may differ depending on your purpose. The purpose may be to present information, to stimulate discussion, to present a solution to a problem, or, perhaps, to persuade a group of the value of a particular view or course of action. Depending on the purpose, you may have to alter the style and content of your presentation.
- *Who else is speaking?* If your presentation is one of several, this may influence the audience's reaction to you (Eisenberg, p. 332). If you are speaking as part of a group, be sure you know what other people will be saying to avoid repeating or anticipating their points.
- *Do your research.* Keeping in mind the purpose of your talk, gather and interpret appropriate and accurate information. Make a point of collecting anecdotes, cartoons, and/or up-to-date statistics that might make your presentation more appealing, colourful, and convincing.

- *Eliminate the dross.* If you have already written a paper on which the presentation is to be based, be aware that you will not be able to communicate everything you have written. Carefully select the main points you wish to tell the audience, and devote attention to the strategies by which those points can be communicated as clearly and effectively as possible.

Selecting your main points

Courtenay (1992, p. 220) makes the following suggestions:

- List all the things you know or have found out about your subject.
- Eliminate all those items you think the audience might already know about.
- Eliminate anything that is not important for your audience to know.
- Keep doing this until you are left with one or two new and dynamic points. These should not already be known to your audience, and they should be interesting and useful to them.

Organizing the material for presentation

- *Choose the right framework.* Ensure that the organizational framework used is appropriate and that it helps make the point of your presentation clear. For example, if your main aim is to discuss potential solutions to homelessness in Vancouver, it might be less than useful to spend most of the time discussing the historical development of social insurance policies in Canada as a prelude to that. If you are presenting as part of a group, ensure that you have agreed on an organizational structure and that each speaker understands fully the place of his or her talk within that structure.
- *Give your talk a clear and relevant title.* An audience will be attracted to, and informed by, a good title. Be sure that your title says what the talk is about.

TIP

To give a successful talk, make sure you know why you are speaking, where, to whom, and for how long, but above all, work out what your central message is.

Organizational frameworks for presentations

Most presentations seem to adopt one of the following five organizational frameworks:

chronological	the history of thought in physics from the 17th century
scale	overview of national responses to unemployment followed by a detailed examination of responses in particular regions
spatial	an account of Japan's trading relations with other countries of the Pacific
causal	implications of financial deregulation on the New Zealand insurance market
order of importance	ranked list of solutions to people's fear of snakes

Structuring your talk

In summary, a great talk will

- start with a clear, memorable statement;
- focus material on a small number of key points;
- be concise, with an even balance of material from one point to another;
- be "signposted"; and
- end with a clear, memorable statement, consistent with the start. (Knight & Parsons, 2003, p. 164)

Let us look at a great talk's structure in more detail. In most cases a talk will have an introduction, a discussion, and a conclusion. The introductory and concluding sections of oral presentations are very important. About 25 per cent of your presentation ought to be devoted to the "beginning" and "end." The remaining time should be spent on the discussion.

The introduction
- *Make your reason for talking and conceptual framework clear.* This gives the audience a basis for understanding the ideas that follow. In short, let listeners know what you are going to tell them, and do this effectively:
  - » *State the topic:* "Today I am going to talk about . . . " Do this in a way that will attract the audience's attention.
  - » *State the aims or purpose:* Why is this talk being given? Why have you chosen this topic? Why should the audience listen?
  - » *Outline the scope of the talk:* Let the audience know something about the boundaries of the presentation. For example, are you discussing attitudes to the environment from an Inuit perspective, or are you offering an accountant's view of Canadian tax law in the 1990s?
  - » *Provide a plan of the discussion:* Let the audience know the steps through which you will lead them in your presentation and the relationship of each step to the others. It is useful to prepare for the audience a written plan (for example, put up an introductory PowerPoint slide) that outlines your intended progression.
- *Capture the audience's attention from the outset.* Do this with a rhetorical question, relevant and interesting quotations, amazing facts, an anecdote, startling statements . . . . Remember that in all likelihood your audience will be your classmates and professor: a *brief* reference to material that has been discussed in class can personalize your talk. Avoid jokes unless you have a real gift for humour.
- *Make the introduction clear and lively.* First impressions are very important. Use visual images if they are appropriate.

TIP

Try to win your audience's attention from the very start of your talk.

The discussion

- *Construct a convincing argument supported with examples.* Remember, you are trying to present as compelling a case as possible in support of your findings.
- Ensure there is a "fluid logic between your main points" (Montgomery, 2001, p. 172).
- *Limit discussion to a few main points.* Lindsay (1984, p. 48) observes that a "rule" of broadcasting is that it takes about three minutes to put across each new idea. Do not make the mistake of trying to cover too much material in your talk.
- *Present your argument logically, precisely, and in an orderly fashion.* Try producing a small diagram that summarizes the main points you wish to discuss. Use this as a basis for constructing your talk. It might also make a useful handout or PowerPoint slide for your audience. If you are giving a group talk, try to prepare a single handout (if appropriate) for the group's entire presentation, rather than separate handouts for each component.
- *Accompany points of argument with carefully chosen, colourful, and correct examples and analogies.* It is helpful to use examples built on the experience of the audience for whom they are intended. In giving a classroom presentation, you have the advantage of presenting to your peers. Analogies and examples clarify unfamiliar ideas and bring your argument to life.
- *Connect the points of your discussion with the overall direction of the talk.* Remind the audience of the trajectory you are following by relating the points you make to the overall framework you outlined in the introduction. For example, "The third of the three points I have identified as explaining . . . "
- *Restate important points.*
- *Personalize the presentation.* This can add authenticity, impact, and humour. For example, in discussing problems associated with administering a household questionnaire survey, you might recount an experience of being chased down dark suburban streets by a large, ferocious dog. Avoid overstepping the line between personalizing and being self-centred by ensuring that the tales you tell help the audience to understand your message.

TIP

Limit your talk to discussion of key points and make clear the relationship of each to the overall trajectory.

The conclusion

- *Cue the conclusion.* Phrases like "To conclude . . . " or "In summary . . . " usually have a remarkable capacity to stimulate audience attention. Less commonly, they may also encourage some audiences to start packing their bags to leave!

- *Bring ideas to fruition.* Restate the main points in words other than those used earlier in the discussion, develop some conclusions, and review implications. Connect your talk with its wider context.
- *Tie the conclusion neatly together with the introduction.* The introduction noted where the talk is going. The conclusion reminds the audience of the content and dramatically observes the arrival at the foreshadowed destination.
- *Make the conclusion emphatic.* Use the conclusion to reinforce your main ideas or to motivate the audience. For instance, if you have been stressing the need for community involvement in reducing greenhouse gas emissions, try to "fire up" the audience so they feel motivated to take some action of their own.
- *End your presentation clearly.* Saying "'thank you," for example, makes it clear to the audience that your talk is over. Try to avoid giggling self-consciously and saying things like "well, that's the end."

TIP

When you tell your audience you are about to finish, you get their attention!

Preparing your text and visual aids

Everyone has his or her unique preferences when it comes to preparing a presentation "script." Some opt for a full script, others for brief notes, and others for graphic images such as a flow chart. The same model is not appropriate for everyone, so heed Montgomery's (p. 171) advice to "design and write out your talk in a manner you feel comfortable with." Having said this, there are a few points worth considering.

KEY CONCEPTS

Preparing notes
- *Prepare well in advance!* The talk is just the tip of the iceberg: the preparation is the much larger submerged section.
- *Prepare a talk, not a speech.* In general, you should avoid preparing a full text to be read aloud. A read-aloud presentation is often boring and lifeless.

If you must prepare a text to be read, remember that a talk needs to be kept simple and logical. Sentences should be kept short and simple. Major points need to be restated. Language should be informal, but should not employ slang and other conventions of café conversation. Because your talk will go past your listener only once, it must also "be very well organized, developed logically, stripped of details that divert the listener's attention from the essential points of the presentation" (Pechenik, 2004, p. 252). Most people speak at between 125 and 175 words per minute (Dixon, 2004, p. 100), though a good speed for formal presentation delivery is about 100 words per minute (Montgomery, p. 171). So, if you feel absolutely compelled to write a script, you will know that a ten-minute talk will require you to prepare about 1,000 words.

EXERCISE

CALCULATING HOW MUCH TO WRITE

1. You have been told that you should prepare a script for a 20-minute presentation. The usual estimate for number of words per page is 250. How many pages of text will you need to prepare?
2. You have written a script that is six pages long. How many minutes will it take you to read it?

Sometimes students write papers that are too formal for a casual **seminar presentation**. If you are accustomed to writing very academic research papers, you might do so, but then go back and turn them into a less formal "script" to be read aloud: add some sentences that are written in the first person ("I became interested in this topic when . . . "), use contractions ("do not" becomes "don't," "cannot" becomes "can't," "will not" becomes "won't"), and write notes to yourself ("slow down!!!," "speak louder!!!," "read this with particular emphasis," "pause and look at the audience here").

TIP

If you use a script for a talk, make sure it is written for speaking, not reading.

Use Pronunciation Prompts

If English is not your first language, it is important to put pronunciation prompts in your "script" if you use one. Remember that no one else will see these prompts, so be sure to develop a system that makes sense to you, no matter how silly it might seem. If you have trouble remembering how to pronounce "Trudeau," for instance, then write "[Troo-doe]" beside it in your text.

TIPS for EAL LEARNERS

NAVIGATING LEARNING CHALLENGES

Find Creative Solutions to Reading Difficulties

If you find reading challenging, do not put yourself in the position of having to read a text aloud. Arrange with the professor to give your speech using index card prompts or PowerPoint slides.

- *Highlight the most important points in your "script."* If you are going to be reading from a text, be sure to highlight the points that are most important. If you find yourself reading more slowly than you had anticipated, you can be sure, if time starts running out, that you at least mention your most important points.

- *Prepare personal memory prompts.* These might take the form of clearly legible notes, key words, phrases, or diagrams to serve as your summary outline of the talk. Put prompts on cards or on notepaper, ensuring that each page is numbered sequentially—just in case you drop them! If you are using PowerPoint for your talk, consider using the "View Notes Page" (PowerPoint) or "Show Presentation Notes" (Keynote) option. This allows you to prepare and print out a set of speaker notes associated with each slide in your show.

- *Revise your script.* Put your talk away overnight or for a few days after you think you have finished writing it. Come back to the script later, asking yourself how the talk might be sharpened.

Preparing handouts

- *Consider preparing a written summary for the audience.* In many disciplines, but not all, an oral presentation should be used to present the essence of some body of material. You might imagine the talk to be like a trailer for a forthcoming movie. It presents highlights and captures the imagination. If members of the audience want to know more, they should come along to the full screening of the film (that is, read the full paper). Depending on the circumstances, it may be helpful, therefore, to prepare for distribution to the audience sufficient numbers of either a full copy of the paper on which a presentation is based or a written summary. Microsoft PowerPoint or Apple Keynote can be very helpful. Either presentation tool includes among its print options a function that allows you to prepare reproducible handout copies of projected images you plan to use during your talk. With such a document, the audience is better able to keep track of the presentation and you are freer to highlight the central ideas and findings instead of spending valuable time covering explanatory detail.

Preparing visual aids

- *Prepare a limited number of useful visual aids.* Slide projections, PowerPoint or Keynote presentations, models, blackboard sketches, video clips, DVDs, maps, and charts help to clarify ideas that the audience may have difficulty understanding, hold the audience's attention, and promote interaction with the audience. Table 15.1 sets out a variety of visual aids and some of their advantages and disadvantages. But do remember not to prepare too many aids as they may defeat these purposes. Flickr (**www.flickr.com**) and Google Images (**www.google.com/imghp**) offer access to many images that may be judiciously incorporated into your presentation or handouts—subject to copyright regulations and with appropriate acknowledgement, of course.

Table 15.1   Advantages and disadvantages of various visual aids

Type	Advantages	Disadvantages
Whiteboard	• Reinforces main points • Allows for use of colour • Good for building up a series of connected ideas • Easy to organize, and can be used outdoors	• Not good for large and/or complicated diagrams • Not useful for large audiences • You usually have to turn your back to the audience • Requires clear handwriting
Flipchart or paper pad stand	• Inexpensive and easily transported • Important material can be prepared in advance • Prompts can be pencilled in beforehand	• Suitable only for small groups • You usually have to turn your back to the audience • Needs a stable easel for support • Requires clear handwriting
Prepared poster	• Provides a brief and striking message • Can include complex colour and design elements	• Can be large and awkward to carry • Can be costly to design well
Overhead transparency projector (OHP)	• Images can be seen by everyone • Good for prepared material using colours or diagrams • Can be prepared from computer-generated slides • No need to turn away from audience • Can use overlays • Can be masked so you can reveal information gradually • Can be stored and reused	• Needs a power source • Needs to be correctly aligned • Projector bulbs can fail without warning • Material can be too small to be read • Transparencies can be awkward to manage
Slides (consider saving slides to a CD or computer as an alternative way of using these images)	• Images are of better quality than with OHP • Better at displaying pictures and photographs than OHP • Can be stored and reused	• Projector needs a power source and a darkened room • Needs careful slide alignment, projector focus and so on. Projectors are notoriously unreliable • Expensive to produce

Type	Advantages	Disadvantages
Computer-generated visual with data projector	• Relatively easy to combine text, graphics, audio, and video • Can generate a sophisticated project relatively cheaply	• Needs a power source • Needs a computer and projector • Technical difficulties in usage are common
Real object	• May be readily available and convenient to display • Audience can see how object works and looks, and it can be used	• May not be suitable for large groups • Potential for damage to object • Not appropriate for large objects
Model	• Works well for large objects • Gives audience sense of scale and of relationships between elements of the object	• May not be to scale • Detail may not be seen by audience • Potential for damage to model • Potentially costly to produce

Source: Street, Hay, & Sefton (2005, p. 177–8)

- *Make visual aids neat, concise, simple, and consistent.* Simple and clearly drawn illustrations on handouts or PowerPoint or Keynote slides are more easily interpreted and recalled than are complex versions. Sloppily produced visual aids suggest a lack of care, knowledge, and interest. Visual aids ought to be consistent in their style but should not be boring.

KEY CONCEPTS

Effective powerpoint or keynote presentations

- *Don't forget to make a title slide.* This might set out your name, the title of your talk, your contact details, and perhaps an outline of the talk to follow. Usually the title itself is larger than most of the text (44 point Arial is the default setting for titles in PowerPoint).
- *Use no more than two or three bulleted points on every presentation slide.* Make each point in as few words as possible (say, about six words per point).
- *Don't plan to just read your slide's text.* Use the slide as a starting place for your discussion or to highlight key points you will be making.
- *Produce large and boldly drawn visual aids.* Visuals that can be seen from about 20 metres should be adequate in most cases.
- *Information shown on presentation slides should be legible.* The font size of all text must be large enough to be easily read. Thirty-point font works well in most instances, although 32-point Arial is the default setting for PowerPoint standard text while 42 is the default size for Keynote. A **sans-serif** font like **Arial** (Arial) or **Verdana**

(Verdana) works best. TRY NOT TO USE ALL UPPERCASE LETTERS; it's easier to read a combination of both uppercase and lowercase text. <u>Avoid underlining</u>: <u>it can be distracting</u> and rarely serves a useful purpose in slide presentations.

- *Use highly visible colours.* For projecting in a dim room, choose a dark, cool colour (green or blue) for the background, with a warm colour (yellow) or white for the text. Use a light background and a dark text for a brightly lit room (Reynolds, "Ten Top Slide Tips").
- *Use line graphs, histograms, and pie charts (and cartoons).* Graphic depictions of information are usually more effective and more easily understood than tables, though tables can be useful if they are easy to read. Well-chosen cartoons can very effectively communicate a message and help to lighten the atmosphere. Do not just cut and paste images; use the program's Insert function.
- *Avoid taking graphs or tables directly from a written paper.* These often contain more information and detail than can be understood readily. Redraw graphs and redesign tables to make the small number of points you wish to convey.
- *Ensure that all of your presentation slides will be displayed through the projector.* Leave some space around the margins of each slide.
- *Keep transitions, animations, or "Smart Builds" between slides simple.* Try to resist introducing the sound of bongos, bubbles, and breaking glass into your presentation; animations such as checkerboarding across, combing horizontally, newsflashing, pushing up, wiping down, shuffling, and thumbing through are lots of fun to use but ultimately distracting for your audience.
- *Spend time thinking about the best order for your slides.* Leave time to change the order, if necessary, using the program's "Slide Sorter" or "Light Table" function (Reynolds, "Ten Top Slide Tips").
- *Check your whole presentation for errors and omissions.* Use the "View Show" or "Play Slideshow" feature to catch mistakes or confusing transitions.
- *Leave a strong impression.* Consider preparing an attractive and relevant final image that can be left on the screen when you have finished speaking and are answering audience questions. It is sometimes useful to include in this final slide a restatement of your talk's title and your name and, if appropriate, contact information.
- *If you are not going to be using your own laptop, be sure that you try out your presentation on the computer that you will be using.* Sometimes there can be unexpected—and usually unwelcome!—changes in formatting when you switch from one computer, or one platform, program version, or operating system to another.

Rehearsing

Few people are naturally gifted public speakers. It is a skill developed through experience. People new to public speaking often speak very quickly or too slowly, belabour minor points, fail to engage with their audience through eye contact, for example, or do not know how to operate audiovisual equipment correctly. You can overcome such problems through practice and useful feedback from other students, friends, or family members.

- *Rehearse repeatedly.* Try rehearsing until there is almost no need to consult prepared notes for guidance—about ten times ought to do it. The intent is not to commit the talk to memory. Instead, rehearsing helps to ensure that you have all the points in the right order and that you have a crystal-clear sense of your talk's key message and its trajectory. This is vital to success. Rehearsing also enables you to practise the pacing and timing of your talk so you don't, for example, spend 90 per cent of your allotted presentation time discussing 20 per cent of your talk's content! It may also allow you to stop, look up, and mark on your "script" pronunciations that you are uncertain about and to work out whether you sound boring or arrogant. Importantly, it also allows you to manage your spoken material, handouts, and audiovisual resources within the time available (Hay, Dunn, & Street, 2005, p. 166).
- *Record rehearsals.* In preparing for the talk, it is often useful to make an audio or, preferably, a video recording of a trial presentation. Digital video cameras do not "pull punches" in the same way that an audience of friends and family, sensitive to your feelings, might. If you are making a group presentation, rehearsing is especially important. Not only does your part of the talk need to go smoothly, but you must also ensure that the links between the presentation's separate parts are clear and clean. Be sure to rehearse several times in advance of the scheduled talk date.
- *Time rehearsals.* Most novice speakers are stunned to find out how much longer their presentation takes to deliver than they expected or felt had elapsed while they were talking. Match the time available for the talk with the amount of material for presentation. Allow for a few extra minutes to compensate for impromptu comments, technical problems, pauses to gather thoughts, or the breathtaking realization that the audience is not following the tale! If your talk is too long, decide what extraneous material can be removed without affecting the main points. It is better to do the pruning beforehand than to be forced to stop your talk, or make the revisions, in midstream. You might consider putting material that you decide to "omit" from your talk in square brackets. That way, if during the presentation itself you start talking more quickly than you did in rehearsal, you will have some "extra" material to reintroduce into your presentation.

TIP

Rehearse your talk using all the prompts you plan to employ.

- *Make full use of the visual aids to be used in the talk.* Visual aids can consume time rapidly as you move from one medium to another, such as from presentation slides to the blackboard. Consequently, pay careful attention to the use of time in the delivery of multimedia presentations.

Final points of preparation

- *Are you dressed and groomed for the occasion?* Although the audience's emphasis should be placed on the intellectual merits of your argument, you need to be aware that your style of dress may affect some people's perceptions of the value of your talk. Dress appropriately. (Wearing something for the first time is not always a great idea when giving a presentation: having a button pop off a pair of pants or a skirt split up the back seam during a presentation will NOT do much for your self-confidence!)

- *Take water.* No matter how well prepared you are, there is a possibility that you will suffer from "cotton mouth" during your talk. This unpleasant affliction causes your mouth to dry up and your tongue to swell to such a size that you can scarcely speak. Water consumed during the talk seems to help.

- *Do the visual aids work and how do they work?* Be familiar with the function of any aid that you will be using. Do not be so unprepared that you must exasperate your audience with questions like: "How do I switch this projector on?" or "Can anyone work the data projector?" You should have checked before your presentation. It's your talk.

- *Be prepared for technical problems.* Ensure that you have a strategy for dealing with computer, data projector, and video glitches. For instance, if you plan on using PowerPoint, take along hard copies of your slides (either multiple copies for distribution or a single copy for your own reference) in case there are problems with your computer or the data projector.

- *Can the audience see you and your visual aids?* Before your talk, sit in a few strategically placed chairs around the room to see whether the audience will be able to see you and your visual aids. Consider where you will stand while talking and take care to *avoid the problem of your silhouette obstructing the audience's view* of a projection screen or the blackboard.

- *Is there a working clock in the room?* If not, make sure you can see your watch, cell-phone clock, or have some other way of checking the time.

- *Is everything else ready?* Are summaries ready for distribution? Are note cards in order?

TIP

Taking a sip of water while you "think over" a difficult question from the audience can also help you collect your thoughts; it can spare you the awkwardness of just standing and staring into the room while you search your mind for something to say.

TIP

When it is your turn to speak, take control: of technology, time-keeping, volume, and vision.

- *Make absolutely clear in your mind the central message you wish to convey. This is crucial to a good presentation.* Knowing your message will give you that confidence your audience will need if they are to have faith in what you are telling them. It also means that if for some unforeseen reason something goes wrong, or you "stall" and lose your place in the talk momentarily, you can take a breath, reflect on your central message, and resume your presentation with the minimum of fuss. Importantly, too, if you do not have the message of your talk firmly established in your own mind, you are unlikely to be able to let anyone else know what the message is.
- *Is your cell phone turned off or to "meeting" mode?* Few things are more distracting than having your cell phone ring while you're in the middle of giving a presentation!

DELIVERING YOUR TALK

TIP

Audiences support speakers who try to do well.

People in your audience, who are most often going to be your classmates, *want you to do well.* They want to listen to you giving a good talk, and they will be supportive and grateful if you are well prepared, even if you do stumble in your presentation or blush and stammer. The guidelines outlined here offer a "target" at which you can aim. No one expects you to give a flawless presentation.

It will make your presentation more convincing and credible if you remember, and act on, the fact that the audience is made up of *individuals*, each of whom is listening to you. You are *not* talking to some large, amorphous body. Imagine that you are telling your story to one or two people and not to a larger group. If you can allow yourself to perform this difficult task, you will find that voice inflection, facial expressions, and other elements important to an effective delivery will fall into place.

- *Be confident and enthusiastic!* One of the most important keys to a successful presentation is your enthusiasm. You have a well-researched and well-prepared talk to deliver. Most audiences are friendly. All you have to do is tell this group of interested people what you have to say. Try to instill confidence in your abilities and in what you have to say. Do not start by apologizing for your presentation. If it is so bad, why are you giving it?
- *Look interested*—or no one else will be. *Talk naturally, using simple language and short sentences.* Try to relax, but be aware that the presentation is not a conversation in a neighbourhood bar. Some degree of formality is expected. Do not use slang or colloquial language unless you have a specific reason for doing so.

- *Speak clearly.* Try not to mumble and hesitate. This may suggest to the audience that you do not know your material thoroughly. You can sometimes make your speech clearer by slowing the rate of delivery.
- *Project your voice.* Be sure that the most distant member of the audience can hear you clearly.
- *Engage your audience.* Vary your volume, tone of voice, and pace of presentation. Involve the audience through use of the word "you" (for example, "You may wonder why we did this . . . ").
- *Use appropriate gestures and movement.* Step out from behind the computer monitor or lectern and move around a little, engaging with different parts of your audience.
- *Try to avoid nervous habits.* Be conscious of distracting behaviours such as jangling money in your pocket, swaying, and pacing back and forth, which you may have detected in your rehearsals. Find alternative, good speaking habits.
- *Make eye contact with your audience.* Although this may be rather intimidating, eye contact is very important. It also allows you to gauge audience response.
- *Face the entire audience.* Do not talk to the walls, windows, floor, ceiling, blackboard, or projector screen. It is the audience with which you are concerned. Remember that you can probably see your slide presentation on the laptop or a printout of your slides in front of you. Avoid turning your back on your audience to look at the screen all the time.
- *Pay attention to audience reaction.*
- If the audience does not seem to understand what you are saying, try rephrasing your point or clarifying it with an example.
- *Direct your attention to the less attentive members of the audience.* Take care not to focus your presentation on those whose attention you already have.
- *Write key words and unusual words on the blackboard.*
- *Avoid writing/drawing on whiteboards, blackboards, or computer writing or graphic tablets for more than a few seconds at a time.* Long periods devoted to the production of diagrams may destroy any rapport or continuity you have developed with your audience.
- *Stop talking when a diagram/slide/map is first shown.* This is to allow the audience time to study the display. Then, take a moment to familiarize your audience with elements of the visual aid (for example, axis labels), remembering that they have never seen the image before. There is no point in telling people what the image means before they have had a chance to work out what it is about (Pechenik, p. 255).

> **TIP**
>
> Pay attention to your audience. Can they hear? Can they see? Are they bored? Do they understand?

- *Point to the audience's screen, not yours.* Some speakers new to PowerPoint will point with their finger to images on the monitor in front of them, believing perhaps that the audience can see what they mean. Others insist on shaking the mouse about and, hence, the cursor in ways that can best be described as nauseating for the audience. These problems can be overcome by pointing with a hand or ruler to the audience's screen. Take care using laser pointers. They can take a slight hand tremble and increase its amplitude significantly (Pechenik, p. 255–6).
- *Do not stand in front of completed diagrams.*
- *Be sure that data projections are high enough for all the audience to see.* As a rule of thumb, make sure the projection is screened higher than the heads of people in the front row of your audience.
- *When you have finished with an illustration, remove it.* In this way, the audience's attention will be directed back at you (where it belongs) and will not be distracted. Do not talk about a topic that is different from the one on your visual display.
- *Switch off noisy machines when they are not being used.* If this is impossible, it may be necessary to speak more loudly than usual in order to compensate for the whirring of electric cooling fans.
- *Keep to your time limit.* Audiences do not like being delayed, but you should take care not to rush at the end. Last-minute haste may leave the audience with a poor impression of your talk. Watch the time as you proceed so that you can summarize if you see that you are running out of time.

COPING WITH QUESTIONS

The post-presentation discussion that typically follows a talk allows the audience to ask questions and to offer points of criticism. It is an important part of the overall presentation, which can completely change an audience's response to you and your work. Take care to be thorough and courteous in your response to comments.

- *Let the audience know whether you will accept questions in the course of the presentation or after the talk is completed.* Questions addressed during a presentation may disturb the flow of the talk, upsetting any rapport developed with the audience, and may anticipate points addressed at some later stage within the presentation. In general, it is wise to ask the audience to keep their questions until the end of the talk. In the case of group presentations, you should have determined before the talk who will answer questions. You may choose a single person to handle all questions on behalf of the group or, preferably, questions can be answered by the person whose part of the talk covered the material being queried. It is sometimes helpful to let the audience know that the group has a leader to whom all questions should first be directed. That person can then turn the question over to the group member best qualified to answer it.

- *Stay at or near the lectern throughout the question period.* Question-time is still a formal part of the presentation. Act accordingly.
- *Control, and be in control of, the question and answer period.* However, if there is a chairperson, moderation of question-time is their responsibility.
- *Address the entire audience, not just the person who asked the question.*
- *Recognize questions in order.* Take care to receive enquiries from everyone before returning to any member of the audience who has a second question.
- *Search the whole audience for questions.* Compensate for blind spots caused by pillars, the lectern, and other barriers.
- *Always be succinct and polite in replies.* You should be courteous even to those who appear to be attacking rather than honestly questioning for two reasons. First, if you have misinterpreted the intent—seeing an affront where none was intended—embarrassment is avoided. Second, one of the best ways of defusing inappropriate criticism is through politeness. If, however, there is no doubt that someone is being hostile, keep your cool and, if possible, move closer to the critic. This reduction of distance is a powerful way of subduing argumentative members of an audience.
- *Repeat aloud those questions that are difficult to hear.* This ensures that you heard the question correctly. Repetition is also for the sake of the audience who may not have heard the question either.
- *Clarify the meaning of any questions you do not understand.*
- *Avoid concluding an answer by asking the questioner if his or her query has been dealt with satisfactorily.* Argumentative questioners may take this opportunity to steal the limelight, thereby limiting the discussion time available to other members of the audience.

> **TIP**
>
> If someone asks a question that is particularly tricky to answer, it is sometimes possible to rephrase it so that it becomes a question that you **can** answer without much difficulty.

> **Repeat Questions**
> If English is not your first language, it is also useful to repeat questions to be sure that you have heard and understood them correctly. It can be very embarrassing to launch into a long answer to a question . . . that no one asked!

- *Deal with particularly complex questions or those requiring an unusually long answer after the presentation.* If possible, provide a brief answer when the question is first raised, but then make it clear that you are happy to discuss matters further after the talk is complete.

- *If you do not know the answer to a question, say so.* In a group, you may be able to seek the assistance of your co-presenters. Do not try to bluff your way through a problem as any errors and inaccuracies may call the content of the rest of the talk into question.

- *You can answer difficult questions by making use of the abilities of the audience.* An enquiry might require more knowledge in a particular field than you possess. Rather than admitting "defeat," it is sometimes possible to seek out the known expertise of a specific member of the audience. This avoids personal embarrassment, ensures that the question is answered, and may endear you to that member of the audience whose advice you sought. It also lets other members of the audience know of additional expertise in the area.

- *Smile.* It is over!

You can use the assessment schedule in Figure 15.1 as a checklist for the criteria important to giving your talk.

FIGURE 15.1   Assessment schedule for a talk

Student name:	Grade:

Assessed by:

The following is an itemized rating scale for various aspects of a formal talk. Sections left blank are not relevant to the talk assessed. Some aspects are more important than others, so there is no formula connecting the scatter of ticks with the final percentage for the talk. A tick in the left-hand box means that the criterion has been met satisfactorily. A tick in the right-hand box means it has not.

If you have any questions about the individual criteria, final comments, final grade, or any other aspects of this assessment, please see the assessor.

First impressions   ✓   ✗

Speaker appeared confident and purposeful before starting to speak

Speaker attracted audience's attention from the outset

Presentation structure

Introduction

Title/topic made clear

Purpose of the presentation clear

Organizational framework made known to audience

Unusual terms defined adequately

Body of presentation

Main points stated clearly

Sufficient information and detail provided

Appropriate and adequate use of examples/anecdotes

Discussion flowed logically

Conclusion

Ending of presentation signalled adequately

Main points summarized adequately/ideas brought to fruition

Final message clear and easy to remember

Coping with questions

Whole audience searched for questions

Questions addressed in order

Questions handled adeptly

Full audience addressed with answers

Speaker maintained control of discussion

Delivery

Speech clear and audible to entire audience

Talk given with impulsion (engagement and enthusiasm)

Presentation directed to all parts of audience

Eye contact with audience throughout presentation

Speaker kept to time limit

Good use of time without rushing at end

Pace neither too fast nor too slow

Visual aids and handouts—if appropriate

Visual aids well prepared

Visual aids clearly visible to entire audience

Speaker familiar with own visual aids (for example, OHTs, blackboard diagrams)

Effective use made of handouts and visual aids

Handouts well prepared and useful

Assessor's comments: was this an effective talk?

GLOSSARY

Arial   A common sans-serif font, often used for PowerPoint presentations.

causal   An organizational framework presenting events to highlight a cause-and-effect relation between them.

chronological   An organizational framework presenting events in the order in which they occurred.

impulsion   Engagement and enthusiasm.

oral presentation   A talk of approximately 20 minutes' duration given by a student within a classroom setting.

order of importance   An organizational framework presenting material from most to least important.

sans serif   Typeface lacking small lines, or serifs, at the end of strokes.

scale   An organizational framework presenting material from both large, comprehensive and small, particular, and specific perspectives.

seminar presentation   See **oral presentation**.

spatial   An organizational framework presenting material with respect to its geographical location.

Verdana   A common sans-serif font, often used for PowerPoint presentations.

SUGGESTED FURTHER READING

Cox, Martin R. (2006). *What every student should know about preparing effective oral presentations*. Needham Heights: Allyn & Bacon.

Gallagher, Michael. (2010). *Speaking out: An introduction to public speaking: A student-friendly guide to public speaking*. Colorado Springs: Meriwether Publishing.

Hay, I. (1994b). Notes of guidance for prospective speakers. *Journal of Geography in Higher Education, 18*(1), 57–65.

Stott, Rebecca, Bryan, Cordelia, & Young, Tory (Eds.). (2000). *Speaking your mind: Oral presentation and seminar skills*. Harlow, Essex: Longman Group.

RELATED WEBSITES

www.canberra.edu.au/studyskills/learning/oral
Academic Skills Program, University of Canberra. "Giving an oral presentation."

www.asc.utoronto.ca/Publications/Oral-Presentations.htm
Perret, Nellie. Academic Success Centre, University of Toronto. "Oral Presentations."

http://it.usu.edu/fact/files/uploads/PP_BestPractices.pdf
"PowerPoint: Best practices: What the experts are saying."

www.cob.sjsu.edu/splane_m/presentationtips.htm
Splane, Mike. "PowerPoint presentation advice: Structuring your talk."

www.toastmasters.org/tips.asp
Toastmasters International. "Ten tips for public speaking."

http://pages.uoregon.edu/tep/technology/powerpoint/docs/presenting.pdf
University of Oregon. "Presenting with PowerPoint."

ANSWER KEY TO EXERCISE

Calculating How Much to Write

1. One hundred words per minute means that you'd need 2,500 words or 10 pages.
2. Six pages at 250 words a page is approximately 1,500 words. If you read 100 words per minute, then it would take 15 minutes to read the script.

16

Showing Off: Communicating with Figures and Tables

If somebody thinks they're a hedgehog, presumably you just give 'em a mirror and a few pictures of hedgehogs and tell them to sort it out for themselves.

Douglas Adams, 1984

WHY COMMUNICATE GRAPHICALLY?

Words or numbers alone are often not sufficient to communicate information effectively. Graphic communication allows you to display a large amount of information succinctly and helps your audience absorb it readily. Effective illustrations can help a reader rapidly achieve an understanding of an argument or issue.

Figures employ human powers of visual perception and pattern recognition, which are much better developed than our capacity to uncover meaningful relations in numerical lists (Krohn, 1991, p. 188). Often, we see things in graphic form that are not apparent in tables and text. Figures (and maps) are important sites for comprehending the world around us.

This chapter outlines the character and construction of different types of illustrative material. First, however, it is important to introduce a few general guidelines for clear graphic communication.

GENERAL GUIDELINES FOR CLEAR GRAPHIC COMMUNICATION

Good graphics are concise

Graphics should present only the information that is relevant to your work and required to make your point. If you reproduce an illustration or table you have found in your research, you may need to redraw or rewrite it to remove irrelevant details.

Good graphics are comprehensible

Your audience must understand what the graphic is about. Provide both a clear and complete title, which answers "what," "where," and "when" questions, and use effective labelling.

KEY CONCEPTS

Labels

Data labels and axis labels should be

- legible and easy to find;
- easily associated with the axis/object depicted—the object and the label should be close together; and
- readable from a single viewpoint—a reader should be able to examine the text without having to turn the page sideways.

(Gerber, 1985, p. 28)

Although you should fully label your graphics, do make sure that data regions are as clear of notes, axis markers, and keys as practicable. In short, the graphed information should be clear and easy to read.

If your graph displays two or more data sets, they must be easily distinguishable from one another. Graphs should include no more than *four* simultaneous symbols, values, or lines (Cartography Specialty Group of the Association of American Geographers, 1995, p. 5), and each line or symbol should be sufficiently different from the others to facilitate easy discrimination.

You can also make a graphic comprehensible by making effective use of the data region (that is, that part of the graph within which the data is displayed). Choose range of axis scale marks that will allow the full range of data being depicted to be included while ensuring that the scale allows the data to fill up as much of the data region as possible. If you take photographs, this principle will be familiar to you. Just as good photos will usually "fill the frame," so a good graph will typically fill the data region. Finally, tick marks on each axis should also be placed at frequent enough intervals for a reader to work out accurately the value of each data point (Pechenik, 2004, p. 162).

Good graphics are independent

Tables and illustrations should stand alone. Someone who has not read the document associated with the graphic should be able to look at the table or illustration and understand what it means. Graphics should also be independent of one another.

Good graphics are referenced

You must acknowledge sources. Use an accepted referencing system to note sources of data and graphics. Each graphic should be accompanied by summary bibliographic details (author, date, page, in the case of an author-date system) or a note identifier allowing the reader to find out where the graph or the data on which it is based came from. A reference list at the end of your work should provide the full bibliographic details of all sources.

Make sure that references are to the source *you* used, and not that of the author of the text you are borrowing from. For example, imagine you are copying a penguin population graph you found in a 1997 book by Dr Emperor. Emperor had, in turn, cited the source of her graphed data as the Argentine Penguin Research Foundation. Following the author-date system, the graph you present in your work would be referenced as "(Argentine Penguin Research Foundation, in Emperor, 1997, p. 12)." The reference would not simply be to Emperor; of course, there would also be a full reference to Emperor's work in the list at the end of your paper. See chapter 14 for further information.

DIFFERENT TYPES OF GRAPHS

Various forms of graphic communication are described in this chapter, with some advice on their construction. In a deliberate strategy, all graphs in this book have been drawn using Microsoft Excel. While other more powerful software packages for producing graphics exist, Excel is a commonly available package that produces adequate figures for most undergraduate assignments. It is readily available in most universities, and students familiar with computers should be able to produce graphics comparable with (or better than) any of those shown in this chapter. Hand-drawn figures can easily be drawn to the same standard. Table 16.1 provides a summary of the major forms of graphics discussed and their nature and function.

Scattergrams

A scattergram is a graph of point data plotted by (x,y) coordinates (see Figure 16.1 for an example). Scattergrams are usually created to provide a visual impression of the direction and strength of a relationship between variables.

The *independent* variable (the one that causes change) is depicted on the horizontal *x-axis*, and the *dependent* variable (the variable that changes as a result of change in the independent variable) is plotted on the *y-axis*. To illustrate the difference between independent and dependent variables, consider the relationship between precipitation levels and costs associated with flooding. Damage costs associated with flooding will usually depend on the amount of rainfall. Thus rainfall is the independent variable (x-axis) and damage costs are dependent (y-axis). Or, the severity of injuries associated with a motor vehicle accident (dependent variable, y-axis) tends to increase with motor vehicle speed (independent variable, x-axis).

Table 16.1   Types of graphic and their nature/function

Type of graphic	Nature/function
Scattergram	Graph of point data plotted by (x,y) coordinates. Usually created to provide visual impression of direction and strength of relationship between variables.
Line graph	Values of observed phenomena are connected by lines. Used to illustrate change over time.
Bar chart	Observed values are depicted by one or more horizontal or vertical bars whose length is proportional to value(s) represented.
Histogram	Similar to a bar graph, but commonly used to depict distribution of a continuous variable. Bar area is proportional to value represented. Thus if class intervals depicted are of different sizes, the column areas will reflect this.
Population pyramid	Form of histogram showing the number or percentage of people in different age groups of a population.
Pie (circle) chart	Circular-shaped graph in which proportions of some total sum (the whole 'pie') are depicted as 'slices'. The area of each 'slice' is directly proportional to the size of the variable portrayed.
Logarithmic graph (log-log and semi-log)	Form of graph using logarithmic graph paper. Key intervals on logarithmic axes are exponents of ten. Log graphs allow depiction of wide data ranges.
Table	Systematically arranged list of facts or numbers, usually set out in rows and columns. Presents summary data or information in orderly, unified fashion.

TIP

Be sure to put
dependent and
independent variables
on the correct axes of
your graph.

After points are located on the scattergram, you might draw a "line of best fit" through the points "by eye" (that is, your visual impression of the relationship). This line may also be calculated mathematically and the regression equation expressed on the graph (see Figure 16.1).

Line graphs

Line graphs are typically used to illustrate continuous changes in some phenomenon over time, with any trends being shown by the rise and fall of the line. Line graphs may also show the relationship between two sets of data. Examples of line graphs are shown in Figures 16.2, 16.3, and 16.4.

Do not use a line graph if you are dealing with disconnected data (Eisenberg, p. 97). For example, if you have air pollution data for every second year since 1945, the information should be graphed using a bar chart because a line graph would incorrectly suggest that you have the figures for each intervening year.

Construction of a line graph

Plot each (x,y) data point for your data set(s). When all the data points are plotted, join the points associated with each data set to produce lines such

Figure 16.1   Example of a scattergram. Life expectancy and total fertility rates, selected countries, 2000–2005

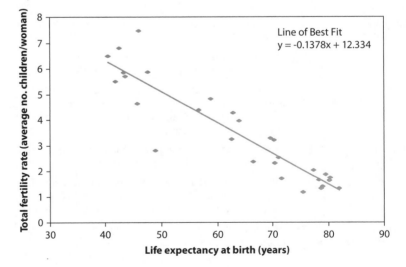

Data Source: United Nations, 2004, pp. 67–77

Figure 16.2   Example of a line graph. Number of sites inscribed on the World Heritage List, 1977–2004

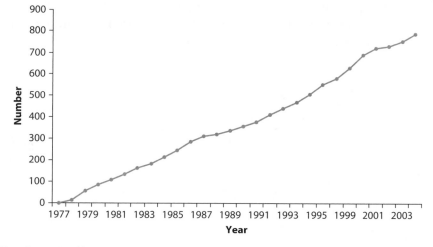

Data Source: World Heritage Centre, 2005, pp. 1–14

Figure 16.3   Example of a line graph. Immigrants and emigrants, Canada, 2008–2009

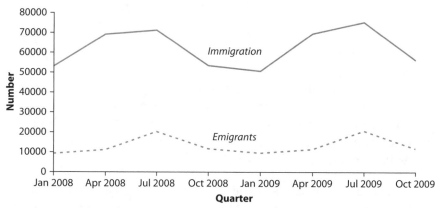

Data Source: Statistics Canada, catalogue no. 91-002-X, tables 4-3 and 4-4. See http://www.statcan.gc.ca/pub/91-002-x/2010003/tablesectlist-listetableauxsect-eng.htm

as those shown in Figures 16.2, 16.3, and 16.4. In some cases it is more appropriate to draw smooth curves than it is to "join the dots" (Mohan, McGregor, & Strano, 1992, p. 284; Pechenik, p. 168) where, for example, a clear trend is disrupted by a single inconsistent data point. Make any such judgments very carefully.

Figure 16.4   Example of a line graph. Mean NDVI (Normalized Difference Vegetation Index)—a measure of vegetation "vigour"—following application of three different herbicides. Figures calculated using Red and NIR (near-infrared) reflectance recordings from 3 × 1 m square test plots (10 plots for each herbicide)

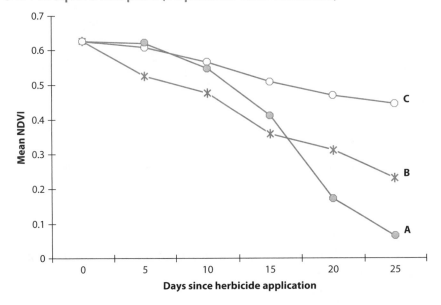

If a number of lines are depicted in one graph, ensure that they can easily be distinguished from one another (see Figures 16.3 and 16.4) by use of colour, dotted lines, or labels.

If you are showing average (mean) values on your graph, you can usefully provide a visual summary of the variation within the data by, for example, depicting the data range or the standard deviation about the mean (Pechenik, p. 171). An example is shown at Figure 16.5.

As Pechenik (p. 172) points out,

> Plots of standard deviations or standard errors are always symmetrical about the mean and so convey only partial information about the range of values obtained. If more of your individual values are above the mean than below the mean, the error bars will give a misleading impression about how the data are actually distributed. If your graph is fairly simple, you may be able to achieve the best of both worlds, indicating both the range and standard deviation (or standard error).

An example is given in Figure 16.6.

If you do include indicators of variation in your graph, make sure that you include details of what you have plotted in any notes that accompany the figure, together with the number of measurements associated with each mean (Pechenik, p. 173).

Figure 16.5 Example of a graph showing variation within data (mean and range). Mean (including trendline) and range (minimum–maximum) of NDVI (Normalized Difference Vegetation Index)—a measure of vegetation "vigour"—measurements. Figures calculated using Red and NIR (near-infrared) reflectance recordings from 3 × 1 m square test plots (10 plots for each herbicide)

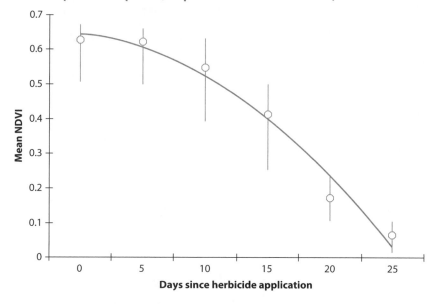

Line graphs will sometimes compare things that have different measurements. This can be done by using vertical axes on the left and right sides of the graph to depict the different scales. Figure 16.7 provides an illustration of the use of multiple vertical axis labels.

Bar charts

Bar charts are of two main types: **horizontal bar graphs** and **vertical bar graphs**. Figures 16.8 and 16.9 show each type, respectively. Horizontal bar graphs usually represent a single period, whereas column graphs may represent similar items at different times (Moorhouse, 1974, p. 67).

In bar graphs, the *length* of each bar is proportional to the value it represents (Coggins & Hefford, 1966, p. 66). It is here that bar graphs differ from histograms, with which they are sometimes confused. Histograms use bars whose *areas* are proportional to the values depicted.

Bar charts are a commonly used and easily understood way of taking a snapshot of variables at one point in time, depicting data in groups, and showing the size of each group (Windschuttle & Windschuttle, 1988, p. 278; Moorhouse, p. 64). Figure 16.10 achieves all these ends in a single graph.

Figure 16.6   Example of a graph showing variation within data (data range, mean, and standard deviation). Variations in NDVI (Normalized Difference Vegetation Index)—a measure of vegetation "vigour"—measurements. Figures calculated using Red and NIR (near-infrared) reflectance recordings from 3 × 1 m square test plots (10 plots for each herbicide)

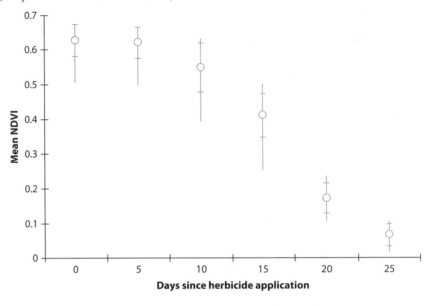

Figure 16.7   Example of a graph using multiple vertical axis labels. Ottawa climate, average monthly precipitation, and daily average temperature, 1971–2000

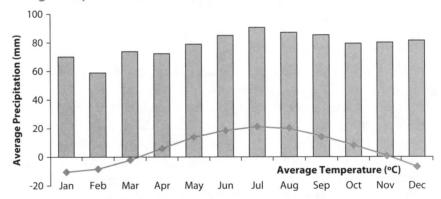

Data Source: National Climate Data and Information Archive (see http://climate.weatheroffice.gc.ca/climate_normals/results_e.html?Province=ALL&StationName=ottawa&SearchType=BeginsWith&LocateBy=Province&Proximity=25&ProximityFrom=City&StationNumber=&IDType=MSC&CityName=&ParkName=&LatitudeDegrees=&LatitudeMinutes=&LongitudeDegrees=&LongitudeMinutes=&NormalsClass=A&SelNormals=&StnId=4337&)

Figure 16.8   Example of a horizontal bar graph. Water volume used per hectare in agriculture in Alberta, by crop type, 2007

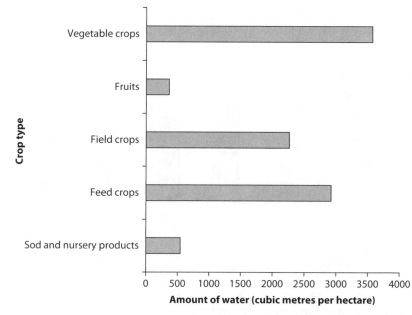

Data Source: Statistics Canada, Environment Accounts and Statistics Division, Agricultural Water Use Survey (survey no. 5145). See http://www.statcan.gc.ca/pub/16-001-m/2009008/t012-eng.htm

Figure 16.9   Example of a vertical bar graph. Prevalence of food insecurity by age group, Canada, 2000–2001

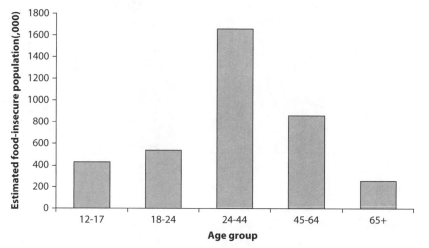

Data Source: 2000/1 Canadian Community Health Survey (cited in Statistics Canada, catalogue no. 82-003. See http://www.statcan.gc.ca/studies-etudes/82-003/archive/2005/7841-eng.pdf)

Bar charts can also be used to show the components of data as well as data totals. See Figure 16.11 for an example of such a *subdivided bar chart*.

Figure 16.10   Example of a bar chart. Male and female death rates from motor vehicle accidents, 1979–2004

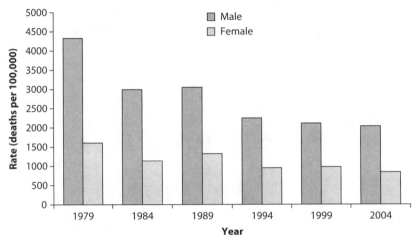

Data Source: Statistics Canada, catalogue no. 82-003-X (see http://www.statcan.gc.ca/pub/82-003-x/2008003/article/10648/t/5202443-eng.htm)

Figure 16.11   Example of a subdivided bar chart. Comparison of employment and unemployment rate in Quebec, 1996–2006

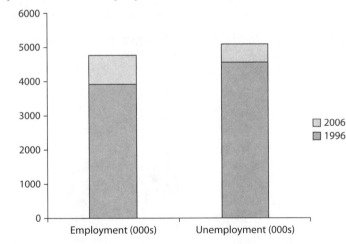

Data source: Statistics Canada, catalogue no. 92-596-XWE

It is possible to go one step further and represent data in the form of a *subdivided 100% bar chart* (see Figure 16.12 for an example). These can be useful to depict figures whose totals are so different that it would be almost impossible to chart them in absolute amounts (Moorhouse, p. 66).

As Figure 16.13 shows, bar charts can be used to portray negative as well as positive quantities.

Construction of a bar chart

Examine the data that are to be graphed and select suitable scales for the graph's axes. In general, scales should start at zero (Coggins & Hefford, p. 66), although this is not critical. Label the axes.

When the chart is being designed, it is important to consider the sequence of items being depicted. In general, the items should be listed in order of importance to the viewer. However, in simple comparisons in a horizontal bar graph format, it is best to arrange the bars in descending order of length from bottom to top. Having said that, you must also be aware that some data sets are listed, by convention, in particular orders. Graphs should typically reflect such customary presentation forms. If you are not sure whether to set up a table in descending order, speak to your lecturer.

The next step is to draw in the bars. Their width is a matter of choice, but should be constant within a graph. If you use different widths within the same graph, some readers may be led to believe that bar width, and hence area, is more important than length. Bars should be separated from one another, reflecting the discrete nature of the observed values (Jennings, 1990, p. 18), and the space between the bars should be about half to three-quarters of their width. However, where the pattern of change is of greater importance than the individual values, no space between the observations is left at all (Coggins & Hefford, p. 66).

Finally, add appropriate title, labels, key, and reference.

Figure 16.12   Example of subdivided 100% bar chart. Household type by province, Atlantic Canada, 2006

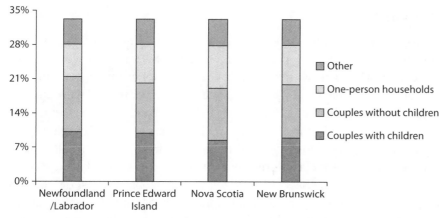

Data Source: Statistics Canada, Census of Population, 2006 (Distribution of households by household structure, Canada, provinces and territories, 2006. See http://www12.statcan.gc.ca/census-recensement/2006/as-sa/97-553/table/t5-eng.cfm)

Figure 16.13   Example of a bar chart depicting positive and negative values. Annual population growth rates for provinces and territories, 2006–2007

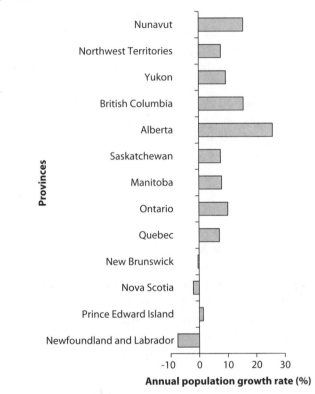

Data Source: Statistics Canada, Catalogue no. 91-215-X (a complete chart also exists, and includes information for 07\08. See http://www41.statcan.gc.ca/2009/3867/grafx/htm/cybac3867_000_2-eng.htm#table)

Histograms

Histograms are mainly used to show the distribution of values of a continuous variable. A continuous variable is one that could have any conceivable value within an observed range (for example, plant height, rainfall measurements, temperature) and may be contrasted with discrete data in which no fractional numbers, such as halves or quarters, exist (for example, plant and animal numbers). For examples of histograms, see Figure 16.14. This figure shows three histograms drawn using the same data set but different **class intervals**. Class intervals are explained shortly.

Histograms may be confused with vertical bar charts or column graphs, but there is a technical difference. Histograms depict frequency through the *area* of the column, whereas bar charts show frequency by column *height*. Thus, histograms usually have bars of equal width because the class intervals are the same. But if the class intervals are different sizes, the columns should reflect this. For example, if one class interval on a graph was $0 to $9 and the second was $10 to $29, the second column should be drawn twice as wide as the first.

The phenomenon whose size is being depicted is plotted on the horizontal x-axis. Frequency of occurrence is plotted on the vertical y-axis. The frequency is the number of occurrences of the measured variable within a specific class interval (for example, number of hotels with rooms available in a given price category).

Construction of a histogram

As Figure 16.14 shows, the method you choose to construct your histogram can have a significant effect on the appearance of the graph you finally produce. Parts (a), (b), and (c) of Figure 16.14 were drawn using the same data (shown in Table 16.2), but each was drawn using different methods of calculating class intervals and frequency distributions. Part (a) splits the data range evenly on the basis of the *number* of x-axis classes desired. Part (b) shows the data on the basis of the desired *size* of the x-axis classes (in this case Can$55), and Part (c) is the product of *minimizing in-class variations* while maximizing between-class variations.

The first two methods of working out class intervals and frequency distributions require that you calculate the range of the data set. Range is

> **TIP**
>
> Range is the difference between the highest data value and the lowest.

Figure 16.14   Example of histograms drawn using the same data but different class intervals. Hotel accommodation costs, Wellington, New Zealand, 1994

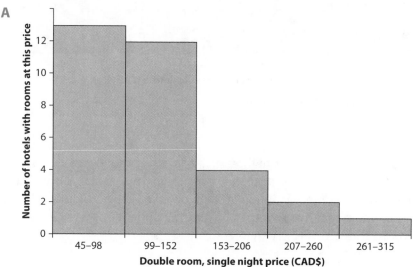

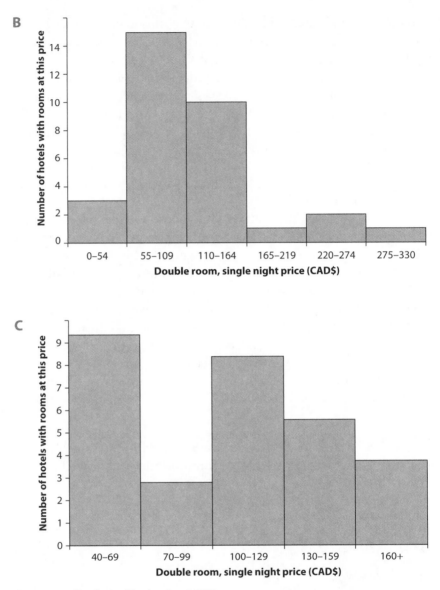

Data source: New Zealand Tourism Board, 1995

the difference between the highest data value and the lowest data value. To illustrate, consider the data shown in Table 16.2, which displays the price of hotel accommodation in Wellington, New Zealand, during 1994.

The most expensive room rate in Wellington in 1994 was CAD$315; the lowest was CAD$45. Therefore, the range is

$315 − $45 = $270

The next step is to calculate class intervals.

Table 16.2 Data set for histogram construction. Single night, double room hotel accommodation rates (CAD$), Wellington, 1994

109	253	118	56
112	124	60	45
95	162	90	59
45	198	100	50
136	156	315	50
156	105	144	65
253	118	101	55
105	152	50	80

Data Source: New Zealand Tourism Board, 1995

Methods of calculating class intervals

1. One common strategy for calculating class intervals is simply to divide the range by the number of classes you wish to portray. The result will be a number of evenly sized classes. For example, the range of the data in Table 16.2 is $315 – $45 = $270. You might have decided that you wish to have a histogram with five classes. Divide $270 by 5 and the result is an interval of $54 (which you might want to round up to $55 for the sake of "tidiness"). Thus we have intervals of

   Class 1 $45–98
   Class 2 $99–152
   Class 3 $153–206
   Class 4 $207–260
   Class 5 $261–315

   The lowest class begins with the lowest value ($45 in this example). To find the *lower limit* of the *next* class we add $54, which produces a figure of $99. We then add $54 to $99 to produce the lower limit of the next class, $153, and so on. The *upper limit* of each class is found by subtracting 1 unit of the measurement form being used (for example $1, 1 cm, 1 m, 0.01 gram, 1 tonne) from the lower limit of the class above. The upper limit of the lowest class in the example is, therefore, $98. Repeat this procedure until the intervals for all classes are calculated. Note that *discrete class intervals* are used (for example, $45–$98, $99–$152, rather than $55–$99, $99–$153). In this way there is no confusion about the class within which any data point is placed (for example, in which class would you put a $99 room charge?). This method was used to produce Figure 16.14(a).

2. An alternative, but closely related, strategy is the one followed in producing Figure 16.14(b). Calculate the data range and then think about the character of the data set to be portrayed. Would it be more useful

to your audience if you divided the range by the class interval you decided on, rather than letting the number of classes determine the size of the interval? Would your audience find it easier to read the data on a graph that uses intervals of, for example, 10s or 50s rather than the 13s, 77s, 54s, and other peculiar numbers that might be achieved in the strategy discussed above? Similarly, would it be useful to begin or end the class intervals at some points other than those fixed by the high and low points of the data set? The following intervals for the data in Table 16.2 were chosen in recognition of such considerations.

Class 1 $0–54
Class 2 $55–109
Class 3 $110–164
Class 4 $165–219
Class 5 $220–274
Class 6 $275–330

3. Yet another technique for working out class intervals is to minimize in-class variations while simultaneously maximizing between-class variations. Look for clusters of data points within the total data set and subdivide the data range into equally sized divisions that best discriminate between clusters. A useful tool in this process is the *linear plot*. Draw a horizontal line and affix to it a scale sufficient to embrace the maximum and minimum values of the data. Locate each of the data points on the scale with a short vertical line. If you are using the linear plot for presentation purposes, rather than for calculation only, you should also label each of the data points and provide a title and source. The plot will graphically portray the data distribution, as in Figure 16.15.

In this example, the data is clustered quite heavily in the range $50–$150. It might be appropriate to produce a histogram that breaks the data into the following ranges:

Class 1 $40–69
Class 2 $70–99
Class 3 $100–129
Class 4 $130–159
Class 5 $160+

This strategy was used to produce Figure 16.14(c).

Figure 16.15   Example of a linear plot, using data from Table 16.2

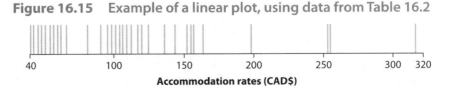

Accommodation rates (CAD$)

There is no definite rule governing the number of classes in a frequency distribution. Choose too few and information could be lost. With a lot of classes, too many minor details may be retained, thereby obscuring major features.

Once you have worked out class intervals, the next step is to construct a **frequency table** to work out the total number of individual items of data that will occur in a particular class.

Construction of a frequency table

A frequency table is simply a tally sheet indicating the number of times observations fall into specific class intervals. Table 16.3 is an example.

Table 16.3   Frequency table of data from Table 16.2

Classes ($)	Tally of occurrence	Frequency
0–54	III	3
55–109	JHT JHT JHT	15
110–164	JHT JHT	10
165–219	I	1
220–274	II	2
275–330	I	1

The observed frequency is then plotted on the y-axis of the histogram and the classes are plotted on the x-axis (see Figure 16.14(b)). The columns that result should touch each other to reflect the continuous nature of the observations.

Population pyramids or age-sex pyramids

A **population pyramid** is a form of histogram that shows the number or, more commonly, the percentage of individuals in different age groups (cohorts) of a population. They also illustrate the female-male composition of that population. Figure 16.16 is an example of a population pyramid.

Construction of a population pyramid

Although a population pyramid is a form of histogram, a few peculiarities bear noting. As Figure 16.16 shows, a population pyramid is drawn on one vertical axis and two horizontal axes. The vertical axis represents age and is usually subdivided into five-year age cohorts (for example, 0–4, 5–9, 10–14 years). The size of those cohorts may be changed (for example, to 0–9, 10–19, or 0–14, 15–19) depending on the nature of the raw data and the purpose of your pyramid. Remember from the discussion of histograms, however, that if you depict different-sized cohorts in the same pyramid, the area of each bar must reflect that variability. For example, a

Figure 16.16   Example of a population pyramid. Age-sex structure of Canada, 2006 (total population = 31,612,895)

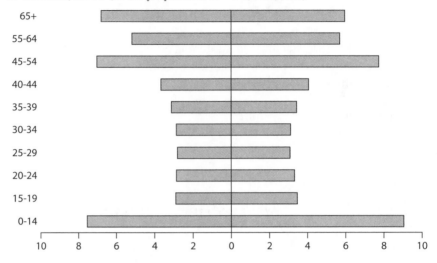

Data Source: Statistics Canada, 2006 Census of Population, catalogue no. 97-551-XCB2006013 (Canada, Code01). See www12.statcan.gc.ca/census-recensement/2006/dp-pd/tbt/Rp-eng.cfm?LANG=E&APATH =3&DETAIL=0&DIM=0&FL=A&FREE=0&GC=0&GID=0&GK=0&GRP=1&PID=88992&PRID=0&PTYPE=889 71,97154&S=0&SHOWALL=0&SUB=0&Temporal=2006&THEME=66&VID=0&VNAMEE=&VNAMEF=

> **TIP**
>
> By convention, a population pyramid shows males on the left and females on the right.

0–14 cohort would be half as wide as a 15–44 cohort on the same graph. On either side of the central vertical axis are the two horizontal axes. That on the *left* of the pyramid shows the percentage (or number) of *males*, while that on the *right* shows the figures for *females*. You will also see from Figure 16.16 that the zero point for each of the horizontal axes is in the centre of the graph. As a final note, it may also be helpful for your reader if you include a statement within the graph of the total population of the place described in your pyramid.

Circle or pie charts

Pie charts show how a whole is divided up into parts and what share or percentage belongs to each part. Pie charts are a dramatic way of illustrating the relative sizes of portions of some complete entity (Windschuttle & Windschuttle, pp. 272–3). For example, a pie chart might show how a budget is divided up and who receives what share of the total. See Figure 16.17 for an example of a pie chart.

Construction of a pie chart

Construction of a pie chart usually requires a little arithmetic. You have to match the 360 degrees that make up the circumference of a circle with the percentage size of each of the variables to be graphed. Do this by multiplying the percentage size of each variable by 3.6 to find the number of degrees

Figure 16.17 Example of a pie chart. Highest level of education of Registered Indians, 2006 (total population = 427,495)

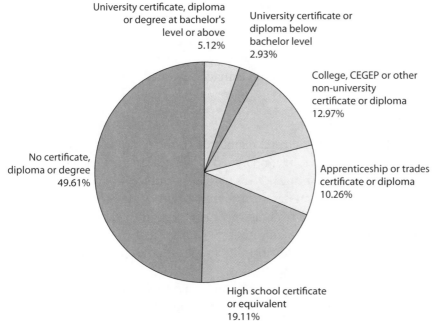

Data Source: Statistics Canada, 2006 Census of Population, catalogue no. 97-560-XCB2006038. See www12.statcan.gc.ca/census-recensement/2006/dp-pd/tbt/Rp-eng.cfm?LANG=E&APATH=3&DETAIL=0 &DIM=0&FL=A&FREE=0&GC=0&GID=0&GK=0&GRP=1&PID=97688&PRID=0&PTYPE=88971,97154&S=0 &SHOWALL=0&SUB=0&Temporal=2006&THEME=75&VID=0&VNAMEE=&VNAMEF=

to which it equates. Obviously, if the values have not already been translated into percentages of the whole, this will need to be done first.

For example, it might be predicted that the population of Victoria, Australia, in 2041 will be 5,750,000 against a national population of 27 million. That is, the population of Victoria might be 21.3 per cent of the national total. If a pie diagram of the Australian population by states and territories were to be drawn, the segment representing Victoria would have an angle of

$$(575\,0000 \div 27000\,000) \times 100 = 21.3\%$$
$$= 21.3 \times 3.6\ 76.7\,\text{degrees}$$

It is best not to have too many categories (or "slices") in a pie chart as this creates visual confusion. Five or six segments is a fair maximum. Generally, no segment should be smaller than six degrees. You may need to group some classes together to achieve this.

The sectors of a pie chart normally run clockwise, with the largest sector occurring first. The starting point for the first sector is created by drawing a vertical line from the centre of the circle to the 12 o'clock position on the circumference.

Pie charts should also advise the reader of the *total value* of categories plotted, as shown, for example, by the statement in Figure 16.17 of the total population of Registered Indians. There is little point in letting a reader know percentages without allowing them the opportunity to determine exactly how much that percentage represents in absolute terms.

> **TIP**
>
> A pie chart should always make clear the total value of all categories it illustrates.

Logarithmic graphs

Logarithmic graphs are used mainly when the range of data values to be plotted is too great to depict on a graph with arithmetic axes (commonly a **scattergram** or **line graph**). National Gross Domestic Product figures are good examples of such data, for national figures range from millions of dollars to billions and trillions of dollars. Similarly, population figures, which might grow from hundreds to thousands to millions, sometimes necessitate the use of a logarithmic graph. Figures 16.18 and 16.19 are examples of logarithmic graphs.

Logarithmic graphs are sometimes also used to compare rates of change within and between data sets. Despite vast differences in numbers,

Figure 16.18   Comparison of same data displayed on (a) semi-log and (b) arithmetic graph paper. **Canada's resident population, 1871–2006**

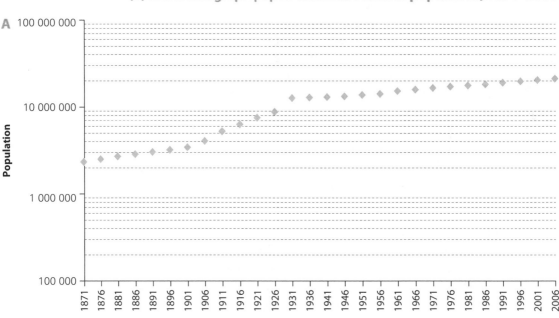

B

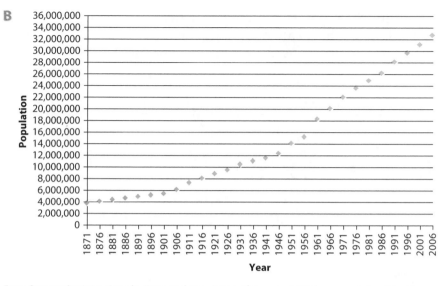

Data Source: Statistics Canada, Estimated Population of Canada, 1605 to present. See http://www.statcan.gc.ca/pub/98-187-x/4151287-eng.htm

if line *slopes* in a logarithmic graph are the same, then the *rates* of change are similar. This might be useful, for example, if you were illustrating rates of historical population growth and trying to argue that despite the fact that the population is now growing at millions of people per year, the rate of change has not actually changed since some earlier period when the population was growing by thousands each year.

Before discussing logarithmic graphs any further, it might be helpful to provide a little useful background information. First, the logarithm of a number is the power to which 10 must be raised to give that number. For example, the log of 100 is 2 because $10^2 = 100$ (that is, 10 raised to the power 2 = 100). Thus the log of 10 is 1; the log of 100 is 2; the log of 1000 is 3; and so on.

Second, simple line graphs and scattergrams typically use *arithmetic* scales on their axes (for example, 1, 2, 3, 4 or 0, 2, 4, 6) where a constant numerical difference is shown by an equal interval on the graph axes. In contrast, **semi-logarithmic** and **log-logarithmic** graphs use a *logarithmic* scale where the numerical value of each key interval on the graph increases *exponentially* (for example 10, 100, 1,000, 10,000) and the lines in each *cycle* (each cycle is an exponent of 10) of the graph become progressively closer together (see Figures 16.18(a) and 16.19 for examples). Figure 16.18(a) is an example of a *semi-logarithmic* graph. It has a logarithmic y-axis and an arithmetic x-axis. (Histograms and bar charts can also be drawn using semi-logarithmic paper if the variable to be depicted by the y-axis has a particularly large range.) Figure 16.19 is a *log-log* graph—both axes are logarithmic.

TIP

Logarithmic graphs are good for depicting vast data ranges.

TIP

Semi-log graphs have one logarithmic axis; log-log graphs have two.

Figure 16.19   Example of a graph with two logarithmic axes (a "log-log" graph). Relationship between gross domestic product and passenger cars in use, selected countries, 1992

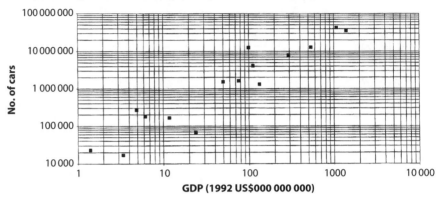

Data source: World Almanac, 1995

Zero is never used on a logarithmic scale because the logarithm of zero is not defined. Scales on log paper start with 0.001, 0.01, 0.1, 1, 10, 100, 1000, 10,000, 100,000 (or any other exponent of 10). If you look at Figure 16.19 as an example, you will see that the x-axis commences at 1 whereas the y-axis commences at 10,000. The determination of the figure with which to start the axis is made on the basis of the smallest data point. For example, if the smallest figure for plotting was 35,000, you would start the axis at 10,000, not 1,000 or 100,000.

Construction of a logarithmic graph

Consider the maximum and minimum values of the data sets to be plotted. In looking, for example, at the population of Canada over the period 1871–2006, the population grew from approximately 3.7 million people to 32.6 million people.

To accommodate this range of data, the graph will need to have three logarithmic cycles, with the first commencing at 10,000, the second at 100,000, and the third at 1,000,000. Because the years are plotted arithmetically, the graph will be drawn in semi-log format. Simply plot data points at their appropriate (x,y) coordinates. Add an informative title and an indication of data source. The same procedures apply for log-log graphs except, of course, that it is necessary to consider the number of cycles for both axes, not just one.

TABLES

Tables present related facts or observations in an orderly, unified manner. They are used most commonly for summarizing results. Tables can be effective for organizing and communicating large amounts of information, especially numerical data, although you should not make the mistake of trying to communicate too much information at once.

The main reasons for using tables are

- to facilitate comparisons;
- to reveal relationships; and
- to save space.

Tables should be self-explanatory. This requires a comprehensive title and good labelling. Data in the table may be referred to and discussed in accompanying text, but should not be repeated extensively. Table 16.4 is an example of a correctly set out table.

Elements of a table

Aside from the information being conveyed, following are the main elements of a table:

- *Table number:* Each table should have a unique number (for example, Table 1) allowing it to be easily identified in textual discussion.

Table 16.4   Example of a table. Population by religion, by province and territory, 2001

Province/ Territory	Religion							No religious affiliation
	Christian	Muslim	Jewish	Buddhist	Hindu	Sikh	Other	
Canada	22,851,825	579,640	329,995	300,345	297,200	278,410	101,525	4,900,090
British Columbia	2,124,615	56,220	21,230	85,540	31,500	135,310	26,175	1,388,300
Alberta	2,099,435	49,040	11,085	33,410	15,965	23,470	13,895	694,840
Saskatchewan	795,935	2,230	865	3,050	1,585	500	7,530	151,455
Manitoba	859,055	5,095	13,040	5,745	3,835	5,485	5,575	205,865
Ontario	8,413,495	352,530	190,795	128,320	217,555	104,875	36,765	1,841,290
Quebec	6,442,430	108,620	89,915	41,380	24,525	8,225	7,295	413,190
Newfoundland	493,480	630	140	185	405	135	245	12,865
New Brunswick	657,880	1,275	670	545	475	90	1,120	57,665
Nova Scotia	780,535	3,545	2,120	1,730	1,235	270	1,720	106,405
Prince Edward Island	123,795	195	55	140	30	0	205	8,950
Yukon	16,660	60	35	130	10	100	520	11,015
Northwest Territories	29,645	180	25	155	65	45	140	6,600
Nunavut	24,855	30	0	15	10	0	105	1,655

Source: Based on data from Statistics Canada, Census of Population, 2001. See http://www40.statcan.gc.ca/l01/cst01/demo30b-eng.htm

- *Title:* The title, which is placed above the table itself, should be brief yet allow any reader to fully comprehend the information presented without reference to other text. The title should answer "what," "where," and "when" questions about the table.
- *Column headings:* These should explain the meaning of data appearing in the columns. If appropriate, specify the units of measurement (for example, $, mm, litres) within column headings. Place a dividing line below the column headings to separate them from the data. The bottom of the table should be marked with a single horizontal line.
- *Notes:* Any notes should appear below the table. These are used to provide supplementary information to the reader, such as restrictions that apply to some of the reported data. Table notes may also be used to explain any unusual abbreviations or symbols.
- *Source:* An indication of the source of the data or table should be provided. See chapter 14 for more information on acknowledging sources.

In the end, always be sure that the way you present a table or figure helps your reader understand it completely and correctly. If you have any doubts, present the figure or table to a friend or your lecturer as a stand-alone document and ask them if it makes sense!

GLOSSARY

class intervals The range of each class of data.

frequency table A tally sheet indicating the number of times observations fall into specific class intervals.

histogram A figure used to show the distribution of values of a continuous variable.

horizontal bar graph A bar chart that usually represents a single period.

line graph A figure used to illustrate continuous changes in some phenomenon over time, with any trends being shown by the rise and fall of the line.

logarithmic graph A figure used mainly when the range of data values to be plotted is too great to depict on a graph with arithmetic axes (commonly a scattergram or line graph).

log-logarithmic graph A figure that has two logarithmic axes.

pie chart This figure shows how a whole is divided up into parts and what share or percentage belongs to each part.

population pyramid A form of histogram that shows the number or, more commonly, the percentage of individuals in different age groups (cohorts) of a population.

scattergram A figure that typically uses arithmetic scales on its axes where a constant numerical difference is shown by an equal interval on the graph axes. See **line graph**.

semi-logarithmic graph   A figure that has one logarithmic axis.

table   A chart used most commonly for summarizing results, which presents related facts or observations in an orderly, unified manner.

vertical bar graph   A bar chart that represents items similar to those of the horizontal bar graph at different times.

SUGGESTED FURTHER READING

Alley, Michael. (1996). *The craft of scientific writing*. New York: Springer Publishing.

Gustavii, Bjorn. (2008). *How to write and illustrate a scientific paper*. New York: Cambridge University Press.

Tufte, Edward. (2006). *Beautiful evidence*. Cheshire, CN: Graphics Press.

Turabian, Kate. (2007). *A manual for writers of research papers, theses, and dissertations: Chicago style for students and researchers* (7th ed.). Chicago: University of Chicago Press.

RELATED WEBSITES

www.ruf.rice.edu/~bioslabs/tools/tools.html
Reformed University Fellowship, Rice University. "Writing and analytical resources."

www.edwardtufte.com/tufte/index
Tufte, Edward. "ET Modern."

http://libguides.usc.edu/content.php?pid=83009&sid=652258
University of Southern California. "Organizing your social sciences research paper."

References and Useful Resources

American Psychological Association. (2010). "APA style blog." http://blog.apastyle.org/apastyle/social-media/

American Psychological Association. "Basics of APA style tutorial." http://flash1r.apa.org/apastyle/basics/index.htm

Australian Government Publishing Service. (1994). *Style manual for authors, editors and printers* (5th ed.). Canberra, AU: AGPS.

Barass, R. (1984). *Study! A Guide to Effective Study, Revision and Examination Techniques*. London: Chapman & Hall.

Barker, J. (17 August 2005). "Evaluating Web pages: Techniques to apply & questions to ask." http://www.lib.berkeley.edu/TeachingLib/Guides/Internet/Evaluate.html

Barrett, H.M. (1982). *One way to write anything*. New York: Barnes & Noble.

Barry, V.E., & Rudinow, J. (1990). *Invitation to critical thinking* (2nd ed.). Orlando, FL: Holt Rinehart & Winston, Inc.

Bate, D., & Sharpe, P. (1990). *Student writer's handbook*. Sydney, AU: Harcourt Brace Jovanovich.

Beck, S.E. "Evaluation criteria." Retrieved 17 August 2005 from http://lib.nmsu.edu/instruction/eval-crit.html

Behrendorff, M. (1995). *Practical aspects of producing a level three report for the Department of Mechanical Engineering*. Adelaide, AU: University of Adelaide.

Berg, L., & Mansvelt, J. (2000). Writing in, speaking out: Communicating qualitative research findings. In I. Hay (Ed.), *Qualitative research methods in human geography* (pp. 161–82). Melbourne, AU: Oxford University Press.

Bernstein, T.M. (1979). *The careful writer: A modern guide to English usage*. New York: Atheneum.

Beynon, R.J. (1993). *Postgraduate study in the biological sciences: A researcher's companion*. London: Portland Press.

Booth, V. (1993). *Communicating in science: Writing a scientific paper and speaking at scientific meetings* (2nd ed.). Cambridge: Cambridge University Press.

Boyd, B., & Taffs, K. (2003). *Mapping the environment: A professional development manual*. Lismore, AU: Southern Cross University Press.

Bryant, J., Baggott, L., & Searle, J. (2002). *Bioethics for scientists*. Chichester, UK: John Wiley & Sons Ltd.

Bundy, A. (Ed.). (2004). *Australian and New Zealand information literacy framework: Principles, standards and practice*. Adelaide, AU: Australian and New Zealand Institute for Information Literacy.

Bunting, T., Filion, P., & Walker, R. (Eds.). (2010). *Canadian cities in transition: New directions in the twenty-first century*. (4th ed.). Toronto: Oxford University Press.

Burchfield, R.W. (Ed.). (1996). *The New Fowler's Modern English Usage* (3rd ed.). New York: Oxford University Press.

Burdess, N. (1991). *The handbook of student skills for the social sciences and humanities*. New York: Prentice Hall.

Burkill, S., & Abbey, C. (2004). Avoiding plagiarism. *Journal of Geography in Higher Education, 28*(3), 439–46.

Calef, W.C. (1964). Canons of reviewing [Course handout]. Normal, IL: Illinois State University.

Cartography Specialty Group of the Association of American Geographers. (July 1995). Guidelines for effective visuals at professional meetings. *AAG Newsletter, 50*(7), 5.

Central Queensland University Library. (2000). "Why do a literature review?" http://www.library.cqu.edu.au/litreviewpages/why.htm

Coggins, R.S., & Hefford, R.K. (1966). *The practical geographer* (2nd ed.). Melbourne, AU: Longman.

Conference Board of Canada. "Employability skills 2000+." http://www.conferenceboard.ca/Libraries/EDUC_PUBLIC/esp2000.sflb

Cottrell, S. (2003). *The study skills handbook* (2nd ed.) Hampshire, UK: Palgrave MacMillan.

Council of Australian University Librarians. (2001). *Information Literacy Standards.* Canberra, AU: Council of Australian University Librarians.

Courtenay, B. (1992). *The pitch.* Sydney, AU: Margaret Gee.

Dane, F.C. (1990). *Research methods.* Pacific Grove, CA: Brooks/Cole.

Day, R.A. (1989). *How to write and publish a scientific paper* (3rd ed.). Cambridge: Cambridge University Press.

Dixon, T. (2004). *How to get a first: The essential guide to academic success.* London: Routledge.

Dwyer, J. (1993). *The business communication handbook.* Australia: Prentice-Hall Inc.

Editors' Association of Canada. (2000). *Editing Canadian English* (2nd ed.). Toronto: Mcfarlane Walter & Ross.

Eisenberg, A. (1992). *Effective technical communication* (2nd ed.). New York: McGraw-Hill.

Endeavor Information Systems. (2005). *ENCompass,* Version 3.6, Endeavor Information Systems Inc.

Engle, M., Blumenthal, A., & Cosgrave, T. (2004). Cornell University. "How to prepare an annotated bibliography." http://www.library.cornell.edu/olinuris/ref/research/skill28.htm

Friedman, S., & Steinberg, S. (1989). *Writing and thinking in the social sciences.* Englewood Cliffs, NJ: Prentice-Hall.

Galanes, G.J., & Brilhart, J.K. (1997). *Communicating in groups: Applications and skills* (3rd ed.). Madison, WI: Brown & Benchmark.

Galanes, G.J., Adams, K., & Brilhart, J.K. (2000). *Communicating in groups: Applications and skills* (4th ed.). Boston: McGraw-Hill Higher Education.

Garnier, B.J. (1966). *Practical work in geography.* London: Edward Arnold.

Gerber, R. (1985). Designing graphics for effective learning. *Geographical Education, 5*(1), 27–33.

Gibbs, G. (1994). *Learning in teams: A student guide.* Oxford: Oxford Centre for Staff Development.

Gould, P. (1993). *The slow plague: A geography of the AIDS pandemic.* Cambridge, MA: Blackwell.

Grantham, D.W. (1987). *Recent America.* Arlington Heights, IL: Harlan Davidson.

Greetham, B. (2001). *How to write better essays.* Hampshire, UK: Palgrave.

Harrison, G.P., & Wallace, A.R. (25 August 2005). Climate sensitivity of marine energy. *Renewable Energy, 30.* www.sciencedirect.com

Hay, I., Dunn, K., & Street, A. (2005). Making the most of your conference journey. *Journal of Geography in Higher Education, 29*(1), 159–71.

Hodge, D. (1994). Writing a good term paper [Course handout]. Seattle: University of Washington, Department of Geography.

Howenstine, E., Hay, I., Delaney, E., Bell, J., Norris, F., Whelan, A., Pirani, M., Chow, T., & Ross, A. (1988). Using a poster exercise in an introductory geography course. *Journal of Geography in Higher Education, 12*(2), 139–47.

International Cartographic Association. (1984). *Basic cartography for students and technicians, 1.* Great Britain: International Cartographic Association.

Jennings, J.T. (1990). *Guidelines for the Preparation of Written Work* (4th ed.). Adelaide, AU: University of Adelaide.

Knight, P., & Parsons, T. (2003). *How to do your essays, exams, and coursework in geography and related disciplines.* Cheltenham, UK: Nelson Thornes.

Krohn, J. (1991). Why are graphs so central in science? *Biology and Philosophy, 6*(2), 181–203.

Language Portal of Canada, Government of Canada. (2010). "Eliminating ethnic and racial stereotypes." http://www.noslangues-ourlanguages.gc.ca/bien-well/fra-eng/style/ethnicracial-eng.html

Larsgaard, M. (1978). *Map Librarianship.* Littleton, CO: Libraries Unlimited.

Lethbridge, R. (1991). *Techniques for successful seminars and poster presentations.* Melbourne, AU: Longman Cheshire.

Ley, D.F., & Bourne, L.S. (1993). Introduction: The social context and diversity of urban Canada. In L.S. Bourne & D.F. Ley (Eds.), *The changing social geography of Canadian cities*. Montreal & Kingston: McGill-Queen's University Press.

Library of Congress. (2005). "How to cite electronic sources." http://lcweb2.loc.gov/ammem/ndlpedu/start/cite/index.html

Lindsay, D. (1984). *A guide to scientific writing*. Melbourne: Longman Cheshire.

Marius, R., & Page, M.E. (2002). *A short guide to writing about history*. New York: Longman.

Mohan, T., McGregor, H., & Strano, Z. (1992). *Communicating! Theory and practice* (3rd ed.). Sydney: Harcourt Brace.

Montgomery, S.L. (2001). *The Chicago guide to communicating science*. Chicago: University of Chicago Press.

Moorhouse, C.E. (1974) *Visual messages*. Melbourne: Pitman.

Moxley, J.M. (1992). *Publish don't perish: The scholar's guide to academic writing and publishing*. Praeger: Westport, CT.

Mullins, C. (1977). *A guide to writing and publishing in the social behaviour sciences*. London: Wiley.

Nadeau, Kathleen. (1994). *Survival guide for college students with ADD or LD*. New York: Magination Press.

Najar, R., & Riley, L. (2004). *Developing academic writing skills*. Tokyo: MacMillan Languagehouse.

New Zealand Tourism Board. (1995). *New Zealand where to stay guide*. Wellington: New Zealand Tourism Board.

Northey, M., & Knight, D.B. (1992). *Making sense in geography and environmental studies*. Toronto: Oxford University Press.

Pechenik, J.A. (2004). *A short guide to writing about biology*. New York: Pearson Longman.

Procter, Margaret. (2010). "Referencing: Why and how across the disciplines." http://www.utoronto.ca/writing/handouts/PDreferencing.pdf

————. University of Toronto. "Understanding essay topics." http://writing.utoronto.ca/advice/general/essay-topics

————. University of Toronto. "Using thesis statements." http://writing.utoronto.ca/advice/planning-and-organizing/thesis-statements

Ramirez, Gerardo, & Beilock, Sian L. Writing about testing worries boosts exam performance in the classroom. *Science 331*(6014), 211–13. doi: 10.1126/science.1100427

Reynolds, Garr. "Ten top slide tips." http://www.garrreynolds.com/Presentation/slides.html

Rudinow, Joel, & Barry, Vincent E. (2004). *Invitation to critical thinking*. Belmont, CA: Wadsworth/Thomson Learning.

Robinson, A.H., Morrison, J.L., Muehrcke, P.C., Guptill, S.C., & Kimerling, A.J. (1994). *Elements of cartography* (6th ed.). New York: John Wiley.

Sim, R. (1981). *Lettering for signs, projects, posters, displays* (2nd ed.). Sydney, AU: Learning Publications.

Simmonds, D., & Reynolds, L. (1989). *Computer presentation of data in science*. Dordrecht, NL: Kluwer Academic.

Singleton, A. (1984). *Poster sessions: A guide to their use at meetings and conferences for presenters and organizers*. Oxford: Elsevier.

Steckley, John, & Letts, Guy Kirby. (2010). *Elements of sociology: A critical Canadian introduction* (2nd ed.). Toronto, ON: Oxford University Press.

Street, A., Hay, I., & Sefton, A. (2005). Giving talks in class. In J. Higgs, A. Sefton, A. Street, L. McAllister, & I. Hay (Eds.), *Communicating in the health and social sciences* (pp.176–83). Melbourne: Oxford University Press.

Sullivan, M.E. (1993). Choropleth mapping in secondary geography: An application for the study of Middle America. *Journal of Geography*, 92(2), 69–74.

Toyne, P., & Newby, P.T. (1971). *Techniques in human geography*. London: Macmillan.

United Nations (2004). *World population prospects: The 2004 revision, highlights*. New York: United Nations Department of Economic and Social Affairs, Population Division. http://www.un.org/esa/population/publications/WPP2004/2004Highlights_finalrevised.pdf

University at Buffalo (2005). "Evaluating resources: How to evaluate periodicals." http://ublib.buffalo.edu/libraries/asl/tutorials/evaluatingperiodicals.html

University of Chicago Press. (2010). *The Chicago Manual of Style* (16th ed.). http://www.chicagomanualofstyle.org/home.html

Vaughn, Lewis, & MacDonald, Chris. (2007). *The power of critical thinking: Canadian edition.* New York: Oxford University Press.

Vujakovic, P. (1995). Making posters. *Journal of Geography in Higher Education*, *19*(2), 251–6.

Williams College Libraries. (2010). "Citation guide." http://library.williams.edu/citing/

Windschuttle, K., & Elliott, E. (1994). *Writing, researching, communicating: Communication skills for the information age* (2nd ed.). Sydney, AU: McGraw-Hill.

Windschuttle, K., & Windschuttle, E. (1988) *Writing, researching, communicating* (1st ed.). Sydney, AU: McGraw-Hill.

Wolvin, A., & Coakley, C.G. (1996). *Listening.* Madison, WI: Brown & Benchmark.

Woodford, F.P. (1967). Sounder thinking through clearer writing. *Science*, *156*(3776), 744.

World Almanac (1995). New York: Newspaper Enterprise Association.

World Heritage Centre (2005). "Properties inscribed on the world heritage list." Paris: UNESCO World Heritage Centre. http://whc.unesco.org/pg.cfm?cid=47

Writing Lab, OWL at Purdue, & Purdue University. (2010). "Purdue online writing lab: Research and citation resources." http://owl.english.purdue.edu/owl/section/2/

Index

bibliographic management programs, 53, 120, 254

bibliography, 260; annotated, 31, 33, 191–3, 209

blackboards, 277

blogs, 141; citing, 253, 259

body: of essays, 168

books: citing, 254, 257; previewing, 41

brainstorming, 24, 33

breaks, from studying, 29–30

bullets: on slides, 272

Business Source Premier, 114

"busy" tasks, 28

Calef, W.C., 204

call numbers, 109, 113, 125

Canadian Oxford Dictionary, 213

capital letters, 237–8

causal framework, 265, 282

cause-and-effect reasoning, valid, 162

cell phones, 16, 276

chairperson (group role), 75

chapters: citing, 257; previewing, 42

charts. *See* graphs

cheating, 101; *see also* academic dishonesty

chronological framework, 265, 282

chunking, 24, 25, 32, 33

circle charts. *See* pie (circle) charts

Cirillo, Francesco, 29

claims, 155, 156, 158

classification systems, 111–13

class intervals, 296, 308; calculating, 299–301

clauses: dependent, 223; independent, 239, 240; punctuation and, 239, 240

clickers, 88, 96, 103

clincher, 144, 151

closed-book exams, 82, 83, 103

CMS (Chicago Manual of Style) system, 249, 260; author-date system, 249, 258–9; bibliography, 258; footnotes and endnotes and, 257–8; notes-bibliography system, 256–8; page numbers in, 257

co-curricular activities, 26–7, 33

colloquial language, 215, 229, 276

colons, 238, 239, 245

Colton, Charles Caleb, 81

column headings: tables and, 308

commas, 240–2, 245; serial, 241, 246

comma splice, 224–5

communication skills, 3

compare, 87, 103, 130, 151

Conan Doyle, Sir Arthur, 154

concentration span, 21, 23

conceptual framework, 86, 209; essays and, 136; in oral presentations, 266; reviews and, 202

conclusion: in essays, 133, 136–7, 168; in presentations, 267–8; in reports, 175, 184–5

conjunction, 224, 229

contractions, 237, 269

contrast, 87, 103, 130, 151

conversations, 16

Copyeditor's Handbook, 245

Cornell note-taking system, 46–9, 53, 54

correction tape, 87, 103

corroboration, 172

Courtenay, B., 265

critical thinking, 57–67; considering evidence, 61–6; defining, 57–61; determining purpose, 58–9; identifying thesis, 60–1; key concepts of, 58; putting information in context, 58; sources of information, 59–60

critique, 59, 67, 202, 209

"crunch" periods, 24, 33

Curve of Forgetting, 83, 103

data, 62, 67

databases, 114–16, 121, 125; citation, 120; full-text, 116, 120; online help with, 120; quality of sources found, 122–3; refining search in, 120; searching, 119–20; summary or abstract, 116

data labels, 285

decision-making: groups and, 77

deductive arguments, 67, 157, 169; misuse of, 161–2

deductive reasoning, 66, 67, 160–2

describe, 130, 151

description, 59, 67; in reviews, 198, 199, 201–4; in summaries, 196

Dewey Decimal Classification system, 111–12, 113, 125

diagrams: in essays, 143; in notes, 45

dictionaries, 41, 119, 146; reading and, 40; writing and, 213, 216, 217

Dictionary.com, 213

disciplines, 3, 17, 60

discrimination: language and, 217–21

discuss critically, 87, 103, 132, 152

discussion: in essays, 133, 136; in presentations, 267; in reports, 173, 189

distance education: online exams and, 83

DOI (Digital Object Identifier), 52, 250, 254, 255, 260

Weekly Study Grid

THE WEEK OF _____

	Monday	Tuesday	Wednesday	Thursday	Friday	Saturday	Sunday
07:00							
08:00							
09:00							
10:00							
11:00							
12:00							
01:00							
02:00							
03:00							
04:00							
05:00							
06:00							
07:00							
08:00							
09:00							
10:00							
11:00							

WEEKLY PLANNER

THE WEEK OF _____

	Monday	Tuesday	Wednesday	Thursday	Friday	Saturday	Sunday
07:00							
08:00							
09:00							
10:00							
11:00							
12:00							
01:00							
02:00							
03:00							
04:00							
05:00							
06:00							
07:00							
08:00							
09:00							
10:00							
11:00							

WEEKLY PLANNER

THE WEEK OF _____

	Monday	Tuesday	Wednesday	Thursday	Friday	Saturday	Sunday
07:00							
08:00							
09:00							
10:00							
11:00							
12:00							
01:00							
02:00							
03:00							
04:00							
05:00							
06:00							
07:00							
08:00							
09:00							
10:00							
11:00							

WEEKLY PLANNER

THE WEEK OF ————————————————————————————

	Monday	Tuesday	Wednesday	Thursday	Friday	Saturday	Sunday
07:00							
08:00							
09:00							
10:00							
11:00							
12:00							
01:00							
02:00							
03:00							
04:00							
05:00							
06:00							
07:00							
08:00							
09:00							
10:00							
11:00							

WEEKLY PLANNER